INTERNATIONAL HANDBOOK OF LAND AND PROPERTY TAXATION

International Handbook of Land and Property Taxation

Edited by

Richard M. Bird

University of Toronto

and

Enid Slack

Enid Slack Consulting, Inc.

Edward Elgar

Cheltenham, UK • Northampton, MA, USA

© Richard M. Bird and Enid Slack

Published by
Edward Elgar Publishing Limited
Glensanda House
Montpellier Parade
Cheltenham
Glos GL50 1UA
UK

Edward Elgar Publishing, Inc.
136 West Street
Suite 202
Northampton
Massachusetts 01060
USA

A catalogue record for this book
is available from the British Library

ISBN 1 84376 647 7 (cased)

Typeset by Manton Typesetters, Louth, Lincolnshire, UK.
Printed and bound in Great Britain by MPG Books Ltd, Bodmin, Cornwall.

Contents

Contributors   vii
Acknowledgements   viii

1   Introduction and overview   1
    Richard M. Bird and Enid Slack
2   Land and property taxation in 25 countries: a comparative review   19
    Richard M. Bird and Enid Slack
3   Reforming property taxes   57
    Richard M. Bird and Enid Slack

PART I   OECD COUNTRIES

4   Property taxation in Canada   69
    Enid Slack
5   Property taxation in the United Kingdom   81
    Enid Slack
6   Property taxation in Australia   91
    Enid Slack
7   Land taxation in Germany   98
    Paul Bernd Spahn
8   Property tax in Japan   107
    Toshiaki Kitazato

PART II   ASIA

9   Property taxation in Indonesia   117
    Roy Kelly
10 Property taxation in India   129
    Gautam Naresh
11 Real property taxation in the Philippines   152
    Milwida Guevara
12 Property tax in Thailand   159
    Sakon Varanyuwatana
13 Land and property tax in China   165
    Xu Shanda and Wang Daoshu

PART III   AFRICA

14   Property taxation in Kenya   177
     Roy Kelly
15   Property rates in Tanzania   189
     Roy Kelly
16   Property taxation in South Africa   199
     Enid Slack
17   Land and property taxation in Guinea   205
     François Vaillancourt
18   Land and property taxation in Tunisia   210
     François Vaillancourt

PART IV   CENTRAL AND EASTERN EUROPE

19   Land-based taxes in Hungary   219
     Almos Tassonyi
20   Land and property taxes in Russia   236
     Andrey Timofeev
21   Property tax in Ukraine   246
     Richard M. Bird
22   Land and property taxes in Poland   253
     Richard M. Bird
23   Real estate tax in Latvia   259
     Richard M. Bird

PART V   LATIN AMERICA

24   Land taxes in Colombia   265
     Richard M. Bird
25   Taxes on land and property in Argentina   281
     Ernesto Rezk
26   Property tax in Chile   286
     Ignacio Irarrazaval
27   Property taxes in Mexico   292
     Richard M. Bird
28   Property taxes in Nicaragua   298
     Richard M. Bird

Index   303

Contributors*

Richard M. Bird, University of Toronto, Canada
Milwida Guevara, Synergia Foundation, Manila, Philippines
Ignacio Irarrazaval, FOCUS, Santiago, Chile
Roy Kelly, Duke University, Nairobi, Kenya
Toshiaki Kitazato, Research Association for Development of Regional Areas and Management of Disasters and Crises, Tokyo, Japan
Gautam Naresh, National Institute of Public Finance and Policy, New Delhi, India
Ernesto Rezk, Universidad Nacional de Córdoba, Argentina
Enid Slack, Enid Slack Consulting Inc., Toronto, Canada
Paul Bernd Spahn, University of Frankfurt, Germany
Almos Tassonyi, Ontario Ministry of Finance, Toronto, Canada
Andrey Timofeev, Georgia State University, Atlanta, USA
François Vaillancourt, Université de Montréal, Canada
Sakon Varanyuwatana, Thammasat University, Bangkok, Thailand
Wang Daoshu, State Administration of Taxation, Beijing, China
Xu Shanda, State Administration of Taxation, Beijing, China

* Affiliation at time of writing.

Acknowledgements

This book originated in a study initially prepared for the World Bank in early 2002 as part of the background work for a report on *Land Policies for Growth and Poverty Reduction*, by Klaus Deininger (published for the World Bank by Oxford University Press, 2003). We are most grateful to Klaus Deininger for the invitation to take part in this work and for the opportunity to discuss our initial findings at regional workshops convened by the Bank in Budapest and Pachuca, Mexico.

We have also benefited greatly both from the comments of discussants at these workshops and from comments and help received from many other colleagues around the world: Olga Lucia Acosta, Julio Francisco Baez-Cortes, Roy Bahl, Nejib Belaid, Jan Brezski, Svetlana Budagovskaya, Zogbelemou Cece, Klaus Deininger, Joseph Eckert, Istvan Feher, Riël Franzsen, Mark Gallagher, Marino Henao, Jose Leibovich, Jane Malme, Arthur Mann, Jorge Martinez-Vazquez, Oliver Oldman, Mudite Priede, Uri Raich, M. Govinda Rao, Ihor Shpak, Martim Smolka, Laura Sour, John Strasma, Wayne Thirsk, Bayar Tummenasan, Dana Weist, Christine Wong, Joan Youngman and Juan Gonzalo Zapata. In addition, Natalia Aristizabal and David Santoyo-Amador deserve special thanks for their assistance in preparing earlier versions of the country studies of Colombia and Mexico, respectively.

Our principal debt of course is to those who have contributed country studies to this book: Milwida Guevara, Ignacio Irarrazaval, Roy Kelly, Toshiaki Kitazato, Gautam Naresh, Ernesto Rezk, Paul Bernd Spahn, Almos Tassonyi, Andrey Timofeev, François Vaillancourt, Sakon Varanyuwatana, Wang Daoshu, and Xu Shanda. Without their efforts, both in preparing the initial country studies and in updating and revising them for publication, there would be no book.

Richard M. Bird
Enid Slack
Toronto, September 2003

viii

1 Introduction and overview

Richard M. Bird and Enid Slack

Taxes on land and property exist all over the world. In both principle and practice, these taxes can have important fiscal and non-fiscal effects. The revenue such taxes produce is often an important source of finance for local governments. In turn, the extent to which local governments have control over property taxes is often an important determinant of the extent to which they are able to make autonomous expenditure decisions. The level, design and control of property taxation are thus critical elements in effective decentralization policy in many countries. From a more general policy perspective, land and property taxes may be viewed as either equitable and efficient ways of raising revenue or regressive and undesirable forms of public finance, depending upon one's assumptions, the environment and how exactly the taxes are designed and applied.

Definitive conclusions on these matters do not emerge easily from an examination of the complex structure of property taxes around the world. Consider, for example, the case of Germany, in which two variants of land tax are imposed on (in effect) four different bases at five different 'base rates' which in turn are modified by locally determined 'leverage factors.' Other than noting that the revenues from this complex set of taxes are small and that reform has proved politically impossible so far, it is hard to say anything very definite about the effects of such a system. Germany is not alone in this respect. Taxes on land and property are among the oldest forms of all taxes. Old taxes need not necessarily be 'good taxes,' as the saying has it, but they almost invariably have over the years become encrusted with various peculiar features that are generally difficult to alter and that often obscure their impact.

The case studies that constitute the bulk of this volume make this point clear. These reviews of the taxation of land and property in 25 countries (five in each of five regions – OECD, Central and Eastern Europe, Asia, Africa, and Latin America) focus on the potential contributions of land and property taxes to the revenues of urban and rural governments and to more efficient land use. Since the ability of the property tax to make such contributions largely depends upon the specifics of the tax (tax base, tax rates and administration), special attention is paid to such characteristics.

The initial terms of reference given to the authors of all case studies were to provide information on four basic items: (1) How much revenue is collected from taxes on land and property? (2) What is the tax base, and who

1

determines it? (3) What are the tax rates, and who sets them? (4) How is the tax administered? In addition, authors were asked to provide relevant information on other land-based taxes, on the frequency of reassessment, on differentiations in taxes on types of property, on enforcement and tax arrears, and so on. Moreover, in each of the five regions noted above, one country – the first listed in each region (Canada, Hungary, Indonesia, Kenya and Colombia, respectively) – was selected for a somewhat fuller study of reform experience. In these cases, authors were asked also to provide some discussion of the rationale, nature and impact of reform efforts.

In total, 15 authors living in 11 countries were involved in preparing these case studies. The great differences from country to country in both practices and the availability of information mean that the results presented here are not uniform from country to country. Some reports are more detailed and comprehensive than others. Some are more factual; others more interpretative. Some, especially those from federal countries, focus on experience in only one part of the country. Some are based on direct fieldwork; others depend more on existing studies. Some focus almost entirely on the property tax; others cast their net more widely. Although all of these case studies were revised and updated by their authors in mid-2003 and have in some cases been further revised by the principal authors of this book, some important information is still missing in some countries because it is simply not available.

Table 1.1 sets out some key characteristics of the 25 countries covered in this book. These countries were selected to cover most regions of the world and also to some extent to depict different 'styles' or practices in taxing land and real property. Although the sample chosen is not representative in any statistical sense, and the information obtained is in any case too diverse and disparate to lend itself to statistical manipulation, many of the conclusions reached on the basis of this study reinforce those of earlier cross-country comparative studies of land and property taxes. Some of these earlier studies focused on developed countries (OECD, 1983), some on transitional countries (Malme and Youngman, 2001), some on developing countries (Municipal Development Programme, 1996; Rosengard, 1998), and some have cast their nets more widely (Youngman and Malme, 1994; McCluskey, 1999; Brown and Hepworth, 2000; Andelson, 2000). Some studies focused on rural land taxation (Bird, 1974; Strasma et al., 1987), some on urban property taxes (Bahl and Linn, 1992), and some on land value taxation as opposed to property taxation more generally (Andelson, 2000; McCluskey and Franzsen, 2001).

Altogether, the various comparative studies cited cover, to varying degrees, land and property tax systems in at least 40 countries in addition to those included in the present book. Moreover, there are, of course, many other

Table 1.1 Some key characteristics of case study countries

Country	Estimated population 2003 (million)	Area (thousand km²)	GDP per capita (PPP 2002 US$)	Exchange rate (local currency = US$)	Central government current revenues, 2000 (% of GDP)	Urban population (% total)	Type of government
Australia	19.7	7 687	27 000	1.8406 dollars	23.6	84.7	Federal
Canada	32.2	9 976	29 400	1.5693 dollars	21.8	76.9	Federal
Germany	83.4	357	26 600	1.0626 euros	31.3	87.1	Federal
Japan	127.2	378	28 000	125.388 yen	20.4	78.5	Unitary
UK	60.1	245	25 300	0.6672 pounds	36.0	89.4	Unitary
Hungary	10.1	93	13 300	257.887 forints	37.4	63.6	Unitary
Latvia	2.4	65	8 300	0.6182 lati	28.5	69.0	Unitary
Poland	38.6	313	9 500	3.99 złoty	29.9	64.8	Unitary
Russia	144.5	17 075	9 300	31.2651 rubles	24.6	77.0	Federal
Ukraine	48.1	604	4 500	5.3266 hrivnia	26.8	67.8	Unitary
Argentina	38.7	2 767	10 200	3.0633 pesos	14.2	89.3	Federal
Chile	15.7	757	10 000	688.953 pesos	22.2	85.2	Unitary
Colombia	41.7	1 139	6 500	2 504.24 pesos	12.6	73.1	Unitary
Mexico	104.9	1 973	9 000	9.656 pesos	14.8	74.0	Federal
Nicaragua	5.1	130	2 500	14.2513 córdobas	31.8	55.5	Unitary
China	1 287.0	9 597	4 400	8.277 yuan	7.2	31.1	Unitary
India	1 050.0	3 288	2 540	48.6103 rupees	12.7	27.8	Federal
Indonesia	234.9	1 919	3 100	9 311.19 rupiahs	18.1	38.8	Unitary
Philippines	84.6	300	4 200	51.63 pesos	15.4	56.8	Unitary
Thailand	64.3	514	6 900	42.9601 baht	16.0	21.0	Unitary
Guinea	9.0	246	2 000	1 950.56 francs	11.7	31.4	Federal
Kenya	31.6	583	1 020	78.7491 shillings	25.8	31.3	Unitary
South Africa	42.8	1 220	10 000	10.5407 rand	26.7	50.0	Federal
Tanzania	35.9	945	630	876.412 shillings	–	30.5	Unitary
Tunisia	9.9	164	6 500	1.4217 dinars	28.6	64.1	Unitary

Sources: Central Intelligence Agency, *The World Factbook 2003*; revenue data and urban share from World Development Indicators, World Bank.

studies of individual countries, as noted in many of the case studies included here. On the other hand, some of the countries studied here have not been covered in earlier studies, and no other study has so systematically attempted to cover the world.

The diversity in the application of land and property taxes even among the 25 countries covered in this volume is striking. There are differences in the determination of the tax base, the setting of tax rates, and the ability to levy and collect the tax. In some countries, one property tax covers all types of property. In others, there are different taxes for different components of real property. Countries may, for example, have separate taxes on land and buildings; separate taxes on residential and non-residential property; or separate taxes in urban and rural areas. Moreover, not only are there significant differences in how land and property are taxed across countries; there are often significant differences within countries.

The greater the degree of local discretion in establishing the tax base and setting the rates, the more diversity there is in property taxes within a country. This is particularly true in federal systems, in which the state or provincial government often provides the legal framework under which municipalities can operate. For this reason, or for reasons of information availability, some case study chapters focus on a specific province or state within the country and may not provide comprehensive information for the country as a whole. Indeed, as a general rule, information on local taxes is often surprisingly difficult to secure and seldom easily comparable even within unitary countries. Furthermore, although recent reform efforts in a few countries are discussed, no doubt other reforms are currently under consideration in these and other countries, so that some of the information included here may already be obsolete.

For these reasons, a certain degree of modesty is obviously called for with respect to what is accomplished in this book. Nonetheless, we are aware of no other recent volume that has attempted to cover the world even to the limited extent we have achieved here. Complexity, diversity, inadequate and imperfect information, and change have long been characteristics of property taxes in many countries. The countries studied here are no exception to this rule. While we venture some generalizations about land and property taxes in this and the next two chapters, we are well aware that the devil in land taxation is in the details, and that the details are often devilishly hard to determine. Still, the more we know, the better we can understand what details may be critical in different situations and how best to tackle the ongoing task of reforming this ancient set of fiscal instruments to cope with the diverse and changing circumstances of the modern world.

In the balance of this chapter we first place land and property taxes in context and then summarize a few major conclusions we have drawn from this study. In Chapter 2 we present a more detailed comparison of the major characteristics of land and property taxes in our 25-country sample.[1] Finally, in Chapter 3 we summarize experience with property tax reform in several of the countries covered in the book.

The role of the property tax

The property tax as a source of revenue

Tables 1.2 and 1.3 provide a useful introductory overview of the role of the property tax as a revenue source. Four key conclusions emerge from these tables and from the Government Finance Statistics (GFS) data that underlie them:[2]

1. Taxes on land and property are at best minor revenue sources in all countries. For the developing countries included in these tables, for example, such taxes accounted for only about 0.4 percent of GDP (Table 1.2) and about 2 percent of total tax revenues in the 1990s, down slightly from earlier decades, although the equivalent share for the OECD countries remained at a bit more than 1 percent of GDP (Table 1.2) and about 4 percent of all tax revenues throughout the period.[3]

2. Nonetheless, as Table 1.3 shows, property taxes are important sources of subnational revenue in many countries, and more so in developing than in developed or transition countries. In the 1990s property taxes accounted for 40 percent of all subnational taxes (rather than the subnational rev-

Table 1.2 Subnational property tax as share of GDP, 1970s–90s (%)

	1970s	1980s	1990s
OECD countries	1.24	1.31	1.44
(number of countries)	(16)	(18)	(16)
Developing countries	0.42	0.36	0.42
(number of countries)	(20)	(27)	(23)
Transition countries	0.34	0.59	0.54
(number of countries)	(1)	(4)	(20)
All countries	0.77	0.73	0.75
(number of countries)	(37)	(49)	(58)

Source: Calculated by Roy Bahl and Bayar Tumennasan, Andrew Young School of Public Policy, Georgia State University, from data in IMF *Government Finance Statistics Yearbook, 2001*.

*Table 1.3   Subnational property tax as share of subnational revenue,
         1970s–90s (%)*

	1970s	1980s	1990s
OECD countries	17.4	17.0	17.9
(number of countries)	(16)	(17)	(16)
Developing countries	27.6	24.3	19.1
(number of countries)	(21)	(27)	(24)
Transition countries	6.7	8.51	8.8
(number of countries)	(1)	(4)	(20)
All countries	22.8	20.4	15.6
(number of countries)	(38)	(48)	(59)

Source: See Table 1.2.

enues shown in Table 1.3) in developing countries, 35 percent (up from 30 percent in earlier decades) in developed countries, but only 12 percent in transition countries. In the same period, property taxes financed a bit more than 10 percent of subnational expenditure in developed and developing countries, although little more than half that much in transition countries.

3. Property taxes are much more important in rich (OECD) countries than in developing or transition countries. Although these details are not shown in the tables, for the last year for which all data were available (1995) the highest property tax to GDP ratio (4.1 percent) was in Canada, followed by the United States (2.9 percent), and Australia (2.5 percent): it seems unlikely to be a coincidence that all three are rich federations. On the other hand, the lowest ratio recorded (0.01 percent) was also in a rich federal country (Austria), and some developing and transition countries (South Africa, Latvia) had relatively high (over 1 percent) ratios. There is clearly more to property tax effort than simply wealth, as we shall discuss later in connection with Table 1.4.

4. None of the characteristics mentioned above has changed much in recent decades, with the exception of a relative decline in the importance of property taxes as a share of subnational revenue (and expenditure) in developing countries.

Dependence on property taxes as a source of local government revenue varies across jurisdictions depending upon many factors, such as the expenditure responsibilities assigned to local governments, the other revenues available to them (such as intergovernmental transfers, user fees and other taxes), the degree of freedom local governments have with respect to property taxation, the size and growth of the tax base available to them, and their willingness and ability to enforce such taxes.

The PT/GDP ratio reported in Table 1.2 may be thought of as the product of the multiplication of a number of other ratios, as follows:

- MV/GDP – the ratio of (market) property values to GDP
- AV/MV – the ratio of assessed base to market values (assessment ratio)
- TV/AV – the ratio of taxable base to assessed base (exemptions)
- T/TV – the ratio of taxes assessed to taxable base (statutory tax rate)
- T*/T – the ratio of taxes collected to taxes assessed (enforcement).[4]

Governments can do little directly with respect to the first of these ratios – although, as noted later, local governments may in some circumstances be able to affect the share of the potential base that is located within their jurisdiction. It may be more meaningful to compare property tax collections not with GDP but rather with (estimated) market values.

This ratio is commonly called the 'effective rate of property tax' (ERPT = T*/MV). In the United States, for example, a recent study found the median effective rate on a house valued at US$150 000 to be 1.2 percent in 1998.[5] The same study found the median ERPT on commercial property to be 2.3 percent and on industrial property to be 1.7 percent. The range from state to state was impressive, however: with respect to residential property, the estimated state ERPT ranged from 0.4 percent to 2.9 percent. The range was almost the same with respect to industrial property (0.4 –3.0 percent), but with respect to commercial property it was considerably greater – 0.7 percent to 6.0 percent.

These numbers suggest two interesting conclusions with respect to the United States. First, property taxes are generally heavier on non-residential (and especially commercial) properties than on residential (single-family) homes.[6] Second, when there is considerable local discretion with respect to property taxes, as is the case in the United States, there are also likely to be great differences in effective tax rates. Relatively little information on effective rates is available for developing and transition countries, but, as discussed later, both these conclusions seem likely to hold much more widely than just in the US case. In addition, the ERPT tends to be considerably lower in most developing countries than noted above for the US. For example, Chapter 11 reports an estimate of 0.07 percent for the Philippines and Chapter 9 shows a range of between 0.1 and 0.2 percent for Indonesia.

Of course, such numbers do not tell us why effective property taxes are so low, but it seems likely that all the administrative factors mentioned above play a role. As noted in Chapter 2, it is clear from the case studies, for example, that the assessment ratio is low in many countries. It is also clear that there are often large exemptions. Moreover, statutory rates are generally low, and collection efforts poor, as evidenced, for instance, by high arrears ratios. All these factors seem especially marked in many transition countries in which in addition land markets are generally not well developed.

As discussed further in Chapter 2, in many – indeed, most – developing and transition countries, local governments as such have very little scope to affect many, or in some cases any, of these factors. Although it is often surprisingly difficult to determine exactly how much 'autonomy' local governments have in fiscal matters, it appears that in many such countries assessment, exemption, rates and sometimes even collection are essentially controlled by higher-level governments.[7] The present and future of subnational property taxes are thus inextricably related to much broader issues related to intergovernmental relations and fiscal decentralization more generally.

Table 1.4   Case study countries: property tax effort, 1995

Country	Subnational property taxes (GFS data) as % of GDP	PT effort
Australia	2.49	2.03
Canada	4.07	3.51
Germany	1.05	0.39
UK	1.43	0.64
Hungary	0.30	0.89
Poland	1.11	2.20
Russia	1.24	1.45
Argentina	0.92	0.84
Chile	0.61	0.76
Mexico	0.31	0.36
Nicaragua	0.13	1.53
India	0.10	0.84
Indonesia	0.32	1.49
Thailand	0.14	1.65
South Africa	0.65	3.82

Note and source: The second column is a measure of 'effort' derived as the ratio of the actual PT/GDP ratio and the 'predicted' ratio based on a regression equation incorporating (in log form) measures of urbanization, population, per capita GDP and decentralization (measured as subnational expenditure as a share of total expenditure). The data reported here are a subset of those reported in Bahl (2001).

Finally, Table 1.4 reports some results from a recent study by Roy Bahl (2002) of the factors determining property tax 'effort' for, among others, some of our case study countries.[8] In this study, the PT/GDP ratio is taken to reflect a number of independent factors – the wealth of the country (as measured by the level of its per capita GDP), its population and its degree of urbanization. A regression equation including these variables explains (statistically) about half of the observed variation across countries and suggests that countries tend to rely more heavily on property taxes as income levels rise and they become more urbanized.

Another specification of this equation, including also the degree of decentralization (as measured by subnational expenditures as a share of total government expenditures) as an independent variable, was used by Bahl (2002) to calculate 'predicted' PT ratios for each country. Property tax 'effort' (as shown in Table 1.4) can then be calculated as the ratio of the actual ratio to the predicted ratio. That is, if a country's actual ratio is exactly equal to the ratio predicted, given the values of the independent variables, then the reported effort would be 1.00. If the actual ratio is greater than the predicted ratio, effort is greater than 1.00, and so on.

While such calculations are obviously crude, Table 1.4 nonetheless suggests two important conclusions:

- Actual ratios are not a good predictor of effort: some countries (for example Canada) have both high ratios and high effort; others (for example the UK) have high ratios but low effort; still others (for example Nicaragua) have low ratios and – at least by this calculation – high effort; and, finally, some countries (for example Mexico) have both low ratios and low effort. How much a country collects in land and property taxes is not, it seems, a reliable guide to how hard it is trying to do so.
- On the other hand, it follows from the same information that countries that make similar efforts may secure very different results (compare, for example, Germany and Mexico on the low side and Canada and South Africa on the high side), and, correspondingly, that countries with similar results (for example Germany and Poland) may be making very different efforts.

From a policy perspective, what this simple exercise suggests is that while countries are inevitably constrained in what they can do by environmental factors, there appears to be considerable leeway for many countries to do better than they have been doing. Low-effort countries such as Mexico and Germany, for example, could clearly collect much more in property taxes if they wanted to do so, although it would be much harder for low-income

Mexico than for high-income Germany to raise, say, an additional 1 percent of GDP in such taxes (Bird, 1976). As is so often the case in fiscal matters, many poor countries could do more than they do in terms of taxing land and property, but no matter how much they do they are unlikely to reap the same relative rewards for their effort as more fortunate countries. To them that hath, it seems, more comes more easily, in this as in other respects.

The property tax as a local tax

The property tax has, historically, been associated with local government in most countries. One reason that taxes on land and property have been considered especially appropriate as a local revenue source is that real property is immovable – it is unable to shift location in response to the tax. Although a change in property tax may be capitalized into property values in a particular community, and in the long run tax differentials may affect where people locate, these effects are of a smaller magnitude than those that would occur with income and sales taxes at the local level.

Another reason why property taxes are considered to be appropriate as a source of revenue for local governments is the connection between many of the services typically funded at the local level and the benefit to property values. Fischel (2001), for example, has argued that the property tax in the United States is like a benefit tax because taxes approximate the benefits received from local services. To the extent that this is the case, local property tax finance of local services will promote efficient public decisions since taxpayers will support those measures for which the benefits exceed the taxes. Both the benefits derived from such local services as good schools and better access to roads and transit, and so on and the taxes used to finance such services are capitalized into property values. Since taxpayers are willing to pay more for better services and lower tax rates, either will translate into higher property values.

Of course, this analysis is based on a number of assumptions, including the following:

- Local property taxes in fact finance services that benefit property values.
- Both tax rates and service levels are decided by local voters.
- Voters who wish to 'buy' other combinations of services and tax rates are free to move to other jurisdictions.
- Voters – impelled by their sensitivity to property values – act rationally in response to such signals.
- Local governments do what voters want them to do.

The strength and validity of many of these links seem suspect in the context of many countries. Moreover, this line of argument seems even more tenuous when it comes to explaining the generally higher taxation on non-residential property observed in many countries. Although we shall not discuss this question further here, as Bird (2003) argues in detail, an income-type value-added tax appears to be a much more sensible way to 'price' local services to businesses than a property tax.

In contrast to this 'benefit' approach, many see the property tax as a tax on capital or, to the extent it falls on housing, as a tax on housing services. Zodrow (2001), for example, argues that the property tax in the United States results in distortions in the housing market and in local fiscal decisions. In particular, since the US property tax, which is based on market value, falls on both land and improvements, it both discourages building and results in the under-utilization of land. The result is that the country ends up with less capital per unit of land than is economically efficient. Homeowners who improve their house, for example, will face higher taxes as a result and will thus be discouraged from doing so. As George ([1879] 1979) said, and as many others have argued since, a tax on land values alone would avoid this economic inefficiency and would indeed stimulate the efficient use of land. We shall return to this point below.

The incidence of the property tax
Who pays the property tax, and is it an equitable tax? There appear to be as many answers to these questions as there are views about the property tax. For example:

- Those who view taxes on residential real property as essentially taxes on housing services tend to think that property taxes are inherently regressive, since, as a rule, housing constitutes a relatively larger share of consumption for poorer people.
- Those who view property taxes as essentially a tax on capital tend to think that such taxes are inherently progressive, since, as a rule, income from capital constitutes a relatively higher share of income for richer people.
- Those who view the portion of the tax that falls on land as being paid out of economic rent consider it to be inherently equitable to tax such 'unearned increments' arising (often) from public actions.
- Those who view property taxes as essentially benefit taxes tend to think that there is no more sense in asking if the 'price' of local public services (the property tax) is regressive than in asking if the price charged for anything else is regressive: voluntary exchange ('taxes' – really generalized user charges – for services) does not, in their view, raise any question of incidence.

Although hardly conclusive, the empirical evidence on capitalization on the one hand and 'tax exporting' on the other, at least in the United States and Canada, suggests that there may be some truth in all of these views.[9] In the end, it seems, what one beholds in the property tax in terms of equity appears to depend to a large extent on what one thinks of the property tax in the first place.

Why property taxes are different

In addition to the obscurity of its incidence, at least four characteristics of the property tax differentiate it to some extent from other taxes: its visibility, its inelasticity, its inherent arbitrariness and, in some countries, the extent to which it reflects local autonomy.

As usually applied, the property tax is a very visible tax. Unlike the income tax, for example, the property tax is not withheld at source. Unlike the sales tax, it is not paid in small amounts with each daily purchase. Instead, the property tax generally has to be paid directly by taxpayers in periodic lump-sum payments. This means that taxpayers tend often to be more aware of the property taxes they pay than they are of other taxes.[10]

Moreover, to a considerable extent, the property tax finances services which are also very visible, such as roads, garbage collection and neighborhood parks. Visibility is clearly desirable from a decision-making perspective because it makes taxpayers aware of the costs of local public services. This awareness enhances accountability, which is obviously a good thing from both an economic (hard budget constraint) and political (democratic) perspective. It does not, however, make the property tax popular. On the contrary, as we discuss further in Chapter 2, it often appears to be harder to raise (or reform) property taxes than other taxes.

The base of the property tax – no matter which of the bases discussed in Chapter 2 is employed – is invariably relatively inelastic, meaning that it does not increase automatically over time. Bahl (2002), for example, notes that the GDP elasticity of the property tax has been close to unity for decades. Property values generally respond more slowly to annual changes in economic activity than do incomes.[11] Taxable area, of course, responds even more slowly. Furthermore, as discussed in Chapter 2, few jurisdictions update property values for taxation purposes on an annual basis.

As a result, in order to maintain property tax revenues in real terms (let alone to raise property tax revenues), it is necessary to increase the rate of the tax. As with visibility, inelasticity leads to greater accountability (taxing authorities have to increase the tax rate to increase tax revenues) but it also leads to greater taxpayer resistance.

Most taxes are based on flows – income or sales. The tax base may sometimes be the source of argument between taxpayer and tax authority, but there is, in principle, a measurable economic activity on the basis of which the tax is levied. In contrast, taxes on land and property are (generally) based on stocks – asset values. Unless the asset subject to tax is sold (by willing buyers to willing sellers) in the tax period, someone has to determine the value that serves as the basis on which to assess the tax.

Valuation is inherently and inevitably an arguable matter. If there is a 'self-assessment' system, owners are likely to undervalue their property; if there is an 'official' (cadastral) assessment system, owners are likely to feel that their property is (at least in relative terms) overvalued. In the end, someone has to determine the tax base for the property tax in a way that is not true for any other significant tax. It is not surprising that the results are often perceived to be unfair and arbitrary. It is also not surprising that the process of obtaining 'good' (close to market, fair) valuations is not likely to be cheap. In short, to administer a property tax at the same level of fairness (non-arbitrariness) as most other major taxes is both a costly operation and one whose results are unlikely to be accepted as fair by most taxpayers.

Finally, to the extent property taxes are levied only by local governments, they obviously act as a major support for local autonomy. The extent to which such autonomy is either desired or attained is very country-specific. Even in such countries as Canada and Australia, with important local governments and important local property taxes, not all taxes on property are levied by local governments. In some countries, such as Latvia and Chile, the property tax is much more a central than a local tax. Indeed, if one defines a 'purely local' tax as one in which local governments can (1) decide whether or not to levy the tax, (2) determine the precise nature of the tax, (3) establish the base on which to tax individual taxpayers, (4) determine the tax rate, and (5) enforce the tax, very few countries have such taxes.

As discussed in Chapter 2, in most developing and transition countries, 'local' property taxes are, in most of these respects, more 'central' than 'local' in nature. Since an essential ingredient of responsible local autonomy – or, if one prefers, of a 'hard' subnational budget constraint – is that tax rates be set locally (and not by a senior level of government),[12] the property tax systems existing in most countries considered here are still far from achieving this goal.

An additional result of the lack of local control over property taxes in Central and Eastern Europe is a disincentive to privatize properties. One reason many cities in transitional countries are unwilling to dispose of properties is that they can control the revenue they receive from leasing them, but they often have no control over property tax revenues. To avoid such distortions, local governments need better control over local tax sources if they are to get out of the land development business, for which they are generally ill suited.

What can property taxes do?

Finance local governments
The property tax generates a significant proportion of local government revenues in a few countries, mainly in the OECD. In most developing and transition countries, however, the property tax yield provides only a small, though not insignificant, share of the revenue available for local governments.

Property tax revenues are low in many developing and transitional economies in part because of the way in which the tax is administered. As shown in detail in this book, as a rule the coverage of the tax is not comprehensive, assessments are low, as are nominal tax rates, and collection rates are also often low. Low tax rates are sometimes imposed by higher-level governments and sometimes by local governments themselves, which find rate increases in this most visible of taxes very difficult to sell politically.

Simply raising the legal tax rate would seldom be considered appropriate, however, because it would place the burden of the increase on 'those few individuals whose properties are on the tax rolls, accurately valued, and from whom taxes are actually collected' (Dillinger, 1991, p. 5). Increased nominal rates are likely to be acceptable only along with such major improvements in tax structure and administration as more comprehensive coverage, better assessments, more frequent assessment revaluations and enforced penalties for late payment.

In general, revenues would be higher if the property tax were based on the value of land and buildings (instead of just on land), if there were few exemptions, if there were no favorable treatment of particular property classes, if the nominal tax rate were set higher, and if the scope for local tax competition were limited.

Despite its many problems, however, as de Cesare (2002, p. 9) has recently said, 'the property tax remains the predominant option for raising revenues at the local government level in Latin America' and, it might be added, elsewhere as well. The potential yield of land and property taxes is unlikely to be huge, revenues from this source will not be very elastic, and administrative costs are substantial. Nonetheless, an expanded property tax is indeed both a logical and a desirable objective for many countries, particularly those in which local governments are expected to play an increasing role in allocating public sector resources. But significant additional revenues from this source can seldom be expected in the short run, and, although property taxes are usually relatively more important in smaller communities, most additional revenues will likely be found in, and accrue to, the larger urban areas.

Affect land use

The instruments used by local governments to raise revenues can have an impact on the nature, location and density of development. Local governments can affect urban form not only with planning tools but also with municipal financial tools. In some cases, municipal financial tools work together with planning tools, but in other cases they may have the opposite effect (Slack, 2002).

The property tax is one fiscal instrument that can clearly influence land use patterns, especially in urban areas. In terms of the impact on the density of development, for example, increases in property tax should be expected to result in a reduction in density (other things being equal). Where the tax is levied on the assessed value of property (land and improvements), any investment that increases the value of the property (such as any improvement to the property including an increase in the density) will increase the assessed value and make the property subject to a higher tax.[13] Higher property taxes thus provide an incentive for less densely developed projects – for example, scattered single-family houses rather than apartment buildings. On the other hand, a tax on land only will provide an incentive for greater density relative to a tax on both land and improvements. The choice of highest and best use as the tax base (rather than current use) is also likely to result in higher densities.

It is important to emphasize, however, that to the extent that property tax differentials are matched by differentials in expenditures on public services, they should not result in a distortionary impact on location or land use. Although the property tax cannot be regarded as a direct 'user fee' through which individuals pay directly for the services they receive, where both tax rates and service levels are determined locally, it can often be thought of loosely as a benefits tax to the extent that public services provided to the property-owner enhance the value of the property and result in higher property taxes. Where such 'matching' does not occur, however, there will be a pattern of positive and negative subsidies that will influence urban development patterns, usually in a way that worsens it. As Oldman et al. (1967) argued some years ago in the context of an analysis of Mexico City's finances, such misallocations are potentially much more damaging in the case of the rapidly urbanizing cities of the developing world. These concerns seem still valid today.

In reality, taxes on land and property are seldom matched by service benefits. For example, non-residential properties are often overtaxed relative to benefits received compared to residential properties; tax competition among municipalities often does not reflect differential service benefits; and favorable tax treatment of farm properties can create distortions.

In summary, a number of policy choices can be made with respect to the structure of the property tax that will have an impact on land use. Such choices include what is included and excluded from the tax base, how property value is defined for different classes of property (for example, residential, farm, commercial and industrial properties), what percentage of the value is taxable, and how effective tax rates vary within and between classes of property.

Unfortunately, the information on many of these aspects available in most countries is inadequate to permit analysis of the effects of the existing – almost certainly non-optimal – tax systems on land use. Given the very low effective tax rates currently applied in most countries, the resulting distortions may not be too high. Nonetheless, given current pressures for further decentralization in many countries and the desirability in most countries of increased land and property taxation as a source of local finance, it is important to ensure that any future property tax reforms take into account not only the need to be politically acceptable and administratively feasible but also that the increased taxes be designed properly from an economic perspective. As argued in Chapter 2, this does not mean that 'gadgets' such as land value increment taxes and progressive land taxes, with their high and perhaps insuperable political and administrative costs, should play a role. On the contrary, what it means in most instances is that more attention should be paid to developing simple, uniform and above all effective local property taxes, with the only differentiation being perhaps somewhat heavier taxation of land than of improvements.

Notes

1. An earlier version of much of the material in this and the next two chapters appears in Bird and Slack (2002).
2. For more data and discussion, see Roy Bahl (2002). We are grateful both to Roy Bahl and to Bayar Tumennasan for providing these data and for permitting us to make use of their work.
3. The data in Tables 1.2 and 1.3 do not include taxes on land and property accruing to central governments. Subnational governments comprise both regional (province, state) and local (municipal) governments. Since in most countries property taxes basically accrue to local governments, we shall often simply refer to them as local taxes.
4. This is a variant of the presentation in Bahl (2002). The ratio T*/T may be broken down in a number of ways. For example, some taxes levied in year 1 may not be collected in that year – arrears. On the other hand, some taxes collected in year 1 may pertain to taxes levied in prior years. Penalties and interest with respect to late payments may be shown as tax collections or as a separate item. Some taxes assessed may be appealed and, if the appeal is successful, refunded. It is thus not always clear exactly what is encompassed in T* in different countries.
5. Data for selected cities in all states (excluding Louisiana) from 50-State Property Tax Comparison Study, Minnesota Taxpayers' Association, January 1999.
6. Multi-family dwellings (apartment buildings) are generally taxed much more heavily than single-family homes, but this important issue cannot be discussed in detail here.
7. By far the most systematic review of this question is OECD (1998, 2001). Unfortunately, similar work has not yet been done for non-OECD countries.
8. Again, we are grateful to Roy Bahl and Bayar Tumennasan for giving us access to the data underlying Bahl (2002).

9. This literature is reviewed in most textbooks. For one example, see Bird and Slack (1993).
10. In some cases, however, mortgage institutions include property tax payments with monthly mortgage payments. This procedure reduces the visibility of the property tax for taxpayers who pay their taxes along with their mortgage payments.
11. There may be exceptions of course, as for example in the case of the well-known 'bubble' in asset prices in Japan in the 1980s, where at one point the effective rate of the fixed property tax in Tokyo was estimated to have fallen to 0.05 percent (Ishi, 2001).
12. This argument is developed in more detail in Bird (2001).
13. This assumes that an increase in the value of the property will be reflected in the value assessed for taxation purposes, which is of course not always the case.

References

Andelson, Robert V. (ed.) (2000), *Land-Value Taxation Around the World*, 3rd edn, Malden, MA: Blackwell.

Bahl, Roy (2001), 'Property Taxation in Developing Countries: An Assessment in 2001,' Lincoln Lecture, Lincoln Institute of Land Policy, Cambridge, MA, 23 October.

Bahl, Roy (2002), 'The Property Tax in Developing Countries; Where are we in 2002?' *Land Lines*, Lincoln Institute of Land Policy.

Bahl, Roy and Johannes F. Linn (1992), *Urban Public Finance in Developing Countries*, New York: Oxford University Press.

Bird, Richard M. (1974), *Taxing Agricultural Land in Developing Countries*, Cambridge, MA: Harvard University Press.

Bird, Richard M. (1976), 'Assessing Tax Performance in Developing Countries: A Critical Review of the Literature,' *Finanzarchiv*, **34** (2), 244–65.

Bird, Richard M. (2001), *Intergovernmental Fiscal Relations in Latin America: Policy Designs and Policy Outcomes*, Washington, DC: Inter-American Development Bank.

Bird, Richard M. (2003), 'A New Look at Local Business Taxes,' *Tax Notes International*, **30** (7), 695–711.

Bird, Richard M. and Enid Slack (1993), *Urban Public Finance in Canada*, 2nd edn, Toronto: John Wiley & Sons.

Bird, Richard M. and Enid Slack (2002), 'Land and Property Taxation Around the World: A Review,' *Journal of Property Tax Assessment & Administration*, **7** (3), 31–80.

Brown, P.K. and M.A. Hepworth (2000), 'A Study of European Land Tax Systems,' Cambridge, MA: Lincoln Institute of Land Policy Working Paper.

De Cesare, Claudia (2002), 'Toward More Effective Property Tax Systems in Latin America,' *Land Lines*, Lincoln Institute of Land Policy, January, pp. 9–11.

Dillinger, William (1991), *Urban Property Tax Reform: Guidelines and Recommendations*, Urban Management and Municipal Finance, Washington, DC: World Bank.

Fischel, William A. (2001), 'Homevoters, Municipal Corporate Governance, and the Benefit View of the Property Tax,' *National Tax Journal*, **54** (1), 157–73.

George, Henry ([1879] 1979), *Progress and Poverty*, New York: Robert Schalkenbach Foundation.

Ishi, Hiromitsu (2001), *The Japanese Tax System*, 3rd edn, Oxford: Oxford University Press.

Malme, Jane H. and Joan M. Youngman (eds) (2001), *The Development of the Property Tax in Economies in Transition*, WBI Learning Resources Series, Washington, DC: World Bank.

McCluskey, William (ed.) (1999), *Property Tax: An International Comparative Review*, Aldershot, UK: Ashgate.

McCluskey, William J. and Riel C.D. Franzsen (2001), 'Land Value Taxation: A Case Study Approach,' Lincoln Institute of Land Policy, Cambridge MA, Working Paper.

Municipal Development Programme (1996), *Property Tax in Eastern and Southern Africa: Challenges and Lessons Learned*, Working Paper No. 2, Municipal Development Programme for Eastern and Southern Africa, Harare.

OECD (1983), *Taxes on Immovable Property*, Paris: OECD.

OECD (1998), *Taxing Powers of State and Local Governments*, Paris: OECD.

OECD (2001), *Fiscal Design Across Levels of Government. Year 2000 Surveys*, Paris: OECD.

Oldman, Oliver et al. (1967), *Financing Urban Development in Mexico City*, Cambridge, MA: Harvard University Press.

Rosengard, Jay K. (1998), *Property Tax Reform in Developing Countries*, Boston: Kluwer Academic Publishers.

Slack, Enid (2002), *Municipal Finance and the Pattern of Urban Growth*, Commentary No. 160, Toronto: C.D. Howe Institute.

Strasma, John et al. (1987), *Impact of Agricultural Land Revenue System on Agricultural Land Usage*, Burlington, VT: Associates in Rural Development.

Youngman, Joan M. and Jane H. Malme (1994), *An International Survey of Taxes on Land and Buildings*, Deventer: Kluwer Law and Taxation Publishers.

Zodrow, George R. (2001), 'The Property Tax as a Capital Tax: A Room with Three Views,' *National Tax Journal*, **54** (1), 139–56.

2 Land and property taxation in 25 countries: a comparative review

Richard M. Bird and Enid Slack

In this chapter, we summarize some of the main findings of the 25 case studies contained in this book. Table 2.1 sets out the main property taxes in each of these countries and indicates their importance as a source of local revenues. We discuss the major policy alternatives with respect to taxing land and property – the choice of tax base, exemptions, methods of determining the tax base, tax rates, differential treatment of different classes of property (farms, residences and so on), and the process of tax administration. We consider more briefly some of the other taxes levied on land found around the world such as land transfer taxes and development charges, unearned increment taxes, and the like. The discussion is organized thematically and illustrated by examples drawn from the case study chapters.

What is taxed?
Property taxes are generally levied on all types of properties – residential, commercial and industrial, as well as on farm properties. Sometimes different categories of property are treated differently. Sometimes certain classes of property, or property owner, or uses of property, are exempt. Sometimes only land is taxed. We shall first discuss the question of taxing land versus land and improvements and then consider exemptions.

Land versus land and improvements
Some countries tax only land. A few tax only buildings. Most tax both land and buildings (or 'improvements'), usually together but in some countries (for example Hungary) separately. Some also tax machinery (or 'tangible business assets'). Table 2.2 summarizes the tax base in our 25 countries. In most of these countries, the property tax is levied on land and improvements. In some countries, however, only the land portion of the property is taxed (for example Kenya and some parts of Australia and South Africa). In Tanzania, unusually, only buildings are taxed. In countries where both land and improvements are taxed, the land portion is sometimes taxed more heavily than improvements.

As mentioned in Chapter 1, the taxation of land only (sometimes called 'site value taxation') may potentially improve the efficiency of land use. In

Table 2.1   Reliance on property taxes by local governments

	Types of property tax	Property tax as % of local revenues
OECD		
Australia	State land tax; municipal rates	37.7[1]
Canada	Property tax	53.3
Germany	Land tax	15.5
Japan	Fixed property tax	25.5
United Kingdom	Council tax (local tax on residential property); business rates (central tax on non-residential property)	33.0[2]
Central and Eastern Europe		
Hungary	Building tax; plot tax; communal tax	13.6[3]
Latvia	Real estate tax	18.2[4]
Poland	Urban real estate tax; agricultural tax; forest tax	9.7
Russia	Land tax; individual property tax; enterprise assets tax	7.0
Ukraine	Land payments and taxes	9.3
Latin America		
Argentina	Property tax	35.0[5]
Chile	Property tax	35.1[6]
Colombia	Unified property tax	35.0[7]

Mexico	Property tax	58.7[8]
Nicaragua	Property tax	6.4
Asia		
China	Urban and township land use tax; house property tax; urban real estate tax; farm land occupation tax	4.9 7.0–41.0[9]
India	Property tax	10.7
Indonesia	Land and building tax	13.4
Philippines	Real property tax	1.4
Thailand	Buildings and land tax; land development tax	
Africa		
Guinea	Rental value tax on housing; local business taxes	32.0
Kenya	Property rates	15.0
South Africa	Rates on property	21.0
Tanzania	Local building tax; national land rents	4.0
Tunisia	Rental value tax on housing; tax on unbuilt land; local business tax	32.4

Notes:

1. Includes only local taxation and not the state tax on land.
2. Includes the local council tax and the local share of national non-domestic rates.
3. Includes other local taxes such as a tourism tax.
4. Percentage of local taxes.
5. This refers only to the municipal tax. There is also a property tax at the provincial level.
6. The property tax is a national tax earmarked for local governments; 40% of revenues remain with municipalities where property is located.
7. Property taxes as a percentage of total Colombian local taxes.
8. Percentage of municipal taxes.
9. The range depends on the state.

Table 2.2 Tax and assessment bases

	Tax base	Basis of assessment
OECD		
Australia	Land or land and improvements	Market value or rental value or combination
Canada	Land and improvements (sometimes machinery included)	Market value
Germany	Land and improvements; farm properties also include machinery and livestock	Market value (rental income/construction costs); area in former GDR
Japan	Land, houses, buildings, and tangible business assets	Market value
United Kingdom	Land and improvements; some plant and machinery	Market value for residential; rental value for non-residential
Central and Eastern Europe		
Hungary	Unimproved value (plot tax); buildings (building tax)	Area or adjusted market value
Latvia	Land and buildings	Market value
Poland	Land, buildings and structures	Area
Russia	Land for land tax; structures for property tax; assets for enterprise property tax	Area; inventory value of structures; value of assets
Ukraine	Land	Area

Latin America		
Argentina	Land and buildings	Market value
Chile	Land and improvements	Area by location for land; construction value for buildings
Colombia	Land and buildings	Market value
Mexico	Land and buildings	Market value
Nicaragua	Land, buildings and permanent improvements	Cadastral value
Asia		
China	Occupied land; land and improvements	Area; market value or rental value
India	Land and improvements	Mostly annual rental value; limited use of area and market value
Indonesia	Land and buildings	Market value
Philippines	Land, building, improvements and machinery	Market value
Thailand	Land and improvements (buildings and land tax); land (land development tax)	Rental value; market value
Africa		
Guinea	Land and buildings	Rental value
Kenya	Land (but can use land and improvements)	Area; market value; or a combination
South Africa	Land and/or improvements	Market value
Tanzania	Buildings, structures or limited development[1]	Market value (or replacement cost, if market value not available)
Tunisia	Land and improvements (rental housing tax); land only (tax on unbuilt land)	Area; rental value

Note: [1] Land belongs to the state and is not taxed; land rents are paid to the national government.

principle, a tax on site value in effect taxes location rents (the returns from a particular location regardless of the improvements to the site). Since improvements to land (such as structures) are not taxed, the owner has an incentive to develop the land to its most profitable use. Compared to a property tax on land and buildings that discourages investment in property, a site value tax thus encourages building and improvements.

Some empirical evidence on the impact of land value taxation on development can be found in a recent US study (Oates and Schwab, 1997). The city of Pittsburgh reformed its property tax in 1979–80 by raising the tax rate on land to more than five times the rate on structures. Although the authors conclude that the subsequent increase in building activity was largely attributable to a shortage of commercial space, the move to land taxation did play a role. By increasing land taxes, which are neutral in terms of development decisions, the city was able to increase its revenues without increasing other taxes that could have had a distortionary impact on development decisions.

Assuming land is in fixed supply (the supply of land offered for development is unresponsive to price changes), a tax on land falls on landowners and cannot be shifted to others. Increased site value taxes will thus be capitalized into lower property values. Since the tax is borne proportionately more by owners of land than is the case with a tax on both land and improvements, and since landownership is unequally distributed, such a tax should be more progressive (borne relatively more heavily by high-income taxpayers than low-income taxpayers).

Site value taxation thus scores well in terms of both efficiency and equity. One problem with taxing land alone, however, relates to the administration of the tax. Accurate land valuation presents a challenge to assessors because most urban real estate sales combine the value of land and improvements. Site value taxation requires the subtraction of the value of the improvements from the value of the property as a whole in order to derive an assessed value for the land. For this reason, some consider that such taxation is unacceptably arbitrary. On the other hand, some authors have argued that valuation of land alone is probably easier than valuation of property (Netzer, 1998). Instead of assessing the value of land and improvements and then subtracting the value of improvements, site values per square meter could, it is argued, be estimated directly from sales and demolition records.

This debate has not been resolved in the literature with respect to developed countries. The original arguments for site value taxation (George [1879], 1979) were made in a context in which cities such as San Francisco were growing rapidly. Land that was worthless one day was worth a fortune the next, owing largely to the rapid influx of population. Along these lines, it has been suggested that valuing land separately may be less of a problem in developing countries in which urban areas are growing rapidly (Bahl,

1998). In many such countries, land and improvements are in practice assessed separately in any case, with land value being estimated on the basis of a land value map and building value in accordance with construction cost tables.

On the other hand, even if assessment is done separately, if the rate is uniform and taxpayers can only appeal the total value, the division between the two components becomes arbitrary. Another problem has to do with the potential revenues that can be collected from a site value tax. Since the tax base is considerably smaller than the value of land and improvements combined, site value taxation can only produce comparable revenues at high rates of tax. Higher rates create greater distortions, however, and it is likely to be politically easier to levy a lower property tax rate on land and improvements than a higher tax rate on the land portion only (Bahl, 1998).

Exemptions

In every country, some properties are excluded from the property tax base. Exemptions may be based on various factors such as ownership (for example government-owned property), the use of the property (such as properties used for charitable purposes), or on characteristics of the owner or occupier (such as age or disability). In some countries, exemptions are granted by the central or state government; in other countries, exemptions are granted locally; in some, both levels can grant exemptions.

Although there is great diversity in the use of exemptions, some properties are exempt in most jurisdictions. For example, property owned and occupied by government is generally exempt from property taxes. Other property types that are often exempt include colleges and universities, churches and cemeteries, public hospitals, charitable institutions, public roads, parks, schools, libraries, foreign embassies and property owned by international organizations. In some countries, agricultural land and principal residences are also tax exempt.

In some instances governments make payments in lieu of taxes on their properties. These payments in lieu are generally negotiated between governments and are often much less than the property taxes would be. In Canada, for example, it is the federal government, and not the taxing authority, which determines the values and rates to be used in the payment in lieu calculation with respect to federal property.

Exemptions have been criticized on a number of grounds. First, to the extent that people working in government buildings or institutions use municipal services just as workers do in other buildings, they should be taxed (Bahl and Linn, 1992, p. 100). Second, the differential treatment means that owners/managers in taxed properties face higher costs than owners/managers of exempt properties. This differential will have implications for economic competition among businesses and between businesses and government (Kitchen and Vaillancourt, 1990). Third, differential tax treatment affects location decisions, choices about what activities to undertake, and other economic decisions. Fourth, exemptions narrow the tax base and thereby increase taxes on the remaining taxpayers or reduce the level of local services that can be offered. Finally, since the proportion of tax-exempt properties varies by municipality, disproportionate tax burdens are created across communities. This result is especially troublesome when higher-level governments determine what is exempt from local taxation.

There may be a case for favoring certain property-holders (such as churches and charitable organizations) to encourage their presence in the local community. If such a case can be made for preferential treatment, it has been argued that these organizations should be rewarded directly with a grant rather than on the basis of their property holdings (Kitchen, 1992). Unlike a property tax exemption, in principle such grants are subject to regular review by elected representatives, although such reviews seem rare in practice.

In any case, it is clear that when property tax exemptions are granted for any reason, in the interest of transparency and accountability all exempt property should still be assessed in the same way as other properties so that the value of the exemption is known. Furthermore, payments in lieu of taxes should be based on the assessed value and should reflect the taxes that could have been collected. Only when this is done – which is unfortunately almost never the case in practice – will the full cost of land use for a particular purpose be taken into account in resource allocation decisions.

How is property taxed?

Once the taxable base has been determined, the next step is to determine the value to which the tax rate is to be applied. In general, two distinct assessment methodologies are used for property taxation: area-based assessment and value-based assessment, with the latter being divided into capital and rental value approaches (Youngman and Malme, 1994). In addition, some countries use a system of self-assessment. The extent to which these approaches are used in the case study countries is summarized in Table 2.2.

Area-based assessment
Under an area-based assessment system, a charge is levied per square meter of land area, per square meter of building (or sometimes 'usable' space), or some combination of the two. Where measures of area are used for both land and buildings, the assessment of the property is the sum of an assessment rate per square meter multiplied by the size of the land parcel and an assessment rate per square meter multiplied by the size of the building. The assessment rates may be the same for land and buildings, or they may be different. For

example, a lower unit value per square meter might be applied to buildings to encourage development.

A strict per unit assessment results in a tax liability that is directly related to the size of the land and buildings. With unit value assessment, the assessment rate per square meter is adjusted to reflect location, quality of the structure, or other factors. Market value has an indirect influence on the assessment base through the application of adjustment factors. For example, the assessment rate per square meter might be adjusted to reflect the location of the property within a particular zone in the city. Although the specific location of the property within the zone is not taken into account, properties in different zones will have different values.

The adjustment factors are derived from average values for groups of properties within each zone and do not reflect the characteristics of each individual property. When the groups are defined narrowly enough, however, unit value begins to approximate market value. For example, a zone could be defined anywhere from an entire city to specific neighborhoods to properties on one side of a street.

As Table 2.2 shows, area-based assessments are commonly used in Central and Eastern Europe, where the absence of developed property markets makes it difficult to determine market value. They are also used in parts of Germany (in the former GDR), China, Chile, Kenya and Tunisia.

In Tunisia, for example, the rental tax (*taxe sur les immeubles bâtis*) requires municipalities to use national values for 'covered' square meters – the area built on – to establish the rental tax roll. The values set by presidential decree vary, depending upon the size of the house and the neighborhood. The municipalities apply four tax rates on an area basis, where areas are classified according to the availability of six services: garbage collection, street lighting, covered roadway, covered sidewalk, sanitary sewers and rainwater sewers. The tax rate is set at 8 percent if there are one to two services; 10 percent if there are three to four services; 12 percent if there are five to six services; and 14 percent if there are other services or better quality services.

Another common example of unit value assessment is in the assessment of agricultural land. In many countries, farm property is assessed at so much per square meter, with the unit value varying with the location (region, accessibility to markets), fertility (irrigation, climatic conditions, soil conditions, hilliness), and sometimes with the crops grown. Such values are sometimes established on the basis of detailed cadastral studies, and sometimes on the basis of sales data on comparable property. In practice, the values for agricultural land often seem, like other presumptive tax bases, to be established on the low side, in part to avoid excessive protest and appeal.

Market value assessment

Market value (or capital value) assessment estimates the value that the market places on individual properties. Market value is defined as the price that would be struck between a willing buyer and a willing seller in an arm's-length transaction.

Three methods are commonly used to estimate market value:

1. The comparable sales approach looks at valid sales of properties that are similar to the property being assessed. It is used when the market is active and similar properties are being sold.
2. The depreciated cost approach values property by estimating the land value as if it were vacant and adding the cost of replacing the buildings and other improvements to that value. This approach is generally used when the property is relatively new, there are no comparable sales, and the improvements are specific. The cost approach is also normally used to assess industrial properties.
3. Under the income approach, the assessor estimates the potential gross rental income the property could produce and deducts operating expenditures. The resulting annual net operating income is converted to a capital value using a capitalization rate. This approach is used mainly for properties with actual rental income.

Market value assessment is used in all the OECD countries studied, as well as a number of others, including Indonesia, the Philippines, South Africa, Latvia, Argentina and Mexico. A variation of the market value approach is used in the United Kingdom. Under the British council tax, the value of each residential property is assessed and placed on a valuation list in one of eight valuation bands. The value assigned to each property only indicates the valuation band and not the actual value of the property. Any change in value because of a change in house prices generally does not affect the banding. Individual properties could be re-banded only under two circumstances: if the local area changes for the worse, all homes in the area may be placed into a lower band. If a house is expanded it will be re-banded only after it is sold; if a home decreases in value because part of it is demolished, it may be re-banded immediately.[1]

Rental value assessment

Under the rental value (or annual value) approach, property is assessed according to estimated (not actual) rental value or net rent. One rationale for using rental value is that taxes are paid from income (a flow) rather than from wealth (a stock) and thus it is appropriate to tax the net rental value of real property. In theory, however, there should be no difference between a tax on market value and a tax on rental value. When a property is put to its highest and best use and is expected to remain there, rental value will bear a predictable relationship to market value – the discounted net stream of net rental payments will be approximately equal to market value.

This relationship does not always hold, however. First, gross rents are often used rather than the economically relevant 'net' rents that build in an allowance for maintenance expenditures, insurance costs and other expenses. Second, most countries tend to assess rental value on the basis of current use. There can thus be an important difference between market value and rental value. A property that is under-utilized – that is, currently used for a purpose less productive than other possible uses – would be assessed at a much lower value under the rental value approach than under the market value approach. From a land use perspective, a tax based on value in highest and best use is more efficient than a tax based on current use because it stimulates use to its highest potential by increasing the cost of holding unused or under-used land (as compared to developed land).

There are some problems with the use of rental value assessment. First, it is difficult to estimate rental value when there is rent control. Controlled or subsidized rents cannot be directly used to assess market rents unless the majority of properties are rent controlled. This has been an important problem in India, as discussed in Chapter 10 below.[2] Second, because vacant land is not taxable under a tax based on rental value in current use (since there is no current use), an incentive is created for low-return uses over high-return uses and it may even become worthwhile to withhold rental properties from the market altogether.[3] If vacant properties are not taxed, the tax has to be higher on occupied properties to yield the same amount of revenue. These higher taxes further discourage investment.

In terms of the administration of the tax, there are some additional difficulties with using rental value (Netzer, 1966). First, rental value is often difficult to estimate because there is little information on the annual rent of comparable properties for such unique commercial and industrial properties as steel mills, for example. Second, it can be difficult to calculate net rents because the distribution of expenses between landlords and tenants differs for different properties. Third, assessors may not have access to rental income information because rental income is not always in the public domain in the same way as are sales prices.

Despite these problems, rental value assessment is used in several countries including, for example, Australia, the United Kingdom (for non-residential property), China, India, Thailand, Guinea and Tunisia. In India, where there are rent controls on older properties, the assessed value is not always related to the market value because it is tied to the controlled rent. Each state has attempted to address the property tax problems associated with rent controls.

In some states, 'reasonable rent' is defined as the actual rent received or the rent receivable, whichever is higher. Other states have defined 'reasonable rent' with respect to certain key variables that contribute to the value, such as location, construction, area, age and nature of use. As noted in Chapter 10, in response to such problems some states in India are moving to a market value system or area-based system.

Area-based versus market-based assessment

Where it is possible to use market value, it is generally regarded as a better tax base. First, the benefits from services are more closely reflected in property values than in the size of the property. For example, properties close to transit systems or parks enjoy higher property values. The benefits from these services are not reflected in the dimensions of the property but rather in the value of the property. Even those services where the benefits may relate more closely to property dimensions (such as sidewalks and street lighting, for example) are related more to front footage than to lot size or building size.

Second, market value has the advantage of capturing the amenities of the neighborhood, amenities that have often been created by government expenditures and policies. Area-based assessments (particularly unit assessment) are unlikely to capture these amenities because they do not take into account differences in the quality of buildings or their location. Consider, for example, the taxes paid by two properties of identical size and age but in different locations. Suppose that one property is located next to a park and the other is adjacent to a factory. Under an area-based assessment system, the same tax would be imposed on both properties. Under a value-based assessment system, the property next to the park would pay higher property taxes. In this example, area-based assessments would not be fair.

Third, area-based assessment results in a relatively greater burden on low-income taxpayers than high-income taxpayers when compared to value-based assessment. The reason is that average household incomes in high-value neighborhoods are higher than in low-value neighborhoods. A tax on area taxes all properties that are the same size the same amount, whether they are in high-income or low-income neighborhoods. Similarly, older houses in a bad state of repair but with a large floor area will pay relatively high taxes.

Furthermore, if a relatively poor neighborhood becomes richer, there would be no tax change. A tax system that fails to take account of changes in relative values over time will result in inequities. If one value per square meter is chosen for all single-family homes, for example, and relative property values change over time as some locations become more desirable over time, then over a period of years inequities in the assessment system will result if the value per square meter is not changed.

One advantage often claimed for unit value assessment is that property taxes on this basis tend to be less volatile than under market value assessment because they do not change when property values change. As just noted, however, this 'advantage' can equally be argued to be a disadvantage, exacerbating inequities.

It has also been argued that unit value assessment is easier to understand and cheaper to administer than value-based assessments, particularly where the real estate market is not well developed, as in many developing and transition countries. However, although unit value may be easier to administer for single-family residential properties, it is difficult to use for the multi-residential rental, residential condominium, commercial and industrial properties that in practice constitute the bulk of the tax base in most such countries.

One problem with such properties, for instance, is what to include for tax purposes. Should atrium floors, servicing shafts, elevator spaces and so on be taxed even though they produce no direct revenue? Issues also arise about whether to include structural elements (such as decorative beams) that project outside of the glass line, as with some office towers.

Another problem is how to allocate shared facilities such as common entrances, halls, exits, aisles, atria or malls, among owners/tenants. For example, common areas can be shared on the basis of the size of each unit relative to the total, the rent charged to each unit, or some other measure.

A third problem in market economies has been the tendency towards the proliferation of multipliers that are applied to the area of improved property to reflect relative differences in value. In the Netherlands, for example, over time the system became so complex through such adjustments that it was finally abandoned (Youngman and Malme, 1994).

At present, many transition countries employ some variant of area-based assessment. To some extent, this choice no doubt reflects the nature of the available information on the physical area of building and land recorded in the old central planning records. Over time, however, as zones become more narrowly defined, it seems both likely and desirable that these systems will evolve into something closer to a market value system.

Self-assessment
Self-assessment requires property-owners to place an assessed value on their own property. In Hungary, for example, the current local tax system is based on the principle of self-identification. Taxpayers are obliged to register and report their tax obligations to the local tax administration. The determination of the tax on buildings and tax on idle land in Hungary requires verification only of the property size and not its market value. In practice, self-registration is not particularly effective because not all owners comply. Consequently,

the number of potential taxpayers or taxable assets is generally unknown. The determination of tax liabilities also requires verification of the self-assessment submitted by the taxpayer. The lack of personnel to make field inspections of each property in Hungary means that verification is inadequate.

The rental value tax on housing in Tunisia is based on the number of square meters. Taxpayers are required to submit a self-declaration form. Some municipalities verify the declared square meters against existing information, for example from the roll for the rental value tax that existed before 1997, but most municipalities do not.

In Thailand, self-declaration of property-owners is made to local assessors, who assess the self-declared value and identification in terms of how well it matches their data. Self-declaration of properties by landowners is also required in the Philippines, once every three years. The local assessor then prepares the assessment roll.

Where properties are assessed at market value and there is self-assessment, the taxing authority in some countries has the right to buy the property at the assessed value.[4] A system where the taxing authority can buy the property will only be credible if it actually can and will buy the property. In practice, this right seems to have been exercised only rarely, presumably because of the political and budgetary impossibility of large-scale property purchases.

Tanzi (2001) has recently made a proposal along similar lines, that people should assess their own properties and then make the self-assessed values public.[5] Anyone who wanted to buy their property at a price that exceeded the declared price, by some margin such as 40 percent, could make an offer. If the owner refused the offer, the bid plus a penalty would become the new assessment. Although appealing to economists, and frequently recommended in the past, such ideas on closer examination seem much less attractive on a number of grounds (Holland and Vaughan, 1970) and have not proven acceptable in practice anywhere.[6]

Nonetheless, self-assessment is an appealing procedure for poor countries with little administrative capacity. It does not appear to require expert assessment staff, and it seems to be easy to implement. Indeed, in some cases, such as Bogotá, Colombia (see Chapter 24), self-assessment has at times appeared to be relatively successful in terms of increasing revenues from property taxes, albeit at a time of rapidly rising property prices.

In general, however, self-assessment seems likely to lead, over time, to inaccurate estimates of property values, with a tendency toward underestimation. It violates the principle of fairness on the basis of ability to pay because people with comparable properties will not necessarily pay comparable taxes. Generally lower-valued properties have a lower rate of underestimation than do higher-valued properties, making this assessment approach regressive (that is, taxes are relatively higher on low-valued properties). Underestimation also obviously erodes the size of the tax base, with the usual detrimental effects on tax rates and/or on service levels. In the end, there is no easy way to get people to tax themselves in the absence of a credible verification process. To minimize the obvious problems of understatement associated with any self-assessment system, the government must be prepared to obtain (costly) expert assessments of individual properties in cases where it believes self-assessment is inaccurate.

At what rate is property taxed?

Tax liability is determined by multiplying the assessed value by the tax rate. Given the size of the tax base, the tax rate determines how much revenue the property tax will generate. Three major issues arise with respect to tax rates. Who sets them? Are they differentiated, and, if so, how? And, finally, how high are they?

Who determines the tax rate?

Tax rates are sometimes determined locally and sometimes by the central government. As shown in Table 2.3, there are very considerable differences between countries with respect to the extent to which local governments are free to determine tax rates. Sometimes (Japan, Ukraine, Chile, Thailand, Tunisia) rates are essentially set by the central government. Sometimes (Hungary, Colombia, the Philippines) there is some local discretion, within centrally set limits. Sometimes (Argentina, Kenya) there is complete local discretion.

Where rates are determined locally, local governments first determine their expenditure requirements. They then subtract non-property tax revenues available (for example intergovernmental transfers, user fees and other revenues) from their expenditure requirements to determine how much they need to raise from property tax revenues. The resulting property tax requirements are divided by the taxable assessment to determine the property tax rate. Even where rates are locally determined, there are often limits placed on them by the central government. In Ontario, Canada, for example, tax rates imposed on non-residential property are effectively 'capped' at present in many localities.

If a local government is to make efficient fiscal decisions, it needs to weigh the benefits of the proposed services against the costs of providing them. If local governments do not finance these services themselves, then the link between expenditures and revenues is lost and the choice of services will not be based on an accurate perception of their cost. Setting tax rates at the local level places accountability for tax decisions at the local level. Local determination of tax rates is particularly important in the many countries in which a senior level of government determines the tax base.

Table 2.3 Characteristics of tax rate setting

	Different tax by property class	Treatment of farm properties	Local discretion over tax rates
OECD			
Australia	Yes	Rates often reduced at local discretion	Yes for local tax; limits on annual increase in revenues
Canada	Yes	Assessed as farm; lower tax rates in some provinces	Yes (restrictions apply in some provinces)
Germany	Yes	Base includes machinery/livestock; no business tax	Central base rates; locally determined leverage factors
Japan	No; assessment differentiation	Assessed as agricultural if outside urban area	Nationally set standard and maximum rates
United Kingdom	Two separate taxes	Exempt	Residential tax only; tax ratios for bands set centrally
Central and Eastern Europe			
Hungary	Yes	Some exemptions	Yes, within legal limits
Latvia	No	Rural land value proportional to average cadastral value	No, but local governments can grant relief
Poland	Yes	Separate taxes on agricultural land and forests	Yes, subject to prescribed minimum and maximum rates
Russia	Yes	Tax rates are different for agricultural land	Yes, within narrow range set by senior governments
Ukraine	No	Tax rates depend on use of land and fertility	No
Latin America			
Argentina	Yes	Value based on location, area, fertility, alternative uses	Yes

Country		Description	
Chile	No	Value in current use	No
Colombia	Yes	Assessed same as urban; tax rates must be the lowest	Yes, subject to central government limits
Mexico	Yes	Land value depends on land use; buildings on unit value of construction; sometimes lower tax rates	Yes
Nicaragua	No	Exemptions may include up to 1 hectare of land	No
Asia			
China	No	Separate tax on farm land occupation based on area	No
India	Yes	Rural similar to urban; lower rates and some exemptions	Yes, subject to state restrictions
Indonesia	No, assessment differentiation	Rural (and low-valued urban) housing mostly exempt	No, but can change valuation deduction
Philippines		Taxed at higher percentage of assessed value than residential	Yes, subject to minimum and maximum rates
Thailand	Yes	Lower rate for land used for annual crops	No
Africa			
Guinea	Yes	Agricultural land not taxed	No
Kenya	Yes, but rarely differentiated	If taxed, typically on the basis of area not value	Yes
South Africa	No; relief mechanisms used	Rural and agricultural properties included in tax base but not taxed	Yes
Tanzania	Yes	Rural property not taxed	Yes
Tunisia	No	Agricultural land not taxed	No

Local tax rates may have to be set within limits, however, to avoid distortions. A minimum tax rate may be needed to avoid distorting tax competition. Richer local governments may choose to lower tax rates to attract business. With their larger tax bases, they can provide equivalent services at lower rates than poorer competing regions. The resulting location shifts are not always allocatively distorting, but they are generally politically unwelcome. In addition, a maximum rate may be needed to prevent distorting tax-exporting, whereby local governments levy higher tax rates on industries in the belief that the ultimate tax burden will be borne by non-residents (Boadway and Kitchen, 1999, p. 373). Such tax-exporting severs the connection between payers and beneficiaries and renders decentralized decision-making about taxing and spending inefficient.

Differentiated tax rates

Many local governments levy rates that differ by property class.[7] Different tax rates may be imposed for different classes of property (residential, commercial and industrial, for example). This system gives local governments the power to manage the distribution of the tax burden across various property classes within their jurisdiction in addition to determining the size of the overall tax burden on taxpayers.

Generally, where such variable tax rates are applied, properties are assessed at a uniform ratio (100 percent or some lesser percentage) of market value. Another and probably more common way to differentiate among property classes is through a classified assessment system, as in the Philippines. Under this system, classifications or types of property are differentiated according to ratios of assessed value, but a uniform tax rate is applied. In terms of accountability, variable tax rates would be more visible and easier to understand for taxpayers than a classified assessment system, which may, unfortunately, be one reason that differentiated rates are less commonly employed than differentiated assessment ratios. Indeed, even when assessment ratios differ substantially among classes of property, the differentiation is more often a matter of practice than of law and can only be determined by special study.

Table 2.3 shows that in many of the countries covered in this book tax rates are differentiated by property class, or there is assessment differentiation or tax relief for some classes of property. Variable tax rates (or other differentiation of property taxes among property classes) may be justified on a number of grounds:

- On the basis of fairness with respect to benefits received, it can be argued that the benefits from local public services are different for different property classes. In particular, a case can be made on benefit grounds for taxing non-residential properties at a lower rate than residential properties (Kitchen and Slack, 1993). Few examples of differentiation in this direction appear to exist, however.[8]

- On efficiency grounds, it has been argued that property taxes should be heavier on those components of the tax base that are least elastic in supply. Since business capital tends to be more mobile than residential capital, efficiency arguments again lead to the conclusion that business property should be taxed more lightly than residential property. In reality, however, as discussed later in this chapter, lower rates are generally applied to residential properties.

- Variable tax rates can also be used to achieve certain land use objectives. Since higher property taxes on buildings tend to slow development and lower taxes speed up development, a municipal policy to develop some neighborhoods instead of others might support differential taxes in different locations as well as for different property classes.

An additional question about property tax rates is whether the tax is levied at a flat or graduated rate. In many countries, as discussed in the case study chapters, some graduation is in effect introduced by exempting low-value properties. In a few instances (for example, some provinces in Argentina) the tax rate increases with the value of the taxed property. In Thailand, the tax rate also increases, although in a peculiar way which has the result that the rates actually end up being regressive. Many countries impose higher taxes on 'idle lands' – though seldom with much effect, as discussed later in this chapter.

Particularly in rural areas some countries have occasionally attempted to use progressive land taxes as, in effect, proxy income taxes by attempting first to aggregate all land owned by a single person and then to impose a graduated tax. Such schemes have generally failed, however, owing both to the administrative difficulty of assembling the information – particularly when properties are located in different jurisdictions – and the political unreality of attempting to, as it were, accomplish 'land reform by stealth' in this way (Bird, 1974).

The level of tax rates
One of the more striking features of land and property taxation in many developing countries is how very low the tax rates are. Even in countries such as Argentina, in which progressive rates are imposed, the top rate (on assessed value) seldom exceeds much more than 1 percent, and it is often lower. In Indonesia, for example, the centrally set land tax rate is only 0.5 percent. Moreover, as noted in Chapter 1, as a rule the effective rate of property taxes is, owing to low assessment ratios and poor enforcement,

much lower than the nominal or statutory rate. Other factors resulting in low effective tax rates in many countries are lags in reassessment and the inadequacy of adjustment for value changes. In the Philippines, for example, where the nominal rate is as high as 2 percent, the effective rate has been estimated at only 0.07 percent (Guevara et al., 1994).

Some special cases
In almost every country, single-family owner-occupied residences are favored, as are farm properties, while non-residential property is subjected to higher taxes.

Owner-occupied residences
Many, perhaps most, countries favor single-family residential owner-occupied properties over multi-residential rental properties and commercial and industrial properties. Favorable treatment of single-family residential properties is achieved in three ways. First, the assessment system deliberately under-assesses single-family residential property compared to apartments or commercial and industrial property of comparable value. In the United States, as an example, the average effective property tax rate on multi-family residences is about 40 percent higher than that on single-family houses.[9] Second, many jurisdictions have legislated lower tax rates on single-family residential property. In many cases, lower-valued houses are simply exempted. Finally, special property tax relief measures are often provided to residential property-owners (and, in some cases, tenants) in the form of tax credits, homeowner grants, or tax deferrals. These measures are not generally available to non-residential properties.

The differential treatment of residences does not reflect the differential use of services by different property types. In many countries, single-family owner-occupied residential properties are presumably favored largely on political grounds: residential homeowners are much more likely to vote in local elections than are tenants.

Non-residential property
Non-residential properties include a wide variety of property uses such as commercial uses (offices, banks, retail outlets, restaurants, hotels), industrial uses (mines, manufacturing plants, shipyards), and special uses (pipelines and railway rights of way).

In most countries, such property is both in law and practice subject to higher taxes than residential property. There is little economic rationale for the higher taxation of non-residential property. Differentially higher taxation distorts land use decisions favoring residential use over commercial and industrial use. A similar rate on both uses would ensure that the choice is based on the highest and best use (Maurer and Paugam, 2000). Special taxation of one factor of production (real property) may also distort productive efficiency by inducing a different choice of factor mix in producing goods and services.

In addition, as mentioned earlier, the ability of non-residential property-owners to export property taxes to residents of other jurisdictions may require the imposition of limits on the local government's ability to determine tax rates on this class of property. The burden of non-residential property taxes is borne by the consumers of the products or services produced utilizing such property to an extent depending on market conditions. If the product or service is exported outside the jurisdiction, consumers in other jurisdictions may bear part of the tax. Such tax-exporting is inequitable because the same benefits of local expenditures require different tax prices in different jurisdictions depending on the degree of exporting. It is also inefficient in distorting development patterns because property taxes paid locally are not related to the benefits received locally. Moreover, it reduces democratic accountability because those bearing the burden of the tax are not the same as those enjoying the benefits.

Lower taxation of particular areas within or between municipalities in order to attract commercial and industrial development will also distort land use decisions. In terms of inter-metropolitan location decisions, business activity is most influenced by market conditions, the availability and cost of a skilled labor force, the presence of necessary production materials, proximity to markets and quality of life. If property taxes account for a relatively small proportion of the total costs of a business, any reduction in the tax is unlikely to be large enough to initiate a relocation decision or to encourage significant business activity. Intra-metropolitan location decisions, on the other hand, may be affected by property tax differentials. Within a large metropolitan area, market conditions and cost variables tend to be reasonably uniform. Lower property taxes in one community will generate lower costs at the margin and higher profits for businesses locating in that particular community. Tax competition among municipalities could lead to lower municipal revenues without any real impact on allocative decisions at the local level (Maurer and Paugam, 2000). One way to minimize such undesirable tax competition is for the central government to set minimum tax limits, as mentioned earlier.

Agricultural land and property
As Table 2.3 shows, in most of the 25 case study countries, agricultural properties tend to be treated on explicitly favorable terms. As noted above, they are also often assessed differently, again probably in a way that ends up treating them favorably. An interesting exception is the Philippines where,

unusually, farm properties are taxed on a higher percentage of market value than residential properties. In most countries, however, rural and especially farm properties are favored in a variety of ways, as indicated in Table 2.3 and discussed in more detail in the case study chapters – for example, through lower assessments, exemptions for part or all of the farm property, lower tax rates on farms, or farm tax rebates. In some countries, as in the African cases included in this book, much agricultural land is simply not taxed.

Rather than assessing farms at their market value (which reflects the highest and best use), farms are often assessed at their value in current use. The value of a farm for tax purposes is thus determined by its selling price if it were to continue to be used as a farm. Alternative uses of the farm (for example as a housing subdivision), or its speculative value, are not considered in the determination of value.

In Ontario, Canada, for example, farms are assessed in current use. Moreover, the farm tax rate is set by provincial law at only 25 percent of the residential tax rate established by the local government. Even when land is being used as farmland simply while awaiting development (urbanization), new values are phased in over stages, with increases being triggered by when the land is registered for subdivision and when a building permit has been issued.

Such favorable treatment of agricultural land is usually designed to preserve it from conversion to urban use. It has been argued, however, that basing the property tax on value in current use is not sufficient to preserve farmland because the resulting tax differential is unlikely, given the generally low effective tax rates on land, to be large enough to compensate for the much higher prices that would be paid if the land were converted to urban use (Maurer and Paugam, 2000).[10] Furthermore, favorable treatment of rural land can increase speculation at the urban fringe and hence end up increasing urban land prices.

There is, of course, an extensive literature on the theory and practice of agricultural land taxation that cannot be discussed in detail in the present book. Bird (1974), for example, argues that refined attempts to impose 'efficient' and 'equitable' land taxes have generally failed for administrative and political reasons. He concludes that a simple uniform tax on a classified area basis is probably the best form of agricultural land tax for most developing countries. Strasma et al. (1987) reviewed subsequent experience and again found little evidence that countries had made much effective use of land taxes in rural areas. More recently, Skinner (1991), Hoff (1991) and Khan (2001) looked in detail at the economics of agricultural land taxation and suggested that the impact of such taxes depended largely upon their effects on uncertainty and on the institutional framework within which production risks are shared. All these authors found that a serious barrier to effective rural land taxation was the high administrative cost of such taxes – a point emphasized also for transition countries by Ott (1999) – thus reinforcing the conclusion cited above from Bird (1974). Of course, as stressed in Chapter 1, the political obstacles to rural land tax reform are also high in many countries.

Tax administration

'Tax administration is tax policy' is a common observation in tax discussions in developing and transitional countries. In no area of taxation does this saying ring truer than with respect to property tax, because no area of taxation is more dependent on administration. How well land and property taxes are administered not only impacts on their revenue but also affects their equity and efficiency. In many countries, poor tax administration is an impediment to implementing the property tax. Often, local authorities do not have the capacity to administer the tax. Many administrative functions are performed manually rather than being computerized. The result is that the revenue base does not include all taxable properties, collection rates are low, and enforcement is almost non-existent. Even in countries with relatively good property tax administration, there are often problems updating values on a regular basis.

Three key steps are involved in the process of taxing real property: (1) identification of the properties being taxed, (2) preparation of a tax roll (which contains a description of the property and the amount of assessment) and responding to assessment appeals, and (3) issuing tax bills, collecting taxes and dealing with arrears. We discuss each in turn.

Property identification

The first step in levying a property tax is to identify the property and to determine the owner (or other person responsible for tax liability). A fiscal cadastre requires the following minimal information for each property: a description, a definition of its boundaries (using cadastral maps), ownership, and the value of land and improvements.[11] The preparation of cadastral maps is an essential element of property identification. It is necessary to establish a complete inventory of all properties and to assign a unique property identification number to each parcel to allow for the tracking of all parcels. Property identifiers also allow for the linking of assessment, billing and property transfer records.

Property identification requires that existing information on properties within the jurisdiction be updated and made consistent. As shown in many of the case studies, at present much of the needed information is held by different agencies – in Latvia, for example, by the State Land Service, the Title Book Service and the State Tax Service. Moreover, in many developing countries, much of the needed information is simply not available to anyone in the 'official' information system. De Soto (2000), for example, argues that, for Latin America, the relevant information is not fully legally recorded for 80 percent or more of land and property.[12] For a property tax to work properly, the information that needs to be collected for each property includes, for example: an assessment roll number of the property, the address, the owner(s) of the property, the area in square meters, the age of the unit, and whether it has been renovated.[13] The information collected has to be reported in a consistent way and a process needs to be established to update it on an annual basis (Slack et al., 1998).

The process of property identification is often very difficult in developing countries and transitional economies. Revenue base information is generally neither up to date nor complete. In Kenya, for example, the fiscal cadastre and valuation rolls include only between 20 and 70 percent of the total taxable land; in Guinea, the tax roll in 1999 covered only about one-third of taxable property. Similarly, the information to support a fiscal cadastre on a consistent nation-wide basis is often fragmented between the central and local governments. In Hungary, for example, the Land Offices of the Ministry of Agriculture manage the legal cadastre but have no information on property values. The Duty Offices at the local level keep transactions records. Tax departments within local governments keep information on residential units. Technical departments within local governments maintain information on building permits, local master plans for land use zoning and information on public utility infrastructure. These databases are not integrated.

Another common problem is often the lack of an adequate system for monitoring and recording land transfers. In the Philippines, for example, the law requires the Register of Deeds, Notaries Public and Building Officials to submit documents on property transfers to the assessors. In practice, however, assessors seem generally to rely on taxpayers for this information. As is not uncommon in developing countries, it is often easier in the Philippines to get (unreliable) information from taxpayers than (probably no more reliable) information from other agencies. In many developing countries property records are not computerized. In Kenya, for example, property records are kept manually and maintained in an *ad hoc* manner. Because it is too expensive for local governments to keep a good record of property identification data in Thailand, taxes are simply not collected on some properties. Thailand is not unique in this respect, of course.

Assessment and appeals
For the costs of local government to be shared fairly among taxpayers, property taxes have to be based on assessments that are uniform within each jurisdiction. Uniform assessments may be easier to achieve where the assessment function is centralized. One study, for example, found that the use of

county rather than local assessors resulted in more uniform residential assessments in US jurisdictions (Strauss and Sullivan, 1998). Another study suggests that, to the extent that there are economies of scale in the assessment function, these are more likely to be achieved at the central (state) government level (Sjoquist and Walker, 1999). Of course, one way to achieve economies of scale while maintaining local assessment might be by contracting out the assessment function (Bell, 1999).

Table 2.4 shows the level of government responsible for the assessment function in each of the 25 case study countries. The assessment function seems to be essentially local in about half the cases and central or regional in the others. In many cases, however, the detailed assessment methodology is established by the central government even when assessment is a local function.

Fair and productive property taxes require not only a good initial assessment but also periodic revaluation to reflect changes in value. Frequent valuations maintain the legitimacy of the tax and reduce the risk of sudden, dramatic shifts in tax burdens from large increases in assessed values. For these reasons, the valuation cycle needs to be fairly short.

In a value-based system where property values are changing, a shorter time frame for reassessments would obviously be better at reflecting current market conditions. Indexing (for example by the rate of inflation) as used in some countries (for example, Colombia) is not as good as reassessment because property values change at a different rate in different neighborhoods and for different property characteristics. Fairness is not achieved when property assessments are merely increased by a common factor on an annual basis. Nonetheless, where financial resources are insufficient to do regular reassessments, indexing may be useful. Indexing (over a three- to five-year period) that reflects relative price changes among locations and property markets can both ameliorate taxpayers' discomfort with large assessment changes and improve information about market trends for assessment administrators.

Table 2.4 shows great diversity across countries with respect to the frequency of reassessment, ranging from annual to infrequent. The general range is from three to ten years. Of course, the time periods mentioned in the table are those specified in the law. In many instances, as discussed in the case studies, the pace of revaluation in the real world has been considerably more dilatory.

As with property identification, the problems encountered with assessment and reassessment often stem from lack of resources and expertise. In Hungary, for example, assessors are not knowledgeable about the technical issues involved in making sales comparisons for estimating market value. In the Philippines, assessment suffers from a lack of technically qualified staff and assessment tools. The same may be said of many other developing and transition countries.

Table 2.4 Assessment and appeals

	Responsibility for assessment	Frequency of reassessment	Appeals mechanism
OECD			
Australia	State government for state and local taxes	Different in each state; ranges from annual to 7 years	State commissioner; courts
Canada	Generally provincial	Different in different provinces	Provincial review board; provincial courts
Germany	Local governments	By law, every 6 years (actually use price-adjusted 1964 values)	Changes in standard assessment are rare
Japan	Local governments based on a uniform national formula	Every 3 years; annually for business assets	Valuation Council and Review Committees
United Kingdom	Central government	No revaluations on res'l; 5 years for non-res'l	Valuation tribunals; High Court
Central and Eastern Europe			
Hungary	Local governments	At local discretion; infrequent	n.a.
Latvia	Central government	Every 5 years	Head of local government council
Poland	Local governments (using information in central registries)	Annual	Local council, regional appeal board, Administrative Appeals Court
Russia	Central government	n.a.	No appeal mechanism
Ukraine	Central government – state tax administration	n.a.	n.a.
Latin America			
Argentina	Provincial and local governments	Periodic adjustments	Formal appeal processes at both gov't levels

Country	Administration	Frequency	Appeals
Chile	National tax administration with local input	Between 3 and 5 years but often postponed	Internal Tax Service, Special Appeals Court on Property Valuation, Supreme Court
Colombia	Local governments	Every 5 years	Cadastral Division, petition tax administration
Mexico	State and local governments jointly	Annual	Fiscal authority, judicial branch
Nicaragua	National tax administration	Infrequent	n.a.
Asia			
China	Local tax office directly under the state council	Once a year for urban real estate tax	Committee
India	Local authorities; some state assessment authorities	Periodic revision of assessments	Appellate Authority; appeal against revision
Indonesia	Central tax department	Every 3 years (annual in cases of rapid development)	Objections to Directorate of Property Tax
Philippines	Provincial and local governments	Every 3 years	Local and Central Boards of Appeal
Thailand	Local governments	Every 4 years	n.a.
Africa			
Guinea	Central government	n.a.	n.a.
Kenya	Local governments	Every 10 years, but generally longer	Objections handled by local councils
South Africa	Local governments	Every 4 or 5 years but not always done	Valuation board and valuation appeal board
Tanzania	Local authorities (funded by central government)	Every 5 years (or longer if approved by Minister)	Appeals Tribunal
Tunisia	Urban municipalities within nationally set ranges	Every 10 years with annual updates	Appeals on tax rate categories

Another problem with keeping assessments up to date in many countries relates to the lack of integration between different government agencies mentioned earlier. If, for example, a property is sold, and the information is recorded in the notarial office or land registry, notification should be sent to the fiscal cadastral system of the new recorded sales value. If a building permit is issued, or a property is subdivided, again the recording office should send notification to the office responsible for maintaining the property tax roll. Such processes do not work well, or at all, in many countries.

Finally, no matter how well designed and implemented it may be, any property tax system may make mistakes. An essential component of a good system is thus an error-correction mechanism, and one critical element of such a mechanism is a process by which taxpayers have an opportunity to appeal their assessment if they think it is wrong. Generally, the appeals process includes an informal review by the valuation office to correct factual errors and differences in views of the assessed value. If differences are not resolved at this stage, they proceed to a valuation review board comprising experts in valuation. In some countries, there is a third stage whereby taxpayers can appeal the decision of the valuation review board to a specialized tax court. This latter stage may require legal representation. Table 2.4 summarizes the assessment appeal mechanisms in the 25 countries covered in this study.

Although appeal systems are both desirable and necessary, in practice they may sometimes result in increasing the inequity of property taxes, simply because they are invariably most utilized by better-off taxpayers who both have more to gain and can better afford to pursue legal redress. In many countries, however, the reality is that, although there may be an appeal system in law, in practice it seems almost never to be utilized – perhaps because the taxes imposed are so small that appealing them is not worth while for those most likely to do so, perhaps because the same (well-off) people may have other, less formal, ways of seeking relief (corruption), or perhaps because the formal system may be so cumbersome and difficult to use that it is not worth pursuing.

Tax collection and arrears

Finally, tax collection involves sending out tax bills, collecting the taxes and ensuring payment. Table 2.5 shows that tax collection is usually, but not always, a local government function. In terms of the formula set out in Chapter 1, at the very least local governments thus almost always have some discretion in determining the size of the last ratio mentioned there – the ratio of taxes collected to taxes assessed. In a few instances, however, such as Guinea and Tunisia (and likely most of francophone Africa) as well as Chile, they cannot even do this.

If the property tax is not paid within a specified time period after the due date, interest and a late fee are generally charged. In cases of long-term delinquency, other enforcement measures are usually taken, eventually leading to the sale of the property to satisfy the tax obligation. Such sales are rare in most countries, however. Often, a more effective enforcement mechanism (at least for properties transferred within the formal legal system) is that property transfers are not permitted unless property taxes are paid.

Tax arrears reduce the revenues generated from the property tax. Table 2.5 shows the extent of tax arrears for those countries for which the information was available. Although tax arrears as a proportion of taxes collectible are low in most developed countries (for example, 3 to 4 percent in Japan and the UK), they can be very large in some developing and transitional countries (for example, 50 percent in parts of Kenya and the Philippines and the stock of overdue payables is almost 70 percent of the estimated annual flow of payables for the land tax in Russia). Tax arrears obviously tend to be highest in countries that do not have sufficient resources, expertise, or will to administer the property tax and where enforcement is weak.

Other taxes on land

The preceding discussion, like the following case study chapters, focused essentially on direct taxes on land and property, and in particular on local property taxes. In many countries, however, many other taxes that to some extent fall on land – transfer taxes, stamp taxes, capital gains taxes, value-added taxes, inheritance taxes – as Table 2.6 suggests.

Perhaps the most common alternative form of land tax is one on land transfers. In fact, land transfers may sometimes be subject to various taxes and charges – land transfer taxes, stamp duties, notarial fees, registry charges, value-added taxes and, in some instances, succession and gift taxes.[14] While it is beyond our scope to discuss these taxes in detail here, it should nonetheless be noted, as David Ricardo pointed out two centuries ago, that taxes on the transfer of property are the ultimate 'anti-market' tax.[15]

Such taxes discourage the development and formalization of land markets. Their existence, often at surprisingly high rates, in a number of countries is presumably attributable primarily to administrative convenience: something happens that comes to the attention of the authorities. The 'taxable event' – the recorded exchange of title – is visible, even if the true value of the transaction usually is not. Any country at all concerned with efficient land use in which land transfer taxes are imposed at high rates, however, would seem well advised to consider lowering such taxes and to make up any revenue loss by, for instance, strengthening basic property taxes.

Many of the other 'non-basic' taxes on land and property noted in Table 2.6 represent attempts to use land taxation for essentially non-fiscal purposes

Table 2.5 Collection and arrears

	Responsibility for collection	Tax arrears as percentage of tax levy
OECD		
Australia	Local governments	n.a.
Canada	Local governments	Generally less than 5%
Germany	Local governments	Less than 1%
Japan	Local governments	2.6%
United Kingdom	Local governments	4% for council tax; 2% for non-domestic rates
Central and Eastern Europe		
Hungary	Local governments	2–11% (includes only partial payments)
Latvia	Local governments	n.a.
Poland	Local governments; national tax office in smaller places	8% for legal entities and 9.5 % for natural persons (Krakow)
Russia	Local branch of federal tax service	Stock of overdue payables 69% of estimated annual flow of land tax payable
Ukraine	Central government	29%
Latin America		
Argentina	Provincial and local governments	20–25%
Chile	Central government	4% in 1991 (owing to amnesty); 29% in 1990
Colombia	Local governments	24.9% in Bogota[1]
Mexico	Local governments	n.a.
Nicaragua	Local governments	n.a.

Asia		
China	Local tax bureaux	n.a.
India	Local governments	33–67% depending on state
Indonesia	Local governments	9% (in urban areas); 15% (in rural areas)
Philippines	Provinces (sometimes delegated to local governments)	53% (cities); 46% (provinces); 23% (municipalities)
Thailand	Local governments	n.a.
Africa		
Guinea	Central government	26%
Kenya	Local governments	40–90%
South Africa	Local governments	n.a.
Tanzania	Local governments	50–60% in Dar Es Salaam
Tunisia	Central government	45%

Note: [1] This is the ratio of the accrued liability relative to collections in 2001.

Table 2.6   Other taxes on land

OECD

Australia
State stamp duties; state fees to developers for infrastructure; water and sewer charges based on land value; capital gains tax (not on principal residence)

Canada
Local improvement charges (same base as property tax); land transfer taxes; municipal development charges; capital gains except on principal residence

Germany
Real estate acquisition tax; state inheritance and gift tax; capital gains tax except sale of owner-occupied residence for reinvestment in another

Japan
City planning tax; prefectural real property acquisition tax; prefectural property tax on business assets,[1] national registration and license tax; inheritance tax, capital gains tax

United Kingdom
Stamp tax on property transfers; property included in base of inheritance tax; capital gains on sale of property is included in income tax

Central and Eastern Europe

Hungary
Land transfer tax; gift and inheritance tax

Latvia
n.a.

Poland
Three transfer taxes; 'adjaceny' fee (betterment levy); tax on increase attributable to land use change on property sale; inheritance and gift taxes

Russia
Federal succession and gift tax

Ukraine
Fee to extend private apartments; hotel fees; resort fees; fees for permission to build residential constructions

Latin America

Argentina
Betterment taxes; national land transfer tax; land and houses included in national tax on personal goods

50

Chile	n.a.
Colombia	Urban outlining tax when construction of new buildings or repair of existing ones occur; registry tax on transfer of land; valorization contribution
Nicaragua	Building licenses
Mexico	Land transfer taxes; development charges; betterment levies; value increment tax
Asia	
China	Business tax on transfer of intangible assets; land appreciation tax on transfer of real estate; deed tax on transferees of land and houses
India	State stamp duty
Indonesia	Land and building acquisition tax; central land transaction tax (revenues shared with local governments)
Philippines	Special education tax; tax on idle lands; special levy on lands benefiting from public works projects; additional tax in Manila for flood control and drainage fund; central government capital gains tax; provincial and municipal land transfer tax
Thailand	Property transfer registration fee
Africa	
Guinea	n.a.
Kenya	n.a.
South Africa	National transfer duty; estate duty or donations tax; capital gains tax; minor local taxes on property tax base, e.g. health rate, water rate, sewerage rate etc.
Tanzania	'Special rate' for capital works that benefit only some property-owners (permitted but never been used)
Tunisia	n.a.

Note: [1] Prefectures can levy a fixed property tax on the asset value of large business assets in excess of municipal taxation limits.

– to reap 'unearned increments' (*plusvalía* in Colombia, for example), to recoup the costs of public investment expenditures (development charges in Canada, special assessments and betterment levies in various countries), or to discourage the holding of 'idle land' (the Philippines and penalty rates in some Latin American countries).

Such non-fiscal objectives of land taxation have received much attention in the literature over the years. In practice, however, such special land tax measures seem to have had little impact. One important point that is not usually noted clearly enough in this respect is that there are two dimensions to the non-fiscal impact (for example on land use patterns) of land and property taxes.

On the one hand, such impacts clearly occur and ought therefore to be taken explicitly into account in designing and evaluating property tax systems. Advocates of land value taxation, for example, argue that taxing land alone is more favorable to investment and growth than taxing land and improvements (Netzer, 1998). The uneven way in which property taxes are often applied within urban areas – with differential taxes on housing and business, for example, and different impacts in older and newer areas – may affect the pattern of urban growth (Oldman et al., 1967; Slack, 2002). Rural development patterns may also be affected by land taxation (Bird, 1974). Sensible fiscal (and land) planning must certainly take such effects into account, and in some instances, as already mentioned in Chapter 1, the design of taxes may be adjusted accordingly.

On the other hand, the temptation to attempt to use special land taxes explicitly to achieve desired non-fiscal outcomes seems generally to be resisted. From Britain to Colombia, from the Philippines to Tunisia, instances of tax design intended primarily to achieve such objectives are easy to find, as illustrated in some of the case study chapters. What is much more difficult to find, however, is any evidence that such tax gadgets produce beneficial results. Indeed, some have argued (Bird, 1974) that in reality the time and effort devoted to designing land taxes intended primarily to achieve non-fiscal purposes has detracted from the more important task of implementing an effective and efficient revenue source for local governments. Rural land reform, the control of urban land speculation, reaping land value increments for public purposes – all these may be worthy objectives but attempting to achieve them indirectly through the clever design of fiscal instruments appears to have been counterproductive.

As an example, the *plusvalía* or land value increment tax found in a number of Latin American countries (Smolka and Furtado, 2001) is no doubt a good idea in principle. But no one, anywhere, has been able to get very far with this approach in practice: witness the account in Hood (1976) of Britain's futile attempts to tax land value increments in the 1950s and 1960s.

Similarly, attempts to adjust rural land taxation to, as it were, achieve land reform by stealth, as has frequently been proposed in India, for example – where the issue is especially salient because of the unfortunate constitutional exclusion of agricultural income from the central income tax – seem doomed. As Hirschman (1967) has noted, what cannot be done openly for political reasons can seldom be accomplished in an indirect manner either, not least when it is adverse to the perceived interests of the landowning élite.

In the end, the only 'non-basic' property tax that really seems worth exploring in most countries is likely some form of special assessment or betterment tax. Countries such as Colombia have had considerable success in recouping some of the benefits to adjacent property-owners from certain public investments through such means. It is not an easy or costless procedure to establish and operate such a system in the conditions of a developing country (Rhoads and Bird, 1970), however. Perhaps for this reason, few countries appear to have managed to do much with this fiscal instrument. Similarly, although development charges, exactions and other forms of 'value capture' have been increasingly employed in some US states and Canadian provinces, and some useful lessons for other countries may perhaps be learned from this experience (Slack, 2002), it seems likely that the role of such devices is also likely to be very limited in the circumstances of most developing and transition countries.

Notes

1. By assigning properties to broad categories rather than assigning a taxable value to each one, the council tax achieves simplicity and stability at the expense of accuracy. Furthermore, because the council tax uses an estimate of market value at a particular point in time (1 April 1991) and then freezes assessments for the foreseeable future, it will have the same implications as any out-of-date assessment system: inequities will increase over time.
2. See also Datta (2002) on the effects of rent controls on Indian property taxes.
3. As noted above, if rental value were based on highest and best use, then vacant land would be taxable; the value would have to be estimated on the basis of other properties. Even if rental value were based on current use, it might be possible to assign a non-zero value to vacant land.
4. Taiwan is an example (Youngman and Malme, 1994, p. 12). This idea is an old one, used in Australia in the nineteenth century, for example, as noted by Bird (1974). It has seldom been effective.
5. Mann (2001) independently made a similar recommendation for Indonesia.
6. For a brief review of the past history of this idea, and the problems with it, see Bird (1984).
7. Property tax rates can also vary according to the services received. The case of Tunisia mentioned earlier is one example. More commonly, in some jurisdictions, there is a general tax rate across the city and a special area rate or additional surcharge in those parts of the city that receive services only provided to them, for example garbage collection, street lighting, transit and so on. Special area rates, which are earmarked for services in those locations, approximate a benefit charge.
8. On the contrary, as Bird (2003) discusses, businesses are usually overtaxed in economic terms.

9. See study cited in note 5 of Chapter 1 above.
10. Note that this is the inverse of the comment later in this chapter with respect to the general ineffectiveness of 'idle land' penalty taxes.
11. We do not discuss cadastres in detail here. For a useful review, see Dale (1976). A useful review of the entire property tax administration process is United Nations (1968). A more up-to-date review is Keith (1993).
12. King (2003) further explores the extensive 'extralegal' world of housing and land titles in Latin America. For a detailed analysis of these and other key questions of land policy in developing and transitional countries, see Deininger (2003).
13. The cost of collecting the information could be added to the tax bill. In some Canadian provinces, for example, the assessment function is performed by a corporation that represents municipalities in the province. The cost of the assessment function is passed on to municipalities who add this cost on to property tax bills.
14. The treatment of land and real property under a VAT is a complex issue. Although every country discussed in this book has some type of VAT, we have information on only a few of them. In Japan, for example, new construction is taxed at the 'standard' VAT rate, while in Canada such construction is taxed at a lower rate, in Germany it is exempted (but subject to an alternative tax), and in the UK, while residential construction is zero-rated, commercial buildings are taxed at the standard rate. All four of the countries mentioned exempt sales of residential real estate, but Canada taxes sales of other real property at a lower rate, Japan does so at the standard rate, and the other two normally exempt such sales (Cnossen, 1996).
15. For an analysis of such 'market-discouraging' transfer taxes, and references to the literature, see Bird (1967).

References

Bahl, Roy (1998), 'Land Taxes versus Property Taxes in Developing and Transition Countries,' in Dick Netzer (ed.), *Land Value Taxation: Can It and Will It Work Today?*, Cambridge, MA: Lincoln Institute of Land Policy.

Bahl, Roy (2001), 'Property Taxes in Developing Countries: An Assessment in 2001,' Lincoln Lecture, Cambridge, MA: Lincoln Institute of Land Policy, 23 October.

Bahl, Roy and Johannes F. Linn (1992), *Urban Public Finance in Developing Countries*, New York: Oxford University Press.

Bell, Michael E. (1999), 'An Optimal Property Tax: Concepts and Practices,' Washington, DC: World Bank.

Bird, Richard M. (1967), 'Stamp Tax Reform in Colombia,' *Bulletin for International Fiscal Documentation*, **21** (June), 247–55.

Bird, Richard M. (1974), *Taxing Agricultural Land in Developing Countries*, Cambridge, MA: Harvard University Press.

Bird, Richard M. (1984), 'Put Up or Shut Up: Self Assessment and Asymmetric Information,' *Journal of Policy Analysis and Management*, **3**, 618–20.

Bird, Richard M. (2003) 'A New Look at Local Business Taxes,' *Tax Notes International*, **30** (7), 695–711.

Boadway, Robin W. and Harry M. Kitchen (1999), *Canadian Tax Policy*, 3rd edn, Toronto: Canadian Tax Foundation.

Cnossen, Sijbren (1996), 'VAT Treatment of Immovable Property,' in Victor Thuronyi (ed.), *Tax Law Design and Drafting*, vol. 1, Washington, DC: International Monetary Fund.

Dale, P.F. (1976), *Cadastral Surveys within the Commonwealth*, London: HMSO.

Datta, Abhijit (2002), 'Rent Control Law and Its Effect on Property Tax in India,' paper presented to national seminar on Reforming the Property Tax, Bangalore, India, February.

De Soto, Hernando (2000), *The Mystery of Capital*, New York: Basic Books.

Deininger, Klaus (2003), *Land Policies for Growth and Poverty Reduction*, New York: Oxford University Press and World Bank.

George, Henry ([1879] 1979), *Progress and Poverty*, New York: Robert Schalkenbach Foundation.

Guevara, Milwida M., Joyce P. Gracia and Ma. Victoria C. Espano (1994), 'A Study of the Performance and Cost Effectiveness of the Real Property Tax,' Manila, July.

Hirschman, Albert O. (1967), *Journeys toward Progress*, New York: Twentieth Century Fund.

Hoff, Karla (1991), 'Land Taxes, Output Taxes, and Sharecropping: Was Henry George Right?' *World Bank Economic Review*, **5**, 93–111.

Holland, Daniel M. and William Vaughan (1970), 'Self-Assessment of Property Taxes,' in Arthur P. Becker (ed.), *Land and Property Taxation*, Madison, WI: University of Wisconsin Press.

Hood, Christopher (1976), *The Limits of Administration*, London: John Wiley.

Keith, Simon H. (1993), *Property Tax in Anglophone Africa: A Practical Manual*, World Bank Technical Paper Number 209, Africa Department Technical Series, Washington.

Khan, Mohammed H. (2001), 'Agricultural Taxation in Developing Countries: A Survey of Issues and Policy', *Agricultural Economics*, **24**, 315–28.

King, Winter (2003), 'Illegal Settlements and the Impact of Title Programs,' *Harvard International Law Journal*, **44** (2), 433–71.

Kitchen, Harry (1992), *Property Taxation in Canada*, Toronto: Canadian Tax Foundation.

Kitchen, Harry and Enid Slack (1993), *Business Property Taxation*, Government and Competitiveness Project, School of Policy Studies, Queen's University, Kingston, Canada.

Kitchen, Harry and François Vaillancourt (1990), 'The Federal Grants-in-Lieu of Property Taxes Program: An Assessment,' *Canadian Tax Journal*, **38**, 928–36.

Mann, Arthur J. (2001), 'Local Government Taxation: Standard International Practices,' paper presented at PEG/USAID Conference on Domestic Trade, Decentralization, and Globalization, Jakarta, Indonesia, April.

Maurer, Robert and Anne Paugam (2000), 'Reform toward Ad Valorem Property Tax in Transition Economies: Fiscal and Land Use Benefits,' Land and Real Estate Initiative, Background Series 13, World Bank, Washington, June.

Netzer, Dick (1966), *Economics of the Property Tax*, Washington, DC: The Brookings Institution.

Netzer, Dick (1998), 'The Relevance and Feasibility of Land Value Taxation in the Rich Countries,' in Netzer (ed.), *Land Value Taxation: Can It and Will It Work Today?*, Cambridge, MA: Lincoln Institute of Land Policy.

Oates, Wallace E. and Robert M. Schwab (1997), 'The Impact of Urban Land Taxation: The Pittsburgh Experience,' *National Tax Journal*, **50**, 1–21.

Oldman, Oliver et al. (1967), *Financing Urban Development in Mexico City*, Cambridge, MA: Harvard University Press.

Ott, Attiat F. (1999), 'Land Taxation and Tax Reform in the Republic of Estonia,' *Assessment Journal*, **6** (January/February), 40–49.

Rhoads, William G. and Richard M. Bird (1969), 'The Valorization Tax in Colombia: An Example for other Developing Countries?' in Arthur P. Becker (ed.), *Land and Building Taxes*, Madison, WI: University of Wisconsin Press.

Skinner, Jonathan (1991), 'If Agricultural Land Taxation is So Efficient, Why is it So Rarely Used?' *World Bank Economic Review*, **5**, 113–33.

Slack, Enid (2002), *Municipal Finance and the Pattern of Urban Growth*, Commentary No. 160, Toronto: C.D. Howe Institute, February.

Slack, Enid, John LaFaver and Ihor Shpak (1998), 'Property Tax in Ukraine: Third Attempt,' *Budget and Fiscal Review*, Second Quarter 1998, Fiscal Analysis Office, Verkhovna Rada, Kyiv, Ukraine.

Sjoquist, David L. and Mary B. Walker (1999), 'Economies of Scale in Property Tax Assessment,' *National Tax Journal*, **52**, 207–20.

Smolka, Martim and Fernanda Furtado (2001), 'Lessons from the Latin American Experience with Value Capture,' *Land Lines*, Lincoln Institute of Land Policy, July, pp. 5–7.

Strasma, John et al. (1987), *Impact of Agricultural Land Revenue System on Agricultural land Usage*, Burlington, VT: Associates in Rural Development.

Strauss, Robert P. and Sean R. Sullivan (1998), 'The Political Economy of the Property Tax: Assessor Authority and Assessment Uniformity,' *State Tax Notes*, 21 December.

Tanzi, Vito (2001), 'Pitfalls on the Road to Fiscal Decentralization,' Working Paper No. 19, Carnegie Endowment for International Peace, Washington, DC.
United Nations (1968), *Manual of Land Tax Administration*, New York.
Youngman, Joan M. and Jane H. Malme (1994), *An International Survey of Taxes on Land and Buildings*, Deventer: Kluwer Law and Taxation Publishers.

3   Reforming property taxes

Richard M. Bird and Enid Slack

Over the last few years, a number of the countries included in this book have implemented, or attempted to implement, property tax reform. The nature and extent of reform have of course been different in different countries, depending on the need for reform and the context in which the reform took place. For example, some countries have made changes to the tax base and tax rates; others have focused reform efforts on improvements to the administration of the tax. In this chapter we briefly review recent experience with property tax reform in six countries: Canada, the United Kingdom, Hungary, Colombia, Indonesia and Kenya.[1]

Reasons for reform

The reasons for undertaking property tax reform vary from country to country. In some countries, property tax reform was part of an overall reform of local government structure and finance. In other countries, it was part of a reform of the overall tax system. In still other countries, property tax reform has been carried out on its own, without being part of other government initiatives.

The main stated reasons for reform in the six countries examined in detail in this book have been (1) to simplify the tax system, (2) to raise more revenues from property taxes, and (3) to remove inequities in the tax system. In almost all cases, particular attention was paid to the reform of the assessment system, either because it was seriously out of date or because there was a desire to move to a value-based system. As mentioned in Chapter 1, however, not only is it not enough to reform assessments, but concentrating on assessment reform may in the end subvert the entire reform effort (Kelly, 1995).

Consider each of the six cases in turn. The property tax reform in Ontario, Canada was introduced in 1998 following 30 years of commissions and reports on the need for reform. The main justification for reform was that the seriously out-of-date assessment system resulted in inequities within and between property classes and across municipalities. These issues had been discussed for years but the situation became urgent when successful appeals of the assessment base increased dramatically in the early 1990s, resulting in a serious erosion of the property tax base. At the same time, a new provincial government was engaged in major reforms of local government such as municipal restructuring and a realignment of services between local governments and the provincial government. Property tax reform was part of an overall reform of local government finance.

In the United Kingdom, property rates were levied on the basis of rental value until 1990. The potential impact of a revaluation from 1973 values to more current values was expected to result in significant (and politically undesirable) shifts among property taxpayers. To avoid the anticipated opposition to a reassessment, the residential property tax was replaced by a poll tax (community charge) in 1990. The poll tax, however, was extremely unpopular. It was felt to be regressive and too expensive to collect, and collection rates were low. The unpopularity of the tax (and the unpopularity of the government that introduced it) combined with low collection rates led to the abolition of the poll tax in 1992 and its replacement with a residential property tax (the council tax). Most recently, the government has announced a revaluation for 2007.

Hungary has not yet had a basic reform but a proposal to implement an *ad valorem* property tax was drafted as an amendment to the Law on Local Taxes by the Ministry of Finance in 1996. Although the proposal was not presented to Parliament, it was tested on a sample of municipalities. The basic reason for the proposed reform was to obtain a sustainable revenue source for local governments in the face of declining central government transfers and reduced revenues from privatization.

In Colombia, following an earlier reform in 1983, another major reform of the property tax regime was made in 1990. This reform was intended mainly to simplify the administration of taxes on land and to raise more revenue from the property tax.

The Indonesian property tax reform began in 1986 and was an integral part of a comprehensive tax reform to simplify the tax code, broaden the tax base, minimize inequities, and increase the efficiency and effectiveness of the tax system to generate government revenues. Before the reform, the property tax was a complex system with seven different land-based tax laws. Each tax had a slightly different tax base and tax rates varied. These taxes were administered by different agencies and by different levels of government. Property tax collections were low and arrears were high. Most property tax information was out of date. Assessed values were much lower than market values and were inconsistent among properties.

In Kenya, property tax reform was part of an overall strategy to reform local government through the Kenya Local Government Reform Programme in 1998. The reform included rationalizing the central–local relationship, enhancing local financial management and revenue mobilization, and improving local service delivery through greater citizen participation. One of the key local government objectives was to establish a sustainable local revenue mobilization capacity to generate more own-source revenues in order (along with other local government reforms) to improve local service delivery, enhance economic governance and alleviate poverty.

Nature of reform

To a large extent, in every case the reform focused on changes to the assessment base. In some cases, there was a move to market value; in other cases, there were administrative reforms to improve the way in which properties are assessed with a view to achieving uniformity in assessment. Improvements to collection and enforcement have also been an essential part of the reform package in some countries.

For example, property tax reform in Ontario, Canada included both assessment and tax policy changes. A uniform assessment base was implemented throughout the province, based on market value. On the tax policy side, municipalities are now permitted to levy different tax rates for different classes of property but they are constrained by provincial ranges of fairness. Municipalities can move towards the ranges of fairness but not away from them. The provincial government also legislated phase-in provisions and tax deferrals to address shifts that would occur within property classes. Even with the initial tax policy reforms and phase-ins, there were large shifts in tax burdens. Further legislation therefore introduced 'capping' of property tax increases on multi-residential, commercial and industrial properties.

In the United Kingdom, the poll tax was replaced by a property tax on residential property. Although the base for the earlier property tax (before the poll tax) was rental value, the base for the council tax is market value. Each property is assigned to one of eight valuation bands. There is no individual valuation. The idea behind banding is to determine the relative values of properties within a particular area at a particular time. Any subsequent changes are not taken into account in the banding. The tax rate differs for each band, with higher rates applying to properties in higher bands.

The draft bill in Hungary defines a range of average unit values for 11 types of residential and commercial property for four types of local governments. Local governments would specify the unit value for the urban zones within the area of a municipality. There are 17 predetermined factors with a given multiplier that can be used to modify the sub-averages (for example age, utilities, building materials and so on). Minimum and maximum tax rates (0.5 percent and 1.5 percent, respectively) are defined in the draft law. The proposal combines an assessment role for both the central and local governments: the central government would define the calculation method through the relative values of different types of property within a class; local governments would define the base or starting point value based on current real property prices. Each property would have a unique value. Frequent reassessments would be required.

Property tax reform in Colombia involved the amalgamation of four taxes (the property tax, park and forest tax, tax on socio-economic strata, and surcharge on the formation of the cadastre) into one unified property tax. Municipalities were permitted, if they wished, to introduce self-assessment (*autoavalúo*) as the tax base. Tax rates were increased to 1.6 percent of the base for land for purposes other than simple possession of the property and 3.3 percent for property not used for the performance of an economic activity.

The Indonesian property tax reform began with the enactment of the Land and Building Tax Law. This law replaced seven different property-related taxes with a single flat tax of 0.5 percent on the market value of land and improvements. It eliminated both a previous concession to residential property and progressive rates for rural land, and it introduced variable assessment ratios, ranging from 20 to 100 percent. The new law broadened the tax base by curtailing exemptions. It also moved from rental value to capital value. It introduced a valuation deduction on the building for all properties, thus in effect exempting most rural housing and low-value urban structures and making the property tax essentially a land tax in rural and low-value urban areas. On the administrative side, strict deadlines and penalties were introduced to ensure timely and accurate property registration and tax payment. The banking sector was assigned responsibility for tax-receiving and accounting components of the collection system. The law stipulated a new division of property taxes among the various levels of government. Further changes in 1994 saw the property valuation deduction extended to land and building value and the assessment ratio changed to 20 percent or 40 percent depending on the value of the property.

Property tax reform in Kenya has focused on tax administration, especially collection and enforcement. The reform was designed to improve the basic management of the property tax system. The property tax management system was part of a new integrated financial management system introduced for local governments. The reform was tested in four local authorities. Two pilot projects were conducted to test a simple and cost-effective field methodology for collecting property information required to extend the tax base, ensure more complete coverage, and develop a computer-assisted mass appraisal (CAMA) valuation model.

Preconditions for reform

The six cases studied demonstrate that, in order to implement property tax reform successfully, some basic elements need to be in place. The preconditions for reform depend, to some extent, on the type of reform that is being implemented. If the reform focuses on the assessment base, for example, a precondition for the successful implementation of that reform is the availability of technical expertise. Other preconditions for property tax reform include the existence of a cadastre, a land registration system, the capacity of local government, and a solid administrative infrastructure. If the reform is expected to result in major tax shifts within or among property classes, some form of phase-in mechanism is almost invariably politically necessary in order to cushion the impact. In this as in other areas of fiscal reform, failure to allow adequately for transitional problems and to cushion burden shifts is generally a fatal defect. And, of course, considerable, and usually sustained, political will is needed to ensure that the reform is implemented.

In the case of property tax reform in Ontario, Canada, political will was definitely an essential element. Successive governments over a 30-year period did not have the political will to implement reform in the face of significant taxpayer resistance. Other preconditions for reform included the introduction of tax relief programs such as phase-ins, deferrals for seniors, and capping of tax increases for some property classes. Taxpayer confidence in assessed values and the process used to derive them was essential to the successful implementation of property tax reform.

Tax reform has not yet been implemented in Hungary. If it were, it would benefit from a centralized assessment system that would enjoy economies of scale and be less vulnerable to local political pressure than the current system. If the property tax is to become mandatory (currently it is optional for local governments), some form of tax relief would likely be needed. Among the impediments to the implementation of a market value property tax is the lack of capacity to administer the tax at the local level. Some of these problems stem from gaps in legislation and some from lack of experience with property taxation. Municipalities do not have enough expertise to appraise the value of all properties in their districts. Furthermore, the legislation does not provide much help with respect to what is meant by terms such as 'market value' or 'comparative sales.' The information to support a fiscal cadastre or mass appraisal on a consistent nation-wide basis is fragmented between two levels of government and often not shared. Information is often not computerized and older information is incomplete and not readily available.

The major precondition for the successful property tax reform in Indonesia was political will. There was also an established property tax culture among taxpayers and the tax administration that had to be changed to make reform possible. It was thus necessary to rationalize tax administration procedures considerably in order to improve taxpayer service, to reduce compliance and administrative costs, to improve equity, and, ultimately, to enhance revenue mobilization. Administrative changes were introduced on a pilot basis to allow the government to field-test procedures, economize on scarce staff and gauge reactions to the new procedures. All methods, procedures and technology were developed to match the available institutional capacity to facilitate implementation. An accurate legal cadastre was not necessary for the property tax reform since the property tax system relies on its own separate fiscal cadastre.

In Kenya, the primary obstacle to implementing property tax reform has been lack of political will and weak administration. Education and incentives are needed for those involved in the revenue mobilization effort. Taxpayers need to receive improved local services and perceive that taxes are being administered fairly. To achieve this goal requires improved tax administration, including property identification and management, valuation and assessment, billing and collection, enforcement, and taxpayer service.

Impact of reform

Unsurprisingly, the impact of the property tax reforms sketched above has been different in different countries, depending upon both the environment and the goal and stage of the reform. In some cases, it is difficult to evaluate the impact of reform. In Hungary, for example, reform has not yet been introduced; in Kenya, new policies and procedures have only been in place for three years and are still not fully implemented. In the other case studies, efforts to introduce market value assessment have had mixed results.

In Ontario, Canada, property tax reform has resulted in improved equity within the residential property class but not much change in equity either between property classes or within the non-residential property classes. Indeed, capping tax increases for the multi-residential, commercial and industrial property classes has perpetuated the inequities in the tax system. The tax system is now more complex and involves much greater provincial government control over the setting of tax rates among property classes than in the past. The result has been to reform the tax system in a way that, on balance, provides more tax stability but at the expense of equity and simplicity.

Tax reform in the United Kingdom has also focused on stability, again in all likelihood at the expense of equity. Although properties were assessed at their market value as of 1991 and placed in valuation bands, these values have not been changed. Because the council tax used an estimate of market value at a point in time and froze it for the foreseeable future, its implications are the same as any out-of-date assessment system: inequities will increase over time. Government reviews of the council tax suggest that it has been widely accepted by taxpayers because it is well understood, predictable and stable. The government is reportedly considering introducing a fixed revaluation cycle such as every six, eight, or ten years to improve the fairness of the tax, however, and has recently announced that there will be a revaluation in 2007.

Property tax reform in Colombia has resulted in an increase in the value of the tax base and an increase in revenues derived from the property tax.

Furthermore, the cadastre registry has been updated. By allowing taxpayers to use self-assessment as the basis for income and capital gains tax purposes, property values in Bogotá were brought more closely in line with market values, at least initially, although this effect now appears to be diminishing.

Property tax reform in Indonesia has also resulted in increased revenues. The policy and administrative framework adopted achieved greater simplicity, equity and ease of administration. At the same time that revenues increased, administrative and compliance costs have decreased. Taxpayer and bureaucratic resistance has been reduced. A remaining critical step, however, is to give local governments some discretion over rate setting to increase local accountability and control over the amount of property taxes collected.

Most of the countries covered in this book use value-based property taxes or are moving towards using value-based property taxes. Because one of the problems with value-based taxes is volatility, the reform of these taxes has often focused on maintaining stability. In Ontario, Canada, for example, properties were classified into several categories to reduce the impact on those classes that would face large increases and a further tax freeze was imposed on increases in multi-residential, commercial and industrial taxes. In the UK, residential properties were placed in valuation bands when the tax was introduced and not changed subsequently. Although taxes were not frozen, assessments were.[2]

Classification of properties is often used to cushion the impact on specific property classes, generally favoring residential properties over non-residential properties. There are several problems with classification (Youngman, 1999). For example, a classified property tax can distort land use decisions in favor of those property classes with lower taxes. To the extent that non-residential properties are overtaxed, there are implications for tax-exporting and the accountability and transparency of local government. There is invariably pressure to increase the number of classes and the complexity of the tax system. Although classification may reduce the threat that homeowners will not be able to pay their taxes by lowering the tax on the residential property class, it favors both high-income and low-income taxpayers. A property tax credit or circuit-breaker program, which is a function of the income of the homeowner (or tenant) would be in general a much more appropriate way to assist low-income property taxpayers, at least in countries with fairly good tax administrations (Bird and Slack, 1978).

Property tax freezes address tax volatility by breaking the link between market values and assessments. In the Canadian case, for example, property taxes for some property classes are based on taxes in the previous year. In the UK case, assessments were frozen. The result of a freeze is that taxes are less uniform and more arbitrary. It also has efficiency and equity implications. Furthermore, as Youngman (1999, p. 1395) notes, it is very difficult to remove a freeze: 'once a freeze is imposed, the process of thawing may be too painful to bear.' She suggests other ways to address volatility, such as reducing tax rates when assessed values increase; payment alternatives such as frequent installments and/or payment by credit cards or debit cards, and tax deferrals.

The reform of land and property taxes
Tax reform is always as much or more a political as it is a technical exercise. The special characteristics of land and property taxes discussed in Chapter 1 make this dictum especially applicable with respect to property tax reform. Setting up and administering a decent property tax is a complex and expensive effort. A recent presentation on property tax reform in developing and transitional countries noted, for example, that the following factors need to be in place for a successful reform: clear goals, strong commitment from all levels of government, careful and detailed plans with respect to legislation, valuation, administration, training, collection and adjudication, and – perhaps most important – political acceptance of the need for the reform (International Property Tax Institute, 2003). Who can argue with this statement? On the other hand, how likely is it that all these conditions are in place in most developing and transitional countries? How much cost in terms of time and effort must be incurred to secure them, and will the expected benefits justify this use of scarce political, technical and economic resources? These are the difficult questions that can only be answered in the circumstances of each individual country.

In practice, as discussed above, property tax reform has addressed different issues in different countries. In some cases, reform was designed to collect more revenues by changing the tax base or improving collection and enforcement. In other cases, the goal was to simplify the tax system by combining several taxes or by improving tax administration. In still other cases, the main aim was to improve the fairness of the tax system by introducing a uniform assessment system.

To implement property tax reform successfully requires a number of preconditions. One of the most important is the existence of a strong tax administration, including a process for property identification, assessment, collection and enforcement. These essential elements are, of course, often weak or missing in many countries. The visibility of the property tax and the inherent subjectivity of determining its base makes it extremely vulnerable to criticism if it is not well administered – and often even if it is.

Such criticisms are important because a critical element in the successful implementation of property tax reform is support from taxpayers. Such support is more likely if taxpayers both feel that they are receiving adequate services for the property taxes that they pay and if they perceive that the process of taxing property is fair and accountable. Unfortunately, local government in general and property tax systems in particular in many countries have a long way to go before these preconditions are likely to be satisfied.

If the major reason for reforming land and property taxes is to increase revenues, many developing and transition countries might perhaps be better advised to follow the paths of two of the more successful property taxing countries, Chile and Latvia, and opt for an essentially centralized property tax on administrative grounds. Of course, if a good property tax is instead being sought as part of a serious decentralization effort, this path is not open.

Whatever the objective, efforts to reform the property tax have met with mixed success in different countries. Some countries have been successful in simplifying the property tax. Others have sacrificed simplicity to achieve other objectives such as stability. Some countries have been successful in increasing revenues from the property tax by increasing the size of the tax base, by raising tax rates, by improving tax administration, or by some combination of the foregoing.

Increasing the fairness of the tax has not always been a stated objective of reform, and even where it has been a goal, it has proved elusive. Moving to a fairer system is usually difficult because it invariably means shifts in taxes among taxpayers. The longer reform is delayed, the bigger the shifts needed, and the more likely that reactions from those adversely affected will be strong. The result in many instances has been the introduction of still more changes to reduce the impact of the burden shift (and hence, in all likelihood, fairness). Even if reform improves the equity, efficiency and ease of administration of the tax, there are invariably winners and losers. Those who benefit from reform tend to remain silent but those who lose tend to be vocal. With a visible tax such as the property tax, increasing the property tax on some taxpayers (particularly more affluent – and usually politically influential – residential homeowners) is very hard to do.[3]

The politics of successful property tax reform thus are not propitious in most countries. Such reform is seldom easy, usually difficult technically, and often not too rewarding in either revenue or political terms. In these circumstances, it is actually somewhat encouraging to see that some countries have in fact been able to achieve considerable success in this difficult task. Experience suggests that, while it may often prove difficult to improve land and property taxes substantially in a short time, it is generally not all that hard to improve them to a meaningful degree if a country really wishes to do so.

Notes

1. Further details on these cases may be found in the respective country chapters.
2. Similarly, the famous Proposition 13 in California substituted time of sale reassessment (market values are only increased at time of sale) for market value and allowed a tax increase of no more than a 2 percent annual inflation adjustment. Even in the face of

subsequent huge state and local deficits, attributable at least in part to this legislation, political factors have made it impossible to revisit the issue. Increasing property taxes is seen to be – and probably is – the kiss of political death in California.

3. In one country in which we have worked (not covered in this book) the spouse of the country's leader was one of the most prominent and public opponents of a (very modest) attempt to improve local property taxes. It should come as no surprise that the proposed reform failed.

References

Bird, Richard M. and Enid Slack (1978), *Residential Property Tax Relief in Ontario*, Toronto: University of Toronto Press.

International Property Tax Institute (2003), 'Reforming Property Taxes for Financing Local Government: Key Lessons Learned,' presentation to World Bank, January.

Kelly, Roy (1995), 'Property Tax Reform in Indonesia: Applying a Collection-Led Strategy,' *Bulletin for Indonesian Economic Studies*, **29**, 85–104.

Youngman, Joan M. (1999), 'The Hardest Challenge for Value-Based Property Taxes: Part II,' *State Tax Notes*, April.

PART I

OECD COUNTRIES

4 Property taxation in Canada

Enid Slack

Canada is a federation with three levels of government: the federal government, ten provincial and three territorial governments and about 4000 local governments. In the urban parts of the country, there are often two levels of local government: an upper tier (county or regional government) and a lower tier (local government). There are also school boards. Generally, the lower tier is responsible for billing and collecting property taxes on behalf of itself, the upper tier and the school boards within its jurisdiction.

Under the Canadian constitution, municipalities are creatures of the provincial government. Provinces can create or destroy municipalities, determine what they can make expenditures on and what sources of revenue are available to them. In terms of the property tax, the provincial governments set the rules for how the tax base and tax rates are determined. Municipalities in all provinces levy property taxes to finance municipal services. In some provinces, the provincial government also levies a property tax to finance some of the costs of elementary and secondary education.

Provincial control over the tax means that there are similarities in the application of the property tax among municipalities within each province but variations across provinces. For this reason, this discussion on property taxes in Canada will focus largely on one province – Ontario, the largest province in Canada, with a population of 10.5 million and 4.2 million properties. Ontario implemented a major reform of the property tax in 1998. This reform was part of an overall reform of local government that included municipal government restructuring (the number of municipalities in Ontario was reduced from over 800 to less than 500 since 1996) and a realignment of services between the provincial and municipal governments.

Revenue importance

Property taxes represent only a small portion of provincial revenues in Canada, but they are the largest source of revenue to municipal governments. As Table 4.1 shows, the property tax accounted for over 53 percent of local government revenues on average across Canada in 2000. Furthermore, reliance on property taxes has increased from 48.6 percent of total revenues in 1988. This increase is largely the consequence of a reduction in provincial grants to municipalities over the same period.

Table 4.1   Distribution of municipal revenue sources, Canada, 1988 and 2000 (%)

Revenue source	1988	2000
Property taxes	48.6	53.3
Other taxes	1.4	1.3
User fees	20.0	21.3
Investment income	6.0	5.0
Other	1.1	1.2
Total own-source revenue	77.1	82.1
Unconditional grants	5.8	2.7
Conditional grants	17.1	15.2
Total grants	22.9	17.9
Total revenue	100.0	100.0

Source: Calculated from Statistics Canada data, Financial Management Systems (FMS), August 2001. Data for 2000 are estimates.

Tax base

In all provinces, the base for the property tax is 'real property,' defined as land and improvements to the land. There is different treatment of machinery and equipment in different provinces; in some cases, machinery and equipment 'affixed' to real property is included and in others it is not. There is also different treatment of minerals, mines, oil and gas wells, pipelines, railways and public utility distribution systems in different jurisdictions.

All provinces assess properties at some percentage of market value (sometimes referred to as actual, real, fair or current value). In Ontario, properties are assessed at their 'current value,' which is defined as the amount of money the fee simple, if unencumbered, would realize if sold at arm's length by a willing seller to a willing buyer. For farms, conservation lands and managed forests, value in current use (not highest and best use) is used. Railway and hydro (electric power) rights of way are taxed on a rate per acre, differentiated by nine geographic regions across the province. These rates are set by provincial statute.

The date used to determine current value is the same for all municipalities across Ontario. For 2001 and 2002, values were determined as of 30 June 1999. For 2003, values are determined as of 30 June 2001. By 2004, current values will be determined each year as of 30 June of the preceding year. Starting in 2005, assessments will be based on average values from successive tax years (referred to as 'rolling averages'). For 2005, a two-year average will be employed (a property's assessment will be the average of the current value for the tax year plus the current value for the previous tax year). For 2006 and subsequent years, property assessments will be based on three-year averages.

Exemptions include churches, cemeteries, Indian lands, public hospitals, charitable institutions and educational institutions. Land or property belonging to the federal, provincial or local governments is not liable for taxation. Instead of paying property taxes, governments make payments in lieu of property taxes to municipalities. The payments are viewed as property taxes since the municipality would have collected property taxes on these properties had they been privately owned. The payments are generally less than the property taxes would be, however.

Tax rates

Property tax rates are generally determined by the amount of property tax revenue that municipalities need to collect (determined by expenditures less non-tax revenues) divided by the taxable assessment base. In most provinces, there is either a differential tax rate between residential and non-residential properties or a classified assessment system which favors residential properties.

In British Columbia, for example, municipalities can set tax rates for nine different classes of property: residential, utilities, unmanaged forest land, major industry, light industry, business/other, managed forest land, recreational/non-profit and farm land. In many municipalities, businesses are taxed at four to five times the residential rate and utilities are taxed even more highly.

Municipalities in Ontario are allowed to levy variable tax rates for different classes of property. The seven main classes of property are: residential, multi-residential, commercial, industrial, pipelines, farms and managed forests. Optional classes which municipalities in Ontario can choose include: new multi-residential, office building, shopping centers, parking lots, professional sports facilities and large industrial. Sub-classes to which rate reductions apply are: vacant commercial (35 percent reduction), vacant industrial (30 percent reduction), farmland pending development and certain theatres in the City of Toronto. Furthermore, the commercial class can be divided into three sub-classes according to value, with graduated tax rates applied to each sub-class. The tax rate on farms and managed forests is legislated to be 25 percent of the residential tax rate.

As noted above, farmland is assessed at its value in current use and the tax rate is legislated to be 25 percent of the residential rate. Tax rates on farmland pending development can be phased in over stages. The triggers for tax increases are: when the land is used solely for farm purposes but has been registered for subdivision and when the land is used solely for farm purposes but a building permit has been issued.

Variable tax rates permit municipalities to shift tax burdens among property classes within provincially determined ranges of fairness. Transition ratios were calculated for each property class to reflect the relative distribution of burden by tax class prior to reform (the 'starting point'). Transition ratios were calculated as the effective tax rate (property taxes relative to market value assessment) for each property class relative to the residential class. The transition ratio for residential properties – the benchmark – was set equal to 1.00. Ranges of fairness were set by the provincial government as in Table 4.2.

Table 4.2   Provincial ranges of fairness, Ontario

Property class	Allowable range of fairness
Multi-residential	1.0–1.1
New multi-residential	1.0–1.1
Commercial	0.6–1.1
Office building	0.6–1.1
Shopping center	0.6–1.1
Parking lots and vacant land	0.6–1.1
Professional sports facility	0.001–1.1
Industrial	0.6–1.1
Large industrial	0.6–1.1
Pipelines	0.6–0.7

Municipalities can set their tax ratios so as to maintain the transition ratios, move towards the range of fairness or vary tax ratios within ranges of fairness. For example, if the transition ratio on multi-residential properties were 4.1, a municipality could reduce it to 4.0 or below or maintain it at 4.1. It could not increase it to 4.2 or beyond. In short, municipalities are not allowed to worsen inequities but they can maintain or reduce them.

Municipal levy increases (that is, year-over-year municipal tax increases) are not permitted on a property class if a municipality's tax ratio for the class exceeds the prescribed threshold ratio. The following threshold ratios (where thresholds represent provincial averages) have been prescribed: commercial – 1.98; industrial – 2.63; and multi-residential – 2.74. Essentially this means that, for those municipalities over the threshold levels for all three property classes, all tax increases resulting from budgetary increases have to be borne by residential property taxpayers.

Tax relief

Some form of property tax relief is provided in most provinces. Direct property tax relief is provided through three types of programs – tax deferrals, property tax credits and direct grants or subsidies. Tax deferrals are administered by provincial and local governments across Canada. Generally tax deferral schemes are only available to seniors and widowed and disabled taxpayers. Under a tax deferral scheme, the owner of the property is permitted to defer a portion of the property taxes, usually up to a maximum specified amount. This amount is recovered either by the province or the municipality, depending on the program. The outstanding amount becomes a lien on the property, payable to the province or municipality when the ownership is transferred. Sometimes a market rate of interest is applied to the deferred amount; sometimes a lower rate of interest is charged.

Property tax credits are refundable tax credits for homeowners and/or renters administered through the provincial income tax system. A credit for property taxes is applied against a property taxpayer's provincial tax liability. It is generally calculated as a portion of property taxes paid (or a percentage of rent in the case of renters) less some percentage of income. The higher one's income, the lower the property tax credit. Tax credits are generally refundable so that if the property tax liability exceeds income taxes payable, a refund is paid to the taxpayer. Credits for renters and homeowners are used in three provinces – Manitoba, Ontario and Quebec.

Grants or subsidies are direct payments from provincial or municipal governments to reduce the burden of the residential property tax. The grant is paid directly to the taxpayer so that the property tax payable is reduced. Grants to residential taxpayers are paid in four provinces – British Columbia, Alberta, Manitoba and New Brunswick.

Tax administration

Municipalities are responsible for the administration of the property tax system in most provinces, including billing and collection. In Ontario, municipalities are also responsible for billing and collecting education taxes (but the tax rate for education is set by the provincial government). The revenues generated by the education portion of the property tax are collected by municipalities and remitted quarterly to their local school boards.

Throughout Canada, assessment is performed by a provincial department or authority. In Ontario until January 1999, regional assessors (provincial officials) were responsible for preparing an assessment roll. Since 1999, preparing the assessment roll has become the responsibility of the Ontario Property Assessment Corporation (OPAC), a non-profit corporation representing Ontario's municipalities. It was renamed the Municipal Property Assessment Corporation (MPAC) in 2001 to reflect its large municipal representation. The responsibilities of MPAC include: the determination of assessed values of properties, classification of properties, determination of properties that are entitled to be exempt, preparation of an annual assessment roll and delivery of the roll to municipalities, and defense of assessment appeals.

The process of levying property taxes

The first element in levying a property tax is to identify the property that is being taxed. There are two systems for people to register interests in land in Canada.[1] Under the registry system, any person can register a document pertaining to title to land in a provincial registry office. Purchasers generally retain a private lawyer to examine all of the registered documents to determine whether a vendor has good and valid title. People can sometimes claim ownership by adverse possession (unchallenged occupation) rather than documents.

Under the land titles system, only the property-owner can register a document in a provincial registry office, with the approval of a provincial official. This system is therefore a registry of titles, rather than deeds and instruments. If an owner wishes to divide land, such as by plan of subdivision or condominium, the land must normally be held under land titles. As of 1998, the electronic registration of real estate transactions in the land titles system became mandatory in certain parts of Ontario.

The difference between the two systems has to do with the guarantee of ownership. The land titles system provides a guarantee of ownership but the registry system does not. The latter is only a system of registration of documents. Efforts are under way in Ontario to convert all properties to the land titles system.

The assessment roll contains the name of the legal owner, the amount of the assessment, and other variables affecting the assessment. The owner must be notified in writing of any change in the assessment affecting the property.

Residential properties are assessed using computer-assisted mass appraisal (CAMA) as well as traditional appraisal techniques. CAMA is a statistical technique used to analyze data in order to predict the value of one variable (market value) from the known value of other variables (such as living area, lot size, quality, location and so on). The task is to examine properties that have actually sold and to identify statistical relationships between the features of these properties and their selling prices. These same relationships are then used to estimate the probable price for properties that have not sold. By using this technique, annual assessment updates are possible without a physical inspection of the property.

Taxpayers in all provinces can appeal their assessment to a quasi-judicial body such as the Assessment Review Board in Ontario. If unsuccessful, they can generally appeal to the courts.

In terms of collection, tax arrears are fairly low in Canadian jurisdictions. In Ontario in 1999, for example, the ratio of tax arrears to the total property tax levy was just over 7 percent.

Property tax reform in Ontario
By the mid-1980s, there was consensus that the assessment system in Ontario was broken and needed to be fixed, even though there has not always been consensus on how to fix it. The assessment systems in a number of municipalities in Ontario were seriously out of date. In Toronto (the largest city in Ontario with a population of 2.5 million), for example, the last reassessment was in 1953 and assessed values were based on 1940 values.

The result of an out-of-date assessment system was three types of inequities: within classes of property, between classes of property and across municipalities. Within classes of property, for example the single-family home class, older properties were under-assessed relative to newer properties. Between classes of property, residential single-family homes were under-assessed relative to apartments and relative to commercial properties. In Toronto, for example, apartments were assessed more than four times higher than single-family homes of equal market value. Across municipalities, similar houses were assessed at different amounts.

These inequities led to a dramatic increase in assessment appeals. A large proportion of the assessment base of Toronto was under appeal each year. To the extent that appeals are successful, the assessment base is eroded. This means that all taxpayers face higher tax rates. The decision on the part of Toronto politicians to favor residential properties by not permitting a reassessment for five decades, combined with a statutory higher tax rate on commercial and industrial properties, meant that taxes on businesses were higher in Toronto than in the rest of the region. This differential provided an incentive for businesses to leave Toronto. For these reasons, reform became urgent.

The change to a uniform province-wide assessment system by itself would have resulted in large shifts in tax burdens within and between classes of property. For this reason, tax policy changes were introduced at the same time. Before the reform, municipalities were required by legislation to levy differential tax rates on residential and non-residential property. Specifically, the residential rate had to be equal to 85 percent of the non-residential rate. The Province moved to the variable rate system described above.

In addition to variable tax rates, the Province legislated phase-in provisions and tax deferrals to address the shifts that would occur within classes of property, especially within the residential property class. Municipalities, at their option, could apply a phase-in for up to eight years for assessment-related tax changes. Interclass subsidization is not permitted. Tax decreases in the commercial class, for example, cannot be used to subsidize tax increases in the residential class. Different schemes can apply to different classes; different phase-in periods can be used for decreases and increases.

Further tax policy reforms
Even with the initial tax policy reforms and phase-in mechanisms, there were still large shifts in tax burdens. In particular, the tax burden on small retail commercial properties increased relative to large office towers because of the recession in office markets in June 1996 (the valuation date). To reduce the shift on to small commercial properties, the provincial government introduced optional classes for office towers, shopping centers and parking lots. It also introduced optional capping. Municipalities could limit tax increases on commercial, industrial and multi-residential properties to 2.5 percent per year for three years (1998, 1999, 2000). This meant that the property tax could not increase more than 2.5 percent on any of these properties over what it was before reform. Furthermore, any tax increases over the three-year period resulting from increased expenditures, for example, would have to be financed from the residential property class.

Only Toronto chose the capping option initially. When it became clear that there were large tax increases on small commercial properties in other municipalities in Ontario, the provincial government introduced another piece of legislation which restricted property tax increases on commercial and industrial properties to 10 percent in 1998, an additional 5 percent in 1999 and an additional 5 percent in 2000. This legislation was not optional but municipalities could decide how to achieve the 10–5–5 target – through phase-ins, capping or some other method.

The result of capping was to freeze the assessment roll based on 1997. In other words, the new assessment roll was not being used for multi-residential, commercial, or industrial properties. Capping also meant that there was no effort to remove or even reduce the inequities in property tax burdens within the commercial, industrial and multi-residential property classes.

For 2001 and subsequent years, municipalities are required to limit the assessment-related property tax increases on commercial, industrial and multi-residential properties to 5 percent per year. A frozen assessment listing is no longer required for the administration of the new 5 percent limit.

Evaluation of assessment and property tax reform
Seven pieces of legislation were needed to reform the property tax in Ontario. The result is a tax system that has not changed much in terms of equity but has changed dramatically in terms of the complexity of administration and degree of provincial control. Current value assessment is being used for

residential properties. The assessment on multi-residential, commercial and industrial properties, however, has virtually been frozen at pre-reform levels. By focusing on tax stability for each tax class, one of the initial goals of the reform – to create a property tax system that is fair – was lost completely. Fairness has not been achieved because inequities between classes of property have not been eliminated and the inequities within the classes (other than residential) have also not been reduced.

Although the assessment function has been downloaded to a corporation comprising mostly municipal officials, the tax-setting process is largely being controlled by the provincial government. Although municipalities have control over the level of taxes, their control over the distribution of taxes among classes of property has been severely constrained by the Province.

There are some lessons that can be learned from the reform of property taxation in Ontario. First, the longer you wait to reform the tax, the more difficult it will be. Annual reassessments for property tax purposes will create far fewer shifts in taxes than a reassessment after 30 years. Second, taxpayers need to have confidence in the assessed values and the process used to derive them. This means taking the time to do the assessment properly.[2] Third, the degree of uniformity in assessment is generally higher when assessment is a provincial function rather than a local function.[3] Although it is too early to evaluate whether there is a lesson to be learned in Ontario, moving the assessment function from a provincial department to a corporation subject to greater municipal control may in time raise questions about the potential to ensure uniformity. Fourth, it is preferable to understand the impact of a reassessment and design appropriate tax policy before implementing property tax reform rather than to undertake the reassessment and then design tax policy in a piecemeal fashion in response to taxpayer resistance. Fifth, as part of the tax policy design, phase-ins and tax deferrals are essential.

More generally, the lesson from the Ontario experience is that, no matter how economically desirable the long-run outcome of any policy change may be, its transitional effects may be sufficiently undesirable in political terms to kill it. From a public choice perspective, the losers from a change in policy tend to be very vocal (even if they are the minority) because they value their losses more than the gainers (even if they are the majority) value their gains. This problem is not unique to property taxes but it is particularly significant because of the visibility of this tax.

Other taxes on land
Other taxes on land include special assessments, land transfer taxes and development charges.

Special assessments

Special assessments (also known as local improvement charges) are compulsory charges imposed on residential, commercial and industrial properties to pay for additions or improvements to existing capital facilities that border on those properties. They are used for capital expenditures to pave or repave streets, install or replace water mains or sewers, construct sidewalks, install street lighting, and so on. The municipality constructs the works and then recoups the cost through a special assessment on the properties that directly benefit from the government expenditure. Although the magnitude of the charge is based on a particular capital expenditure in a particular year, the costs may be spread over a period of years.

The most common base for special assessments is the front footage of those properties that abut the capital works in question, but the charges can also be levied on the basis of size of lot, assessed value of property or by zone.

Land transfer taxes

Land transfer taxes are levied at the time of sale of a property and are calculated as a percentage of the value of the property transferred. The tax, which must be paid before the transfer is registered, is like a sales tax payable by the purchaser and calculated as a percentage of the purchase price. The tax rate sometimes increases with the value of the property; in some cases, taxes are higher on non-residents. Six provinces in Canada impose land transfer taxes. In all cases, provincial governments legislate the parameters of the tax. The exception is Nova Scotia, where municipalities have the authority to impose the tax. Only in Nova Scotia and Quebec are the revenues retained locally.

In Ontario, for example, the rate is 0.5 percent of the first $55 000 of purchase price; 1 percent on the amount from $55 000 to $250 000; 1.5 percent on the amount from $250 000 to $400 000; and 2 percent on the amount over $400 000. A refund is provided for first-time homebuyers of newly built homes which applies to the entire tax payable up to a maximum of $2000. The refund is calculated according to the amount of financial interest the purchaser has in the home. In British Columbia, the tax is 1 percent on the first $200 000 of purchase price and 2 percent on the amount over $200 000. Similar schemes exist in other provinces.

In 1974 Ontario levied another type of land transfer tax, known as the land speculation tax. This was a provincial tax on the gains realized on the disposition of real property, including buildings and fixtures. The stated purpose of this tax was to restrain the rate of increase of land and housing prices by curbing speculation and also to recover for the public a major share of the windfall gains from land speculation. The tax rate of 20 percent applied to realized capital gains, with some important exceptions.[4]

A study of the land speculation tax found that, although the tax caused a temporary reduction in the price of houses, it left the upward trend in house prices unaffected (Smith, 1976). Furthermore, the tax was argued to increase concentration in both the construction industry and in the ownership of residential investment properties, thus reducing competition. The tax was also said to encourage the deterioration of residential investment properties and to reduce the availability of funds for investment in real property. Finally, the tax was found to be costly to administer and it was not clear if it generated sufficient revenue to cover its administrative costs. Since the tax was found to eliminate most taxable transactions in Ontario, revenues were small. (At the extreme, of course, if the tax succeeded in eliminating 'speculation' there would be no revenues at all.) For all these reasons, the tax was eventually eliminated.

Development charges
Development charges (also known as exactions and lot levies) are levied by local governments on developers to cover the growth-related capital costs associated with new development (or, in some cases, redevelopment). These charges provide revenues from the private sector to municipalities to finance infrastructure needs arising from growth. Development charges are levied for officially mandated programs and the funds collected have to be used to pay for the infrastructure made necessary by the development.[5] Development charges are levied by local governments in British Columbia, Alberta, Saskatchewan, Ontario, Quebec and the Yukon and Northwest Territories.

Development charges are structured according to a set of rules. Local governments in Ontario, for example, are required to calculate the need for the services to be financed by development charges, where the need for services depends on the forecasted growth over the next ten-year period and the existence of excess capacity. Future capital expenditures have to be specified by category of expenditure and a determination made of what portion is growth-related. The calculation of the development charge cannot be based on a level of service that exceeds the average level of service provided in the municipality over the last ten years.[6]

Although the charge can be levied on a uniform basis across a municipality or on a development-by-development basis, most municipalities in Ontario levy a uniform charge. Municipalities in British Columbia, however, favor a development-by-development approach.

Other exactions (formal or informal) on the developer that are part of the subdivision approval process include, for example, land dedications that require the developer to set aside land for roadways, other public works, school sites or for environmental reasons; parkland dedications that require a portion of the land used for development to be set aside for parkland or that a cash payment in lieu of parkland be made; density bonusing whereby developers are granted higher densities than are permitted by planning regulations in return for meeting conditions such as providing day care, preserving an historic building and so on, connection fees to permit developers to buy into existing capacity of water and sewer facilities; and oversizing provisions (sometimes called front-end financing) that require developers to provide more infrastructure than is required for their development. The municipality, in some cases, agrees to recover part of the costs on behalf of the developer from future benefitting owners.

Notes

1. For a useful earlier overview of cadastral systems in Canada, see Dale (1976).
2. In another Canadian province (British Columbia), market value assessment was introduced in 1978, four years after the assessment authority was created. Over the four-year phase-in period, the authority kept two rolls (a phase-in roll and a market value roll). This allowed time to prepare the market value and conduct impact studies. The first market value roll was not released to the public until 1978.
3. Studies in the United States suggest that the degree of uniformity in assessment is higher when county assessors (rather than local assessors) are used and when the state government establishes and enforces assessment standards.
4. Exceptions included principal residences, developed industrial and commercial property sold to government, residential investment property owned by the transfer for at least ten years and containing a structure worth at least 40 percent of the total value; farm property owned by the transferor for at least ten years, included in a registered plan of subdivision and wholly or partially serviced by the transferor.
5. Municipalities in Canada have, historically, required developers to provide or pay for on-site services such as streets, street lighting, sidewalks and other public facilities within the subdivision. More recently, municipalities have extended the responsibility to developers to pay for the off-site costs associated with new development. Although most municipalities specify the on-site costs that are required to be made by developers, not all municipalities make developers pay for the off-site costs. Development charges only apply to the off-site costs.
6. The estimated capital costs have to be reduced by an amount that reflects a municipality's excess capacity and by an amount that reflects the benefit to existing development. Furthermore, legislation requires that the capital costs be reduced by 10 percent for infrastructure other than water supply, wastewater, stormwater drainage, services related to highways and electrical power, police and fire protection services.

References

Boadway, Robin, W. and Harry M. Kitchen (1999), *Canadian Tax Policy*, 3rd edn, Toronto, Canada: Canadian Tax Foundation.

Dale, P.F. (1976), *Cadastral Surveys within the Commonwealth*, London: HMSO.

Slack, Enid (2001), 'Property Taxation,' in Mila Freire and Richard Stren (eds), *The Challenge of Urban Government: Policies and Practices*, Washington, DC: The World Bank Institute, pp. 269–79.

Slack, Enid and Richard Bird (1991), 'Financing Urban Growth Through Development Charges,' *Canadian Tax Journal*, **39**, 1288–304.

Smith, Larry (1976), 'The Ontario Land Speculation Tax: An Analysis of an Unearned Increment Tax,' *Land Economics*, **52** (1), 1–12.

5 Property taxation in the United Kingdom

Enid Slack

The United Kingdom is a unitary kingdom consisting of four parts: England, Scotland, Wales and Northern Ireland. The structure of local government varies across the UK. In England, there are four types of government structure. First, in the London area, there is the Greater London Authority (which includes the Metropolitan Police Authority, the London Fire and Emergency Planning Authority, Transport for London and the London Development Agency), the London boroughs and the City of London. Second, metropolitan districts deliver services in the six metropolitan areas (Greater Manchester, Merseyside, South Yorkshire, Tyne and Wear, West Midlands and West Yorkshire). Third, areas outside of London and the metropolitan areas are called shire areas. Most of these have two tiers of local authority – shire districts (the lower tier) and shire counties (the upper tier). In some shire areas there is a third tier known as a parish or town council. Fourth, there are 46 unitary authorities in the shire areas.

Property taxes on residential property (known as the council tax) are set locally; business rates on non-residential property (also known as non-domestic rates) are set nationally. This chapter reviews council taxes and business rates separately and discusses the reform of each of these taxes in 1993. Although national taxation is the same in all parts of the UK, there are variations in local taxation. Most of the discussion here is based on how these taxes are applied in England.

Revenue importance

Council taxes and business rates are an important source of revenue to local authorities, accounting for about 33 percent of local revenues in England in 2000–2001. This proportion has increased from about 29 percent in 1995–96. The council tax accounted for almost 16 percent of the income of local authorities in England in 2000–2001 and business rates accounted for about 17 percent. The breakdown of local government revenues by source for 2000–2001 is shown in Table 5.1. Business rates are shown under grant income because, as will be noted below, these tax revenues are pooled by the central government and redistributed to local authorities.

Table 5.1   Local government income, England, 2000–2001

Source of income	£ million	Percentage of total income
Grant income:		
Redistributed business rates	15 400	17.1
Revenue support grant	19 437	21.6
Other grants	19 637	21.8
Total grant income	54 474	60.4
Locally funded income:		
Council tax	14 292	15.9
Sales, fees and charges	8 143	9.0
Other	7 365	8.2
Total locally funded income	29 800	33.1
Other income	5 905	6.5
Total gross income	90 179	100.0

Source: Office of the Deputy Prime Minister (2003).

Council tax
Before 1989 in Scotland and 1990 in England and Wales, all residential and non-residential properties were subject to property taxes ('rates') on the value of occupation. The value was measured by nominal rent. These taxes were replaced in 1990 by a poll tax (known as the community charge). The community charge was then replaced by the council tax on 1 April 1993. The reasons for these two reforms are discussed later in this chapter.

Tax base for the council tax
The council tax is a tax on the occupant of the dwelling. One council tax is imposed per dwelling. The full council tax bill assumes that there are two adults living in the dwelling. If there is only one adult, the council tax bill is reduced by 25 percent. The tax is reduced by 50 percent if the dwelling is not the main home of someone or if it is empty or a second home. Students and severely mentally impaired people are not counted among the number of adults resident in a dwelling.

The tax base is the capital value, defined as what each dwelling might reasonably have been expected to realize if it had been sold in the open market by a willing vendor on 1 April 1991, taking account of any significant change to the property between then and 1 April 1993.

Table 5.2   Council tax bandings (England)

Band	Range of values (at 1 April 1991)	Ratio to Band D
A	Up to £40 000	6/9
B	£40 001 to £52 000	7/9
C	£52 001 to £68 000	8/9
D	£68 001 to £88 000	1
E	£88 001 to £120 000	11/9
F	£120 001 to £160 000	13/9
G	£160 001 to £320 000	15/9
H	Over £320 000	2

Source: Valuation Office Agency of the Inland Revenue.

Each property is assigned to one of eight value bands ranging from A to H as shown in Table 5.2. The list shows only the band to which the dwelling has been allocated and not its actual value. In other words, there is no individual valuation. Although there are legislative provisions for changing the banding of a property (for example, banding can be updated upon sale), this has not generally been done. The idea behind banding is to determine the relative values of properties within a particular area at a particular date. Any changes since then are not normally taken into account.

Banding establishes a dwelling's value relative to other dwellings in the local area. Any change in value because of a change in house prices generally will not affect the banding. Individual properties may be re-banded only under a few circumstances. If the local area changes for the worse, all homes in the area may be placed into a lower band. If a home is expanded, it will be re-banded only after it is sold; if a home decreases in value because part of it is demolished, it may be re-banded immediately. If the property increases in value because the occupier has carried out improvements, such as an extension, it will re-banded but, again, not until it is sold.

Initially, it was envisaged that there would be frequent revaluations of property and amendments to banding ranges to keep the base up to date. There has been no revaluation of the council tax since its introduction in 1993, however. The present government has announced a revaluation for 2007 based on 2005 values. There is also pressure to increase the number of bands from the current eight and to change the balance of tax paid from band to band as a way to increase the progressivity of the tax.

Exemptions to the tax base include properties which are: vacant or undergoing structural or other major works; owned by a charity and unoccupied for less than six months; vacant for less than six months; unoccupied because owners/tenants are in prison, mental care, hospital or nursing home, or are dead; prohibited for occupation; kept for occupation by ministers of religion; empty because the resident is elsewhere to take care of others; occupied by students; in possession of a mortgagee; occupied or managed by an educational establishment or charitable body and used predominantly for study; part of armed forces accommodations; in possession of a trustee in bankruptcy; consisting of a pitch or mooring not occupied.

Council tax rates

Local authorities set the council tax rate so as to balance their spending priorities against their own-source revenues, grants and what they will be permitted to borrow. Each billing authority determines its own level of tax but the central government has the power to cap the level of tax for an authority under certain circumstances.

The council tax bill for each of the different bands differs according to a fixed ratio set out in the legislation. In particular, higher rates apply to properties with higher band values. Tax ratios are shown for England in Table 5.2, where ratios are calculated relative to Band D. For example, if the council tax for a dwelling in Band D is £180, the bill for one in Band A would be £120 (6/9 times £180) and the bill for a dwelling in Band H would be £360 (2 times £180).

Tax administration for the council tax

The council tax is administered by billing authorities (such as district councils, unitary authorities, metropolitan councils, a London borough council and so on). They are responsible for notification, collection and enforcement of the tax. Banding is the responsibility of the central government valuation officer.

Valuations are carried out by the listing officer at the Valuation Office Agency (part of the Inland Revenue). Taxpayers can appeal their assessment to the listing officer in their area, for a limited time, but only on a few grounds. Grounds for appeal include, for example, that the wrong person was billed, that the dwelling should be exempt, that the amount of bill is incorrect because a discount should apply, and so on. A taxpayer can appeal the banding of their home if he or she is a new taxpayer for the property, or if there has been a material increase or reduction in the value of the dwelling, or where the dwelling begins to be or stops being used for a business.

If the listing officer agrees with the appeal, the valuation list may be altered. If the listing officer does not agree, the appeal is referred to a valuation tribunal as a formal appeal. Valuation tribunals are judicial bodies, independent of the local council and the listing officer. Normally the valuation tribunal's decision is final but there can be an appeal to the High Court on a point of law.

Table 5.3   Council tax collection rates, England, 2001–2002

	Receipts of 2001–2002 council taxes by 31 March 2002 as percentage of net collectable debit
Inner London boroughs (incl. City of London)	91.1
Outer London boroughs	94.9
London boroughs	93.7
Metropolitan districts	95.3
Unitary authorities	95.3
Shire districts	97.4
England total	96.1

Note: The annual collectable debit is the council tax that authorities would collect if everyone liable paid (net of discounts, exemptions, disabled relief, transitional benefits and council tax benefits).

Source: Office of the Deputy Prime Minister (2003).

Table 5.3 shows collection rates for the council tax in various parts of England for 2001–2002. Overall, the receipts of council taxes as a percentage of the net collectable debit were more than 96 percent; the arrears are just under 4 percent.

Business rates
Business rates were introduced in 1990 to replace the former locally determined business rates.[1] The tax is levied on businesses and other occupiers of non-domestic property. The income from business rates is paid into a central pool and then redistributed to local authorities on the basis of population.

Tax base for business rates
The base of the tax is the occupation of a property. Each property is assessed for tax on the basis of its 'rateable value,' which is the annual rent that the property could have been let for on the open market at a particular date (known as the antecedent date). For the 2000 list, the antecedent date was 1 April 1998. Rateable values are reviewed every five years. The next valuation will be effective from 1 April 2005. In the intervening years, the rates collected change by the amount of inflation. Some plant and machinery may also be rateable.

There are two types of rating lists: local rating lists relate to all properties within a billing authority's area; the central rating list applies to network-type properties such as gas, water and telecommunications, which can be difficult to apportion among the local lists. Government properties have been included in local rating lists since 1 April 2000. Before 2000, they made payments in lieu of taxes on a notional rateable value.

New lists are compiled every five years following a revaluation of non-domestic properties. Within the five-year period, lists are maintained and updated to reflect changes in properties; new properties are added to the lists; demolished properties are removed and other changes are made.

Exemptions are based on the use to which the building is put and not the ownership. Exemptions include: agricultural land and associated buildings; places of public religious worship; property used by the disabled; fish farms; sewers; certain properties of Trinity House; public parks; swinging moorings; road crossings over watercourses; properties in enterprise zones; and properties occupied by visiting forces.

Business tax rates
Assessments are multiplied by a uniform business rate (UBR), which is set nationally. This rate, known as the tax multiplier, is a single figure determined by Parliament each year. There are different rates in England, Scotland and Wales. The tax applies to occupiers of the property (tenants or owners); the rates are 50 percent for unoccupied properties. No rates are set for properties used for warehousing or industrial purposes.

Rate relief can be provided by local authorities who are responsible for assessing rates bills and collecting taxes. Rates can be reduced for charities and other non-profit-making bodies; businesses in rural areas such as the sole village general store or post office; unused properties; or, in limited circumstances, businesses suffering hardship. Legislation limits annual tax increases to the retail price index (RPI), having regard to changes in the total rateable values.

Since the revaluation in 2000 resulted in shifts in property taxes, the central government implemented a self-financing transitional relief scheme. This scheme sets ceilings on the amount by which business rate bills may increase. The cost of the relief is paid for by limiting the decreases. The limit for real increases in business rate bills in 2000–2001 in England was 12.5 percent for large properties, and 5 percent for small properties; decreases were limited to 2.5 percent for large properties and 5 percent for small. Limits also apply to increases and decreases in following years over the life of the scheme until the taxpayer is paying the full amount of the tax liability.

Tax administration for business rates
The Valuation Office Agency of the Inland Revenue is responsible for determining the rateable value of all properties and maintains the rating lists on

which tax payable is assessed. Local authorities are responsible for assessing rate bills and collecting business rates payable on properties within their authority. Income from properties on local rating lists is collected by billing authorities and paid into a national pool (one for England and one for Wales). Income from properties on the central list is paid directly into the pool. The money in the pool is redistributed to local authorities on a per capita basis. There are special arrangements for London.

Occupiers of property are required to complete a form which indicates the lease terms. Ratepayers can appeal their assessment to the valuation tribunal. If they are dissatisfied with the outcome, they may appeal to the lands tribunal. The latter is a more formal hearing where ratepayers need to be represented by legal counsel. Tribunal fees, in addition to costs of lawyers and expert witnesses, can be very high.

Table 5.4 shows the collection rates for the business rates in England for 2001–2002. Collection rates are almost 98 percent.

Table 5.4   Business rates collection rates, England, 2001–2002

	Receipts of 2001–2002 non-domestic rates by 31 March 2002 as percentage of net collectable debit
Inner London boroughs (incl. City of London)	97.9
Outer London boroughs	97.1
London boroughs	97.6
Metropolitan districts	97.4
Unitary authorities	97.9
Shire districts	98.2
England total	97.9

Note: The net collectable debit is the business rate for the relevant year that authorities would collect if everyone liable paid (net of relief or voids).

Source: Office of the Deputy Prime Minister (2003).

Tax reform
Before 1990, all properties (residential and non-residential) were subject to rates. The tax was levied on the occupants of all buildings and each building was assessed by a central government agency on the basis of its rental value. The last revaluation in England was in 1973. Local authorities set the tax

rates but, with the introduction of rate capping in 1985, some municipalities were constrained. Rate rebates were made available to low-income households.

The residential property tax was abolished in 1990. In its place, local authorities were permitted to levy a community charge (poll tax) on all adults 18 years of age and over. Exemptions included people who were severely mentally handicapped, convicted prisoners, people living in homes and hostels, and 18-year-old schoolchildren. Full-time students in higher education got an 80 percent exemption. Low-income households could qualify for rebates of up to 80 percent. At the same time, the non-residential property tax was to be retained but at a uniform rate. Payments were to be paid into a pool and distributed on a per capita basis.

Part of the reason for abolishing the residential property tax stemmed from the estimated impact of a revaluation from 1973 values. Any revaluation of this type means that there will be winners and losers. Moving to a poll tax eliminated this particular impact. Furthermore, the community charge was introduced to expand the tax base to finance local government services – it widened the tax base to include everyone over 18. Under the old rating system, only the owner or the occupier of property was liable for the tax. The change to a poll tax increased the number of taxpayers from 20 million to 40 million.

In 1992, the community charge was eliminated and replaced by the council tax. Non-domestic rates (business rates) were maintained. The council tax was introduced following problems with the community charge. The community charge had been introduced to achieve accountability. It was felt that everyone would be paying some part of the tax in the local authority area and would thus have an interest in how local authorities spent their funds. Collection rates were initially low, however, and the tax was expensive to collect because many people failed to register and many who were registered refused to pay. Unlike property, which is highly visible and in a fixed location, individual taxpayers were able to escape full reporting of the total number of taxable occupants. The community charge was also unpopular because it was felt to be regressive (borne relatively more heavily by low-income households than high-income households).

The council tax was more like the previous property tax (known as domestic rates). The main difference was that the valuation base changed from annual rental value to capital value. By assigning properties to broad categories rather than assigning a taxable value to each property, the council tax attempted to achieve simplicity and stability. This was done at the expense of accuracy, however.

Government reviews of the council tax suggest that it is working well as a local tax.[2] It has been widely accepted by taxpayers because it is well understood, predictable and stable. Because the council tax uses an estimate of market value at a particular point in time (1 April 1991) and then freezes assessments for the foreseeable future, however, it will have the same implications as any out-of-date assessment system: inequities will increase over time. Although there are no plans to change the council tax, the government is considering the introduction of a fixed cycle for revaluation such as every six, eight, or ten years to improve the fairness of the tax. The first such revaluation is currently scheduled for 2007 (to be based on 2005 values).

A recent review of business rates suggests that the government is also considering some changes in this tax (UK Department for Transport, 2000). First, the government is considering allowing local authorities to levy a supplementary local rate in addition to the central tax. However, the amount of the tax and the allowable annual increase would be controlled by the central government. Second, it has been suggested that there should be mandatory relief for small businesses. Third, the government is seeking advice on changing the frequency of revaluations from five years. Fourth, the government is considering changes to the transitional relief arrangements.

Other taxes on real property
A stamp tax is imposed on property transfers. Immovable property is included in the base of the inheritance tax, and capital gains on the sale of immovable property are subject to income tax. The inheritance tax is a tax on the receipt of property by means of an inheritance; it also taxes certain transfers made during the lifetime of the taxpayer. The capital gains tax is a tax on any gains of the sale of an asset realized after 31 March 1982. The private residence of the taxpayer is exempt from the capital gains tax. All these are national taxes.

Although many attempts have been made in the past to institute various forms of land value taxation, betterment taxes and other fiscal devices intended to capture increments in land value attributable to public policy changes (such as planning permissions or infrastructure development), such policies have proved both politically highly contentious and administratively complex.[3] At present, no such special taxes exist.

Notes
1. Non-domestic rating is the oldest tax in the UK, dating back to 1601 (Brown and Hepworth, 2002, p. 332).
2. See UK Department for Transport, Local Government and the Regions (2000), ch. 5. For a less sanguine view of the new tax, see Giles and Ridge (1995).
3. See Connellan and Lichfield (2000) for a review. On the administrative aspects, see the classic study by Hood (1976), pp. 94–114.

References

Brown, P.K and M.A. Hepworth (2002), 'A Study of European Land Tax Systems,' Cambridge, MA: Lincoln Institute of Land Policy Working Paper.

Owen Connellan and Nathaniel Lichfield (2000), 'Great Britain,' in R.V. Andelson (ed.), *Land-Value Taxation Around the World*, 3rd edn, Malden, MA: Blackwell, pp. 239–57.

Giles, C. and M. Ridge (1995), 'The Council Tax: An Examination of the New Local Property Tax in Britain,' *Journal of Property Tax Assessment and Administration*, **1** (2), 40–59.

Hood, C.C. (1976), *The Limits of Administration*, London: John Wiley.

King, David N. (1988), 'Accountability and Equity in British Local Finance – The Poll Tax,' University of Stirling, Discussion Papers in Economics, Finance, and Investment.

Office of the Deputy Prime Minister (2003), *Local Government Financial Statistics*, England, No. 13.

Smith, Peter (1991), 'Lessons from the British Poll Tax Disaster,' *National Tax Journal*, **44** (4), 421–36.

UK Department for Transport, Local Government and the Regions (2000), *Modernising Local Government Finance: A Green Paper.*

Youngman, Joan and Jane Malme (1994), *An International Survey of Taxes on Land and Buildings*, Deventer, The Netherlands: Kluwer Law and Taxation Publishers.

6 Property taxation in Australia

Enid Slack

Australia is a federation with three levels of government: federal, state and local. There are six states (divided into local government areas) and two territories (in which there is only one level of government). There are 143 urban municipalities and 579 regional and rural municipalities in the country. Constitutional responsibility for local governments rests with the states and territories. They provide the legal framework in which local governments operate. They also oversee their operations. States and territories mandate the local electoral system, establish municipal boundaries, and regulate local services. Local governments in each state (as well as the territorial governments) are authorized by state or territorial legislation to levy rates on property. Municipal rates vary across states/territories.

Property taxes comprise the land tax, municipal rates, financial and capital transactions and other property taxes levied. Table 6.1 shows a breakdown of the level of government that levies each of these taxes. This chapter focuses on the state land tax and municipal rates, with a particular focus on one state – New South Wales.

*Table 6.1   Distribution of property tax revenues, by level of government,
Australia, 1999–2000 (%)*

	Commonwealth	State	Local
Land tax	0.0	100.0	0.0
Municipal rates	0.0	1.6	98.4
Financial and capital transactions	0.0	100.0	0.0
Other property taxes	1.6	98.4	0.0

Source: Based on information in National Office of Local Government (2001).

Revenue importance

Table 6.2 provides a breakdown of the sources of revenue to local government in Australia in 2000–2001. It shows that local governments received an average of 37.7 percent of their revenues from taxes (municipal rates). The circumstances of individual councils within states and between states and the Northern Territory vary considerably from the national average, however. For

Table 6.2   Sources of local government revenue, Australia, 2000–2001

Revenue sources	$ millions	% of total revenues
Taxation	6 388	37.7
Sales of goods and services	5 433	32.1
Interest	433	2.6
Grants and subsidies	2 147	12.7
Other revenue	2 530	14.9
Total revenue	16 930	100.0

Source: Australian Bureau of Statistics, Government Finance Statistics, cat. No. 5512.0 as reported in National Office of Local Government (2003).

example, the use of municipal rates ranges from a low of 26.7 percent of local revenues in the Northern Territory to a high of 57.4 percent in South Australia (National Office of Local Government, 2003, p. 12).

Over the last 40 years, there have been changes in the distribution of municipal revenues. In particular, municipal rates are now a smaller proportion of local government revenues; user fees are larger; Commonwealth transfers have increased; and state transfers have remained roughly the same as they were in the 1960s (Commonwealth Grants Commission, 2001, p. 170).

Tax base

The land tax is a state tax on the ownership of land (including vacant land or a flat or home unit). The land tax is levied on the unimproved value of taxable land in the state governments and the Australian Capital Territory. It is not levied in the Northern Territory. In all states except Victoria, the taxpayer's principal residence is exempt from the land tax. Expensive parcels may receive only a partial exemption or no exemption, however. Land owned by religious bodies and schools is exempt from the land tax in all states and territories. Land designated for primary production is exempt in all states except Tasmania.

In New South Wales, land used for the principal place of residence (up to a threshold level), primary production, maintaining endangered animals and birds, retirement villages and nursing homes, non-profit associations, some government or semi-government bodies, and Aboriginal land councils are exempt from the state land tax.

Municipal rates are levied on a variety of tax bases in Australia. Local governments can levy a property tax on any one of the following bases (Youngman and Malme, 1994, p. 85):

- unimproved land value: the amount which the fee simple of the land might be expected to realize if sold, assuming any improvements had not been made;
- land value or site value: similar to unimproved value except that improvements such as clearing, excavating, or grading are not disregarded in determining value;
- improved value of land and buildings: the market value which the property might be expected to realize if sold;
- rental value of land and buildings: gross annual rental value that the land and buildings might realize if leased.

The following summarizes the tax base for municipal rates used in each state:

- New South Wales: land value (replacing unimproved value in 1978) is used for residential property and assessed annual value is used for non-residential properties.
- Victoria: 61 municipalities use capital improved value, 11 municipalities use net annual value and 6 municipalities use site value.
- Queensland: land value (unimproved value) is used for urban and rural areas.
- Western Australia: gross rental value is used in metropolitan and non-metropolitan local government authorities; unimproved land values are used in rural areas and some outer metropolitan areas for non-residential land.
- South Australia: four councils tax land values and the remainder tax improved values.
- Tasmania: the base is annual rental value.

As noted above, a combination of bases is used in some states. Moreover, a combination of bases can be used for different types of property. For example, rental value for land and buildings can be used for commercial and industrial properties while only unimproved land is taxed elsewhere. In valuing property, reliance is mostly placed on the comparable sales method.

Exclusions include machines, tools or other appliances not affixed to the property (or which could be removed). Exemptions are determined by the state or territorial governments. Although there is some variation in the use of exemptions, the most common ones are publicly owned land, public hospitals, libraries, cemeteries, charities, church lands, universities, schools and foreign embassies. A number of states exempt the owner's principal place of residence either entirely or up to some threshold value.

Tax rates

For both land taxes and municipal rates, different rates are used for different land uses. Often rates are reduced on agricultural land at local discretion. For example, primary producers pay half the rates payable by non-primary producers. This tax policy encourages land speculation by rural enterprises such as market gardens and nurseries, which still enjoy windfall profits when land is re-zoned to a higher use (Hornby, 1999).

The land tax is levied by states on the unimproved value of the land at its highest and best use either by a flat rate or a progressive rate. In New South Wales for 2003, the land tax rate was 1.7 percent applied to the total value of property assessed beyond the land tax threshold (which was $261 000 in 2003).[1] This means that taxpayers are liable if the aggregate value of the land they own, other than a principal residence, has a total value of $261 000 or more. The land value threshold is linked to the annual increase in the value of commercial, industrial and residential land across New South Wales. The premium property tax for 2003 only applies to principal residences where the land value is $1.68 million or more.[2] The land value threshold for the premium property tax is indexed according to the average change in residential land values in the Sydney statistical division. The threshold will not fall if land values fall, however. There is also an early payment discount of 1.5 percent for full payment if the land tax is paid within 30 days of receipt of the tax notice. The other states and the Australian Capital Territory levy progressive fixed rates or percentages on various ranges of value.[3]

Municipal tax rates are determined on the basis of local budgetary requirements and include general rates on all property-owners or specific rates imposed for a special purpose, for example, for infrastructure improvements. In New South Wales, ordinary rates cover the basic costs of local councils; special rates are charged for services provided by councils or for special purposes such as water supply, sewerage and drainage. Ordinary rates can vary for different types of land. There are four categories of land (residential, farmland, business and mining), and sub-categories may be established under each of these categories.

Both ordinary rates and special rates may be assessed entirely on land values or with a two-part structure in New South Wales. The two-part structure comprises a base amount and an amount calculated using land value. The base amount must not produce more than 50 percent of total revenue from a particular category or sub-category of rate. The base amount for ordinary rates is generally determined by administrative and general operational costs; for special rates, the rate is determined by administrative services costs. Municipalities may also charge a minimum rate on each parcel of land. The state government sets a limit on the percentage increase in income that municipalities can achieve from rates each year.

Concessions are available for eligible pensioners. In the inner suburbs of Sydney, local councils allow either rebates or rate reductions for pensioners (for example, tax deferrals). Other concessions are also available for vacant land, where zoning anomalies exist or for heritage properties. Municipalities can also reduce the rates in cases of genuine hardship.

Administration

The titling system in Australia (the Torrens system) is administered by the Registrar of Deeds and the Registrar of Titles and ensures certainty of rights in property (McCluskey and Franzsen, 2001, p. 25). The state governments prepare the assessment rolls and submit them to the local governments who set the tax rates, administer, and collect the taxes. Valuations are established by each state's valuer-general for both the land tax and local government rates as well as government land acquisitions, rentals and transfers between agencies. Valuations are also used for stamp duties, land transfer taxes, or water rates based on land values.

The valuation cycle differs among states, ranging from annual reassessments (in New South Wales) up to seven years. In some states, such as South Australia, an equalization factor is applied between general valuations to adjust the land value for the land tax to reflect more current market values and achieve greater uniformity. The valuer-general determines the equalization factor each year for each zone in each local government area. The factor, applied to the nominal land value, approximates the value that would have been applicable had a general valuation taken place. Assessed annual value is nine-tenths of the fair average annual value of the land with the improvements or $10, whichever is greater.

Throughout all of the states in Australia, emphasis is being placed on more frequent revaluations. Although the State of Victoria has moved to a two-year cycle, there is a trend towards annual revaluation in some cases at the state level (for example, Western Australia) and in some cases at the city level such as Melbourne, Brisbane and Cairns (McCluskey and Franzsen, 2001, p. 42).

In New South Wales, the valuations for the state land tax are made by the Chief Commissioner of State Revenue on 1 July preceding each land tax year. These valuations are not the same as those made by the valuer-general for rating purposes (which are made approximately every three years). An allowance, or reduction in land value, may be applicable where expenses for land improvements have been made by an owner, occupier or lessee.

Assessments can be appealed to the Chief Commissioner of State Revenue within 60 days of receiving an assessment. A review of this decision to the Administrative Decisions Tribunal or the Supreme Court can be requested. A review of a land value decision can only be made to the Land and Environment Court.

As noted above, local governments are responsible for collecting the taxes. Tax arrears vary across municipalities but 'the collection ratio is presumed to be very high' (Youngman and Malme, 1994, p. 87).

Other taxes on land
Stamp duties are levied by state and territorial governments, usually as a percentage of the transfer price. The stamp duty is paid by the purchaser of the property on the basis of the value of the property transferred. All states have stamp duty concessions for first-time homebuyers and some states have concessions for any principal residence. An exemption is available for designated government authorities, some educational authorities and registered charities.

In New South Wales, for example, there is a tax on the transfer of land or business. Duty is payable by the transferee or the purchaser. The rate of duty is calculated according to Table 6.3.

Table 6.3   Calculation of duty on the transfer of land or business, New South Wales

Dutiable value of the dutiable property subject to dutiable transaction	Rate of duty
$0–$14 000	$1.25 for every $100 or part thereof
$14 001–$30 000	$175 plus $1.50 for every $100 or part thereof
$30 001–$80 000	$415 plus $1.75 for every $100 or part thereof
$80 001–$300 000	$1290 plus $3.50 for every $100 or part thereof
$300 001–$1 000 000	$8990 plus $4.50 for every $100 or part thereof
over $1 000 000	$40 490 plus $5.50 for every $100 or part thereof

Source: Office of State Revenue, New South Wales Treasury.

Most states charge fees to developers to compensate local governments for improvements in infrastructure necessitated by the development. In some states, water and sewer availability charges are based on rateable land values.

A capital gains tax was introduced in Australia in 1985. It applies to all assets acquired after 20 September 1985 with the exception of a principal residence.

Notes
1. This is up from $220 000 in 2002 – an increase of 18.6 percent.
2. This is up from $1.414 million in 2002 – an increase of 18.8 percent.
3. For example, in Western Australia in 2002–2003, there are nine value categories not

including the category of unimproved values under $50 000 for which there is no tax. For values between $50 000 and $100 000, the rate is $75 plus 0.15 cents for each $1 in excess of $50 000; for values between $100 000 and $190 000, the rate is $150 plus 0.25 cents for each $1 in excess of $100 000; for values between $190 000 and $325 000, the rate is $375 plus 0.45 cents for each $1 in excess of $190 000 and so on up to values exceeding $5 million, where the rate is $96 782.50 plus 2.50 cents for each $1 in excess of $5 million. In addition, there is a rate of 0.15 cents for each $1 of unimproved value of taxable land situated in the metropolitan region only. The land tax rate is reviewed annually (Government of Western Australia, 2003, p. 4).

References

Commonwealth Grants Commission (2001), *Report on State Revenue Sharing Relativities, 2001 Update*, Canberra.

Government of Western Australia (2003), *Land Taxes 2002/2003*, Department of Treasury and Finance, Office of State Revenue.

Hornby, David (1999), 'Property Taxes in Australia,' in William McCluskey (ed.), *Property Tax: An International Comparative Review*, Aldershot, UK: Ashgate Publishing, pp. 313–36.

McCluskey, William J. and Riël C.D. Franzsen (2001), 'Land Value Taxation: A Case Study Approach,' Cambridge, MA: Lincoln Institute of Land Policy, Working Paper.

National Office of Local Government (2001), *1999–2000 Report on the Operation of the Local Government (Financial Assistance) Act 1995*.

National Office of Local Government (2003), *2001–2002 Report on the Operation of the Local Government (Financial Assistance) Act 1995*.

Youngman, Joan and Jane Malme (1994), *An International Survey of Taxes on Land and Buildings*, Deventer, The Netherlands: Kluwer Law and Taxation Publishers.

7 Land taxation in Germany

Paul Bernd Spahn

Germany is a federal country consisting of 16 autonomous states (*Länder*) of which three are city-states (Berlin, Hamburg and Breme) that exercise both state and municipal functions and a strong municipal sector represented by roughly 14 000 municipal governments. The municipal sector consists of county-free cities (*kreisfreie Städte*), counties (municipalities of mainly rural areas forming so-called *Kreise*) and the municipalities themselves (*Gemeinden*).

The three levels of government are mainly financed by shared taxes. In addition, there are some federal excise taxes and minor state taxes. These taxes are subject to federal legislation and are uniform in structure and tax rates. The municipal sector also participates in shared taxes (VAT and personal income tax). There is also an important local business tax and less important land taxes where local governments have the right to vary their municipal 'leverage factors' (see below) and thus enjoy some limited taxing autonomy.

The basic framework of the German land tax

The legal basis of the German land tax is the federal land tax law (*Grundsteuergesetz*) of 7 August 1973 and subsequent modifications. The tax code is uniform across the Federation although the tax is a municipal tax.[1] Municipalities are however entitled to 'leverage' the land tax (see below for explanation), they collect the tax, and they appropriate its full proceeds. The administration of the tax is split between the state (for assessing the rateable value of the property and determining the appropriate 'base rates' according to federal legislation) and the municipality (for applying a municipal leverage ratio as determined by the local council, and for collecting tax revenue). If a property extends over the territory of more than one municipality, the tax base is apportioned appropriately.

The object of the land tax is domestic land and buildings, including agricultural land and forests. Exemptions exist for public land (such as parks, cemeteries), land and buildings of public authorities, of the federal railways, of churches, hospitals, scientific and educational institutions, military compounds and municipal corporations. The owner/beneficiary of the property is liable to pay the tax. The tax refers only to the nature and value of land. Personal circumstances of the owner/beneficiary are totally disregarded.

Tax base and rates

German tax law is peculiar in that a 'standard tax' (*Steuermessbetrag*) is determined by the state tax administration on uniform rules for all municipalities. This standard tax is obtained by multiplying the 'rateable value' (*Einheitswert*) by a 'base rate' (*Steuermesszahl*). The assessment is made for every single piece of land registered in the cadastre (*Grundbuch*). The state tax administration notifies the owner/beneficiary and the municipality in whose jurisdiction the property is located. Changes of this standard assessment are extremely rare and occur only in cases of sale or change in the use of the property (or change in federal legislation). For the five states that constituted the former East Germany the procedure is slightly different in that more recent rateable values are not available (see below). The tax is therefore based on a 'surrogate rateable value' instead.

The assessment of the standard tax by the state tax administration is the basis for levying the municipal tax. The municipality applies a 'leverage ratio' (*Hebesatz*) to this standard tax. The ratios may vary among municipalities.[2]

The land tax is thus calculated as follows:

At the level of the state:

(Rateable value or surrogate rateable value) × (base rate) =
(assessed base value for tax purposes), with standard rules for all
municipalities.

At the level of the municipality:

(Assessed base value for tax purposes) × (municipal leverage ratio) =
(assessed municipal land tax).

For instance, if the rateable value of a two-family house is €40 000 (not an unrealistic figure), the base rate would be 0.31 percent, and the assessed base value for tax purposes €124 per year. If the leverage ratio of the municipality is 300 percent, it would assess a municipal land tax of €372 per year.

Two variants of the land tax

The law distinguishes two categories of land: agricultural land and forests; and other real property. This leads to two variants of the land tax: land tax A (for agricultural businesses and forestry), and land tax B (for other land, including improvements).

The tax base of land tax A includes all business-related objects that serve to maintain the agricultural or forestry business – not only land, but also buildings, machinery and livestock. This is why it is often seen to be, in effect, the 'business tax of farmers.'[3] Land tax B includes buildings and ancillary structures, but *not* machinery and business-related objects, even though they may represent fixed capital. Land tax B also covers leaseholds and owner-occupied dwellings.

The division of the land tax into two categories allows not only the separation of tax assessment and collection but also the application of different leverage ratios to each variant of the tax. Variations of the leverage ratio for different types of properties *within* each tax variant are not allowed, but some differentiation occurs through the base rates.

Rateable values

The rateable value of land is determined by a specific federal law on valuations (*Bewertungsgesetz*). This law is not only the basis for assessing the value of the land tax, but also for all other property-related taxes (such as the (suspended) net wealth tax, and the gift and inheritance taxes).

According to the valuation law, the rateable value (*Einheitswert*) is defined as the 'price that could be realized ... in the case of a sale' without regard to personal circumstances. The value includes buildings and ancillary structures, and in the case of agricultural land, machinery and livestock.

Up to 1973 the rateable values were based on the totally outdated census data of 1935. In 1964 there was a comprehensive census in West Germany, which established rateable values for land in accordance with the law. Rateable values were obtained on the basis of capitalized gross returns (rental income) or, where these figures were not available, as in the case of owner-occupied dwellings, on the basis of construction costs.

The values were established as follows:

- Land on the territory of West Germany is valued at its rateable value of 1964.
- Agricultural and forestry land in the territory of East Germany, the former German Democratic Republic (GDR), is valued at a surrogate rateable value (*Ersatzwirtschaftswert*) for 1964.
- Other land in the territory of the former GDR, for which a rateable value for 1935[4] is available, is established at this value.
- For apartments and one-family houses on the territory of the former GDR built before 1991, and for which a rateable value of 1935 is not available, a surrogate assessment basis (*Ersatzbemessungsgrundlage*) is used. It consists of a monetary amount estimated at arm's length on the basis of square meters and conforming quality indicators.
- For dwellings in the territory of the former GDR built between 1981 and 1991 there was a ten-year exemption from the land tax.

From 1974 on, the census data of 1964 were used in West Germany (with a general adjustment factor of 1.4 in order to account for price increases during the preceding decade). According to the law on valuations, the rateable value is to be updated every sixth year. But the census originally planned for 1970 never took place, nor were there any other revisions of rateable values. The 1964 data (price-adjusted for 1974) have thus been used until now without further update. In East Germany, valuations go back to the census year 1935. For new buildings and structures since 1964, valuation is done on the basis of costs at prices of the standard valuation date 1974.

This treatment of land valuation has led to an unacceptable privilege of landowners compared to other forms of holding wealth.[5] However, there has been little inclination by federal and state politicians to alter the situation. This has led to a constitutional challenge based on the equality-of-treatment clause of the Constitution. The Federal Constitutional Court forced the government to amend the tax law on inheritances and gifts with respect to the valuation of land,[6] and to suspend the net wealth tax altogether from 1997 on. However, the land tax remained unaffected by this ruling because *all categories* of land are undervalued similarly, which is less problematical in view of the equality-of-treatment clause.

The base rates
As mentioned before, the state tax office calculates the base value for tax purposes (*Steuermessbetrag*), and notifies the municipality accordingly. This value is established by law as the rateable value/surrogate rateable value multiplied by the base rate for tax purposes (*Steuermesszahl*). The base rates for tax purposes are uniform for all municipalities. They are:

- 0.6 percent for agricultural land and forestry.
- 0.26 percent for one-family houses for the first €38 346.89, and 0.35 percent above this amount.
- 0.31 percent for two-family houses.
- 0.35 percent for other real estate with/without buildings.
- real estate in the territory of the former GDR evaluated by the (unadjusted) rateable value of 1935 is assessed with rates between 0.5 and 1 percent in accordance with the land tax law of 1 July 1937.

The differentiation of the base rates is motivated by social policy objectives. For instance, an incentive is embedded for (smaller or lower-cost) one-family dwellings and two-family houses. The higher rate for agricultural land is explained by two factors: a lump-sum correction for the usually low rateable value; and some compensation for the exemption from the local business tax that non-agricultural businesses have to carry.

The leverage factors

At the local level, the base value for tax purposes is multiplied by a municipal leverage factor (*Hebesatz*). Municipalities are free to determine this factor. Therefore the effective rate of the land tax differs between municipalities. The land tax law fixes no maximum limit for the leverage.

Normally, there are two leverage factors to distinguish in accordance with the tax object: one for agricultural and forestry enterprises (land tax A), and one for private and business real estate (land tax B). The weighted average of municipal leverage factors by state is shown in Table 7.1.

Table 7.1   The weighted average of municipal leverage factors for the land tax by State, Germany, 2000 (%)

State	Land tax A	Land tax B
Baden-Württemberg	320	332
Bavaria	323	333
Berlin	150	600
Brandenburg	229	342
Bremen	248	530
Hamburg	225	490
Hesse	263	320
Lower Saxony	315	358
Mecklenburg–West Pomerania	233	343
North Rhine–Westphalia	202	401
Rhineland–Palatinate	277	328
Saarland	244	332
Saxony	280	385
Saxony–Anhalt	272	354
Schleswig–Holstein	250	303
Thuringia	227	324
National average	278	367

Source: Federal Statistical Office.

Tax revenue

The share of the land tax relative to municipal tax revenue has been declining significantly over the last 50 years (34.8 percent in 1951, and 15.5 percent in the year 2000). This is mainly due to the outdated and basically unadjusted tax base. In particular, land tax A for agricultural land is virtually stagnating. Revenue of land tax B has been increasing somewhat due to alterations in the use of land (for instance through adding constructions) and consequent revaluations, and to a general increase of leverage ratios. But since the tax base does not include a price adjustment element (all prices and costs being discounted to 1974), the tax will never become buoyant without a major reform. Some reform proposals are discussed below, but they have all been put on hold.

The revenues of the land tax are shown in Table 7.2.

Table 7.2   Germany: land tax revenues, 1997–2000 (in € million)

	1997	1998	1999	2000
Land tax A	328.7	326.7	327.9	332.8
Land tax B	7 597.8	7 970.5	8 307.8	8 516.1
Total revenue of municipalities	48 273.1	53 749.5	56 333.9	57 136.2
Land tax revenues as a percentage of total municipal revenues	16.4	15.4	15.3	15.5
Land tax revenue as a percentage of GDP	0.42	0.43	0.44	0.44

Source: Federal Ministry of Finance; own currency conversions.

The reasons why politicians are reluctant to reform the land tax are mainly linked to their inability to tackle complex valuation rules (which even made them abandon the net wealth tax altogether rather than reforming the assessment rules), and fear of causing unrest because the tax is typically a cost element of housing rents. As most Germans live in rented dwellings, this poses an unnecessary political risk for federal politicians. Moreover, neither the federal nor the state governments have any interest in the tax because its yield falls exclusively to municipalities. Municipalities appear to be more accountable for the tax when using their leverage factors.

It is also important to understand that the land tax plays only a minor role in municipal budgets. Municipalities can count on the much more important business tax, on a share in the more buoyant personal income and value-added taxes, as well as on transfers from their respective state governments (and even some from the federal government).

Tax assessment

At the beginning of the year, the municipality sends a land tax assessment to taxpayers. For taxpayers who have to pay the same amount as in the previous year, the municipality can assess the tax by public announcement. This is cheaper than an individual assessment, and is therefore done more and more frequently. On the day of the publication the land tax is fixed, payable in quarters on 15 February, 15 May, 15 August and 15 November. On request, it is possible to pay the tax in smaller amounts at other dates.

The person to whom the rateable value was attributed (normally the owner) is liable to pay the tax. In addition, the user of the property (usefructor) can be rendered liable to pay the tax. The owner is identified by the cadastre, and transfers of property are monitored by the property transaction tax (see below) where the notary is required to send a copy of the sales contract to the state tax authority.

The land tax is payable to the municipality. If a taxpayer does not pay in due time the municipality can levy fees and penalty supplements. Taxpayers can avoid this problem by automatic debit authorization. This allows the municipality to charge the amount directly to the bank account of the taxpayer. Data on tax arrears are not available, but due to the low tax burden and automatic payment arrangements, arrears are insignificant in Germany (less than 1 percent of taxes paid).[7]

Reform proposals

The German land tax is clearly old-fashioned and based on data that have not (or have only partially) been updated during a quarter of a century. Therefore ten years ago a Working Group of the Conference of State Finance Ministers was assigned the task of developing new rules for assessing the tax base of the land tax. Two models were discussed: (i) a simple tax on area (land and buildings); and (ii) a combination of land and building values. The first proposal found support only from Bavaria, and the majority vote was in favor of the second approach. Other proposals discussed (but not taken up by the Working Group) were a tax on the value of land only, and a tax on a combination of land value and building areas. Although the Group presented its findings in May 2000, neither the federal legislature nor the states (through an initiative of the Second Chamber of Parliament, the *Bundesrat*) have taken any step to start a reform.

Instead, the states of Bavaria and Hesse have proposed transferring legislation of the land tax from the Federation to the states, which would end the uniform federal tax law allegedly required by the 'uniformity-of-living-conditions' clause of the Constitution. The states would then be free to determine both the tax base (rateable value) and the base rates in accordance with their own preferences. If this proposal ever becomes reality, it is unlikely that the

structure of the tax (with the rateable value as a base, the (then state-legis-
lated) base rates for determining the standard tax, and the municipal leverage
ratios) will be changed because the Federation will insist on the need for a
'framework law' that would define the tax structure uniformly, albeit not its
elements in detail.

The two states also proposed transferring all other land tax competencies
to municipalities, including the right to assess the tax based on (then state)
legislation. This would end the split in the administration of the tax according
to which the state assesses the rateable value and the base rates, while
municipalities apply their leverage ratios and collect the tax.

Given the controversial nature of the proposals (the latter would require a
constitutional amendment) and the unwillingness of politicians to tackle the
intricacies of the German land tax in general, it is highly unlikely that these
reform proposals will bear fruit in the near future.

Other land-based taxes

Other land-based taxes are as follows:

- There is a tax on the acquisition of real estate, covering transactions of
  land (with or without buildings), parts of buildings, rights to build,
  rights to parts of buildings, and so on. The tax rate is 3.5 percent of the
  gross value of the transaction (purchase price). Vendors and buyers are
  legally jointly liable to pay the tax, but most sales contracts stipulate
  that the tax be carried by the buyer.

  The real estate transactions tax is a state tax, but municipalities may
  receive a share of the revenue according to state legislation. The total
  receipts of the tax were €5.24 billion (or 0.26 percent of GDP) in the
  year 2000.
- Before 1997, land was also taxed in the context of a net wealth tax at
  rates of 0.5 percent (0.6 percent for corporations). Following a ruling
  of the Federal Constitutional Court of 22 May 1995, the tax was
  declared unconstitutional. It was therefore suspended with effect from
  January 1997. A revised version of the wealth tax law was under
  discussion at the time of writing.
- Land is also taxed within the context of the inheritance or gift tax (see
  text at note 6 above). This tax is a state tax in Germany.
- Finally, capital gains on land are taxed within the income tax and
  corporate tax laws. For businesses, all real property on the balance
  sheet is taxed at market values upon realization (or an assessed market-
  related value upon transfer into private property). For private individuals,
  the capital gains tax applies only for property sales realized within a
  time span of ten years from acquisition. After the elections of 2002 the

federal coalition government announced its plan to extend that time span to infinity, but legislation on this is still pending. The tax base is the sales price minus the purchase price and property-related (and income tax deductible) expenditures incurred during that same period. There is an exemption for homeowners who use the proceeds of the sale of the owner-occupied home for reinvestment in another owner-occupied dwelling.

Notes

1. In principle, municipalities do not have to levy a land tax, but all do.
2. It is difficult to speak of a 'tax rate' for the German land tax. If the rateable value were considered the tax base, the conventional tax rate would be the composite of the base rate multiplied by the municipal leverage ratio. However, as the state administration assesses not only the rateable value, but also the standard base rate for the property, which together form the basis of municipal taxation, the unconventional term of leverage ratio is used here instead of tax rate.
3. In Germany, there is a separate municipal business tax for commercial enterprises, but not for farmers.
4. The last census of real estate before 1964 took place in 1935.
5. A study done by the Wissenschaftlicher Beirat beim Bundesminister der Finanzen found that the average rateable value was 1231 DM/hectare compared to an average market (sales) price of 32 852 DM/hectare in 1996 (or less than 4 percent of market value).
6. For idle land the valuation used is established by the municipality (*Bodenrichtwert*), with an arm's-length reduction of 20 percent (30 percent for industrial land). For business properties, the value is taken from the balance sheet (which is usually low because it is based on the purchase date). For constructed land the value is a multiple of the annual rental income, corrected by an obsolescence factor based on the age of the building. One- and two-family housing also benefits from a rebate of 20 percent.
7. There are a few cases of land tax arrears that are worth mentioning, but these were caused by inappropriate tax administration and uncertainties surrounding the taxation of land in the former GDR (East Germany). It is also noteworthy that municipalities in the East do not have an incentive to levy the tax due to the fact that their lack of own fiscal revenue is almost completely compensated by intergovernmental transfers.

8 Property tax in Japan

Toshiaki Kitazato

Japan has a three-tier governmental system that consists of the national government, 47 prefectures (middle-level governments), and 3219 municipalities (cities, towns and villages).

The Local Tax Law at the national level gives municipalities the legal basis to levy various local taxes, including the fixed property tax. Municipalities levy the fixed property tax on (a) land, (b) houses and buildings, and (c) tangible business assets by passing their own by-laws in accordance with the Local Tax Law. Table 8.1 outlines the principal characteristics of this tax.

Table 8.1 Japan: outline of fixed property tax, 2002

Tax authority	Municipalities (cities, towns and villages) assess, levy and collect the tax. For 23 special wards of Tokyo, the tax is levied by the Tokyo Metropolitan Government.
Object of taxation	Land, buildings and tangible business assets Land: 178 million plots Building: 60 million buildings
Taxpayer	Owners of land, buildings and depreciable property Land: 38 million persons Buildings: 36 million persons Tangible business assets: 4 million persons
Tax base	Value (fair market value) as of 1 January Land and buildings are reassessed every three years
Tax rate	Standard tax rate: 1.4% Maximum tax rate: 2.1%
Tax revenue	9.065 trillion yen as of 2001 45.3% of total municipal taxes 25.5% of total local taxes

Revenue

The yield of the fixed property tax is shown in Table 8.2, along with that of the city planning tax levied by 785 municipalities to finance city works. The

Table 8.2   Japan: taxes on property as share of total local taxes, 1997–
2001 (trillion yen)

	Total municipal taxes (a)	Fixed property tax (b)	(b)/(a), %	City planning tax (c)	(c)/(a), %
2001	20.019	9.065	45.3	1.320	6.6
2000	19.961	8.955	44.9	1.318	6.6
1999	20.440	9.244	45.2	1.375	6.7
1998	20.603	9.020	43.8	1.352	6.6
1997	21.208	8.752	41.3	1.326	6.3

base of this tax is land and buildings. Municipalities can set the tax rate as
high as 0.3 percent.

In addition to these two municipal taxes on real property, a real property
acquisition tax is levied by all prefectures. This tax is levied on the property
tax assessment value at the time of acquisition of land and buildings. The tax
rate is 4 percent. Table 8.3 shows the yield of this tax, while Table 8.4 shows
the relative importance of these taxes in total subnational taxation.

Table 8.3   Japan: prefectural tax on property, 1997–2001 (trillion yen)

	Total prefectural taxes (a)	Real property acquisition tax (b)	(b)/(a), %
2001	15.530	0.537	3.5
2000	15.585	0.567	3.6
1999	14.586	0.580	4.0
1998	15.319	0.635	4.1
1997	14.948	0.731	4.9

Tax base of the fixed property tax
In addition to land and buildings, taxable fixed property includes tangible
business assets that are depreciable for the purposes of the income tax and
corporation tax.

The tax base is the assessed value of the taxable fixed property as listed
in the fixed property tax register book compiled by each municipality.
Although the assessment is administered by municipalities, a unified formula for the assessment of the value of taxable fixed property is determined

Table 8.4   Japan: local taxes, 2001 (trillion yen)

Prefectural Taxes	Amount	%
Prefectural inhabitants' tax	4.382	28.2
(Individual)	2.369	15.3
(Corporation)	0.837	5.4
(Interest rate)	1.176	7.6
Enterprise tax	4.328	27.9
(Individual enterprise tax)	0.226	1.5
(Corporation enterprise tax)	4.102	26.4
Real property acquisition tax	0.537	3.5
Prefectural tobacco tax	0.278	1.8
Automobile tax	1.771	11.4
Local consumption tax	2.474	15.9
Automobile acquisition tax	0.450	2.9
Light-oil delivery tax	1.190	7.7
Miscellaneous	0.120	0.8
Total prefectural taxes	15.530	100.0

Municipal taxes	Amount	%
Municipal inhabitants' tax	8.185	40.9
(Individual)	5.996	30.0
(Corporation)	2.188	10.9
Municipal fixed property tax	9.153	45.7
Municipal tobacco tax	0.851	4.3
City planning tax	1.320	6.6
Miscellaneous	0.510	2.5
Total municipal taxes	20.019	100.0

by the national Ministry of Public Management, Home Affairs, Posts and Telecommunications. With this uniform formula the assessment by each municipality is basically unified all over Japan in order to ensure that the system is fair and equitable.

The assessed value of land is determined by taking into account actual market prices of several similar tracts of land. A certain number of standard plots of land for each type (such as residential land, agricultural land, forest and so on) in different areas of each municipality is selected, and an assessed value is assigned to the land facing the main roads. Then the value of each plot is assessed in relation to the value of the standard plot of land, taking into consideration the surrounding conditions.

Agricultural lands are assessed in the same way as residential lands, starting with the selection of a standard plot for assessment as agricultural land in each area. Agricultural lands in 'the urbanization area' of the city planning area are basically assessed as if the lands were residential lands. However, for agricultural land designated as an 'agricultural green area' currently used for harvesting agricultural products, the tax is levied as if on agricultural land even if the property is located in the 'urbanization area.'[1]

For purposes of housing policy, the tax base for residential land is taken to be one-sixth of the assessed value for the portion up to 200 square meters (m^2), and one-third of the assessed value for the portion exceeding 200 m^2. Taxable assets valued at less than the following amounts are exempt from tax: for land – 300 000 yen; for buildings – 200 000 yen; and for tangible business assets – 1 500 000 yen. Fixed property used as public roads or cemeteries, or for educational, religious, social welfare, and other purposes stipulated in the Local Tax Law is exempt from the fixed property tax. Fixed property owned by the national government, prefectures, municipalities, and embassies and consulates of foreign countries is also exempt from the fixed property tax.

The value of a house or building is determined by taking into account the cost of replacement as well as depreciation for the years in use.

Again in furtherance of housing policy, the amount of tax for certain houses is reduced in the following manner:

(a)   For new houses built by 31 March 2004 with floor space of 50 to 280 m^2, the tax amount is reduced by 50 percent for floor space up to 120 m^2 for the first three taxable years.

(b)   For new fire-proof residential buildings with three or more stories built by 31 March 2004 with floor space of 50 to 280 m^2 (for apartment buildings for rent, the range of space is 35 to 280 m^2), the tax is reduced by 50 percent for the first five taxable years.

The taxable value of tangible business assets is determined by taking account of the cost and amount of depreciation.

Tax rate
In the Japanese local tax system, the Local Tax Law stipulates the local taxes that prefectures and municipalities can levy. The standard tax rate is also stipulated in the Law and each local government is expected to adopt this rate when they levy local taxes. The standard tax rate for the fixed property tax is a flat rate of 1.4 percent of the taxable value. In addition to the standard tax

rate, the maximum tax rate is also stipulated in the Law, which gives each local government the power to levy fixed property tax at up to 2.1 percent instead of the standard rate 1.4 percent. Out of 3219 municipalities, 276 have adopted a tax rate over 1.4 percent.

The same tax rate is applied to land and buildings in each municipality.

Tax administration

The fixed property tax is collected by municipalities. For 23 special wards of Tokyo, however, the Tokyo Metropolitan Government levies and collects the tax. As of FY 2001, the tax collection rate of the fixed property tax (the ratio of the fixed property tax collected against the tax due) is 97.4 percent.

The fixed property tax is levied by the municipalities in which the taxable property is situated as of 1 January. Persons, irrespective of whether resident or non-resident, who are listed as owners of taxable fixed property in the tax register book as of 1 January of each year, are required to pay the fixed property tax. This tax is paid in four installments, usually in April, July, December, and the following February. Each municipality sends taxpayers a tax form that includes the amount of the tax due as of 1 January. Taxpayers must pay the tax either through banks or post offices or directly to municipal offices. Those municipalities that levy the city planning tax in addition to the fixed property tax send the tax form of the city planning tax with that of the fixed property tax.

Each municipality must compile a tax register book for taxable fixed property. These registers used to be compiled in the form of paper documents. Now, however, under a new provision of the Local Tax Law, digital disks or other electronic devices can be considered as tax register books.

The tax register book for taxable fixed assets is exhibited to taxpayers from 1 April every year. Taxpayers are allowed to examine the tax register book and make objections to the Fixed Asset Valuation Council on the assessed value of their fixed assets. There are very few formal appeals to Assessment Value Review Committees: out of 760 000 taxable properties in Nagoya, for example, only 114 appeals were filed on land values and 17 on building values (Youngman and Malme, 1994, p. 152).

The assessed value of land and houses or buildings listed in the tax register book is revised every three years according to a survey of the market price of land and the cost of replacement of houses or buildings. Since reassessment in 1994, the assessed valued of residential land has been set at 70 percent of the official valuation price of land. When reassessment is carried out all over Japan every three years, sometimes the assessed value of land rises considerably. In order to avoid abrupt increases in the tax burden, the increment in the taxable value of the land in the period from FY 2000 to FY 2002 is limited to a certain extent by adjustment rates which are determined by the ratio of the taxable value to the real assessed value of land.

The assessed value of tangible business assets in the tax register book is revised annually. Owners of taxable tangible business assets must report to the municipalities in which they are situated the details needed to assess the value of such tangible business assets.

Citizens can register their rights to the land or building in order to protect them when they purchase or transfer the fixed property. The Ministry of Justice keeps fixed property registry files of its own. Regarding such purchases or transfers, it is convenient for municipalities to use this file to check their tax register book for the fixed property tax. For example, they can check whether there are any discrepancies as to who the real owner is, or what land a taxpayer owns. On the other hand, the branch offices of the Ministry of Justice must inform each municipality of the acquisition or transfer of fixed property located in the municipality.

Other taxes on land

In addition to the acquisition tax mentioned earlier, prefectures can also levy a prefectural fixed property tax on the part of the assessed value of large business assets in excess of municipal taxation limits. The owner of business assets whose assessed value exceeds the municipal taxation limits prescribed by the Local Tax Law is liable for the fixed property tax imposed by the prefecture in which the assets are located. Accordingly, in such areas the owner will pay two taxes on his/her business assets, the prefectural fixed property tax and the municipal fixed property tax. The tax base of the prefectural fixed property tax is the amount of the assessed value in excess of municipal taxation limits.

Land in Japan is (or has been) subject to several other taxes. Until 2003, when they were abolished, two 'special land-holding' municipal taxes were imposed. One of these taxes was imposed on the acquisition of real property at a rate of 3 percent of acquisition cost for land (against which the prefectural tax on acquisition was creditable); the other was imposed at a rate of 1.4 percent of acquisition cost for land held less than ten years (with the property tax payable on land creditable against it).

Finally, several national taxes affect land transfers such as a registration and license tax based on assessment values at a rate of 0.5 percent and an inheritance tax levied at progressive rates on the (different) assessment value for inheritance tax.[2] Capital gains taxes with rates varying with the time of holding are also applied to land transfers.

Reforms in land taxation

Following a prolonged boom in land prices, the whole system of land taxation was reviewed in detail in a special report in 1990. The nominal rates of the basic property taxes, as noted earlier, were 1.4–2.1 percent of assessed value for the property tax plus 0.3 percent for the city planning tax and an additional 1.4 percent (on acquisition cost) for the special land-holding tax. But the effective tax rate of the property tax alone in 1990 was only 1 percent of official valuations (as set each year) and for all three taxes on land hold-ings, the effective rate was only 1.5 percent, largely as a result of the relief for residential land mentioned above and especially the marked undervalua-tion of assessed values for tax purposes compared to official valuation prices. The national average assessed/official value ratio in 1991 was only 36.4 percent (with a coefficient of variation of 34.2). The effective rates relative to market prices were even lower, with a figure as low as 0.05 percent being cited for the Tokyo metropolitan area.

One result of the 1990 report was some reforms in assessment which led to a rise in the assessed/official ratios to 2.4 percent and 3.3 percent respectively by 1995. Nonetheless, as Professor Ishi (chair of the committee which wrote the report) subsequently noted, there was very strong resistance to raising local taxes:

> local authorities strongly maintained that the property tax should not be employed to levy a heavier burden on land-holdings as a means of reducing the asset value of land. This reflected their basic attitude of benefit taxation. They believe that the property tax should be collected by municipal governments to cover the cost of local public services to the inhabitants. Such a tax has no direct bearing upon the increased asset value of land caused by price hikes. As a consequence, a lower value of property tax assessment was rationalized on the ground that it should basically differ from either the market price or the official valuation price of land. (Ishi, 2001, p. 232)

For this reason, the principal fiscal recommendation of the 1990 commit-tee, in addition to strengthening the capital gains tax on land, was to introduce a new national land value tax, which was duly done in 1992, at a rate of 0.2 percent. This rate was raised to the planned 0.3 percent in the following year. Collections from this tax fell steadily, however, accelerated by a cut in the rate to 0.15 percent in 1996, until it was abolished in 1998, following a prolonged decline in land prices as Japan entered into an ever deeper reces-sion. Interestingly, agricultural land was exempted from this tax, which was levied only on land exceeding a high basic deduction (the greater of 1 billion yen or 30 000 yen per m^2).

Notes
1. The effects of this special treatment of agricultural land during the 'boom' period of the 1980s are discussed in Ishi (2001), p. 230.
2. On the exceptionally complex Japanese inheritance tax, see Ishi (2001), ch. 12.

References

Ishi, Hiromitsu (2001), *The Japanese Tax System*, 3rd edn, Oxford: Oxford University Press.

International Bureau of Fiscal Documentation (2001), *Asia Pacific Taxation*, Supplement No. 197, January.

Youngman, Joan M. and Jane H. Malme (1994), *An International Survey of Taxes on Land and Buildings*, Deventer: Kluwer Law and Taxation Publishers.

PART II

ASIA

9 Property taxation in Indonesia

Roy Kelly

The Republic of Indonesia, with a population of over 230 million, is the world's largest archipelago nation, consisting of over 17 000 islands, which straddle the equator, stretching 4500 km across the Indian and Pacific Oceans. Indonesia is a unitary country, with two levels of local government: Level I regional government consists of 27 provinces, two special regions and the capital city of Jakarta, while Level II regional government consists of 357 districts (regencies). Under the recent decentralization reforms in 2001, the 357 Level II districts are now the key administrative units for providing most government services. Under the Level II governments, Indonesia is organized into 4000 sub-districts (*kecamatan*) and 70 000 villages.

Role of property taxes in Indonesia[1]

Property taxes in Indonesia in FY 2001 generated about Rp 5.3 trillion (or approximately US$530 million). In 2001, property taxes represented 0.35 percent of GDP, 2.9 percent of total government tax revenues and roughly 11 percent of local government revenues.

The property tax in Indonesia is structured as a central government tax, whose revenues are shared with the local governments. As such, the property tax plays an important role in local government finance. As Table 9.1 indicates, the property tax has increasingly become a more important source of own revenues at both levels of local government. The property tax provided about two-thirds of all local-level tax revenues (67 percent), 50 percent of non-grant revenue and 11 percent of total local revenues in 1999–2000. At the provincial level, it plays a less important role – providing 26 percent of tax revenue, 22 percent of non-grant revenue and 11 percent of total provincial revenues.

As Table 9.2 indicates, property tax revenues have grown substantially over time – with a major shift in revenues from the rural sector to the urban and mining sectors. In 1969–70, the rural sector generated 75 percent of total revenue; it now generates less than 8 percent of total revenues. This sectoral shift is largely explained by the rapid urbanization rate and the new valuation system used for oil-producing properties within the mining sector.

In addition to the annual property tax, the government enacted a land and building acquisition tax in 1997. A tax of 5 percent is now applied to the 'acquisition value' of the property minus a valuation deduction of up to Rp 60

Table 9.1   Indonesia: regional government revenue structure, 1987–88 and 1999–2000

	1987–88		1999–2000	
	Rp billion	%	Rp billion	%
Provincial government level (Level I)	2 791	100	11 871	100
Central grants	2 112	75.7	6 041	50.9
Property tax	58	2.1	1 277	10.8
Level I taxes	459	16.4	3 632	30.6
User charges	58	2.1	268	2.3
Government enterprises	19	0.7	102	0.9
Other revenues	75	2.7	336	2.8
Loans	11	0.4	215	1.8
Property tax as % of total revenues		2.1		10.8
Property tax as % of non-grant revenues		8.5		21.9
Property tax as % of total tax revenues		11.2		26.0
Local government level (Level II)	1 414	100	26 935	100
Central grants	911	64.4	21 176	78.6
Property tax	146	10.3	2 893	10.7
Level II taxes	74	5.2	1 416	5.3
User charges	152	10.8	971	3.6
Government enterprises	7	0.5	75	0.3
Other revenues	71	5.0	301	1.1
Loans	54	3.8	103	0.4
Property tax as % of total revenues		10.3		10.7
Property tax as % of non-grant revenues		28.9		50.2
Property tax as % of total tax revenues		66.3		67.1

Source: National and Regional Government Budget Database, 2001.

million – a threshold that is determined by the regional government. The exception is for internal family transactions that have a maximum valuation deduction of Rp 300 million. In FY 2001, this acquisition tax was expected to generate about Rp 1.1 trillion.[2]

Tax base

The property tax in Indonesia is known as the 'land and building tax' (*Pajak Bumi dan Bangunan*, or PBB). It is levied upon the capital value of land and

Table 9.2   Indonesia: property tax revenue, by sector, 1992–2001 (in Rp billion)

Year	Rural	Urban	Estate	Forestry	Mining	Total
1969/70	5.9	0.8	0.7	–	0.5	7.9
1972/73	10.5	1.9	1.0	0.1	1.6	15.1
1975/76	22.7	5.9	3.7	1.6	2.0	35.8
1978/79	30.7	9.9	6.6	9.1	7.7	64.0
1981/82	36.2	20.6	11.2	12.5	15.1	95.6
1984/85	49.6	45.6	15.5	19.1	36.8	166.6
1987/88	76.8	95.1	32.3	7.0	104.8	316.0
1990/01	116.3	169.6	47.0	59.2	378.9	771.0
1993/94	154.0	382.0	55.0	129.0	767.0	1486.0
1996/97	227.0	768.0	87.0	207.0	1148.0	2438.0
1999/00	267.0	1040.0	201.0	175.0	1584.0	3267.0
2000*	267.0	1084.0	199.0	132.0	1879.0	3562.0
2000* (adj.)	356.0	1445.0	265.0	176.0	2505.0	4749.0
2001	322.0	1712.0	245.0	170.0	2838.0	5287.0

Note: In 2000, the Government of Indonesia changed the fiscal year to the calendar year. Thus, FY 2000 only includes nine months. The extrapolated 12-month equivalent is shown in 2000* (adj.).

Source: Government of Indonesia, Directorate of Property Taxation, 2001.

buildings. The tax liability is defined broadly to fall upon either the owner and/or beneficiary of the land and/or building. This broad definition is used to facilitate tax administration in light of unclear or incomplete legal cadastre and property titles.

The property tax is based on the sales value for each property as determined by the tax department. Property valuations are to be carried out every three years, except in areas of rapid development, where the exercise can be carried out on an annual basis. The tax department is given flexibility in choosing the valuation technique. With the exception of unique, high-value properties, rural and urban properties are valued through a simple mass appraisal system which uses land value books for land and a building classification system for buildings, while the estate, forestry and mining sectors are valued using a modified income approach.

The mass appraisal process for land is based on a 'similar land value zone' approach, where land is divided up into various zones – each with an average sales price per square meter as determined by the tax department. All land parcels located within that zone are valued by multiplying the land area by the average per unit price. The buildings are valued based on a cost approach using cost tables determined by the tax department. The total property value is the summation of the land and building values.

Although the tax department is responsible for property valuation, it works closely with the local government officials in determining the land value books. All these books are discussed with the local authorities and signed off by the regional head before being authorized for property tax purposes. This review process ensures a degree of quality control, ownership and transparency in the land values used for taxation. Beginning in 2000, the tax department began undertaking selective assessment/sales ratio studies in a few local governments to determine the accuracy of the valuations. It is expected that these sorts of quality control studies will be continued.

Property tax rates
The tax rate is set by the national law at 0.5 percent, assessed on the capital value of land and improvements. This tax rate is uniform throughout Indonesia – applied equally to all property types. Local governments do not have any discretion in setting the property tax rate.

The property tax law provides for an assessment rate that is applied to the property value to determine the final taxable value upon which the 0.5 percent tax rate is applied. This assessment ratio can range from 20 to 100 percent and is set by presidential decree. In 1986, the assessment ratio was set at a uniform nationwide rate of 20 percent. In 1994, the assessment ratio was increased to 40 percent for urban properties valued over Rp 1 billion. In 2000, the assessment ratio was increased to 40 percent for all urban and rural properties valued over Rp 1 billion and for all properties within the forestry and estates sector. Mining sector properties and rural and urban properties under Rp 1 billion continue to have an assessment ratio of 20 percent. Applying the assessment ratio with the tax rate generates an effective legal tax rate ranging from 0.1 to 0.2 percent.

The PBB Law also provides for a valuation deduction, an amount deducted from the property value before the application of the assessment ratio and tax rate. In 1986, the valuation deduction was applied only to the building value. The valuation deduction was initially set at a uniform Rp 2 million so as to exempt most rural housing and the majority of low-income urban housing, allowing the tax office to concentrate its scarce resources on higher-value property improvements. This valuation deduction structure essentially made the PBB tax a land tax in the rural areas and lower-value urban areas. The valuation deduction was set as a flat unit amount, thereby introducing a degree of progressivity into the tax system.

In 1989, the valuation deduction was increased to Rp 3.5 million and further increased to Rp 7 million in 1991. In 1994, the valuation deduction was increased to Rp 8 million, and the PBB Law was changed to apply the valuation deduction on both land and buildings and to provide only one such deduction per taxpayer.[3] The apparent reason for this change was an attempt to reduce the tax on the poor.[4] In 2001, the valuation deduction was increased up to Rp 12 million, and the law was changed to provide local governments with discretion in setting the actual valuation threshold.

Since the tax rate and the assessment ratio are set centrally, local governments only have the policy option of changing the valuation deduction to affect the revenue yield. In 2001, 210 local governments continued to use a valuation deduction of Rp 8 million, 17 increased the valuation deduction, while 114 reduced the valuation deduction. The 17 local governments that increased the valuation deduction tended to be richer regions, while those local governments that reduced the valuation deduction appeared to be those that needed to increase property tax revenues.

Property tax administration
Property tax administration is the responsibility of the central government. The tax is administered through 106 regional field offices under the Directorate of Property Tax within the Directorate General of Taxation, Ministry of Finance. These 106 regional offices are staffed by 6700 employees, administering the property tax for about 50 million taxpayers and 79 million properties. In the capital city of Jakarta, the property tax is applied to 1.6 million properties, paid by about 1.2 million taxpayers.

The Directorate of Property Tax is organized along functional lines with separate sub-directorates responsible for property information (data collection), valuation, assessment, collection, and objections and tax reduction. In addition, there is a special group of property valuers assigned to each regional office to assist with the property valuation functions.

Tax administration has been highly automated since 1991, as part of the property tax reform. The tax department uses a property tax information management system (SISMIOP) which integrates information processing with the administrative procedures necessary to manage comprehensively all aspects of the property tax – namely, property information management, valuation, assessment, billing and collection, enforcement, taxpayer service and appeals. SISMIOP was introduced in 1994 throughout Indonesia and currently manages over 78 million properties (Kelly, 1996). Each of the 106 offices has its own computer-assisted SISMIOP system to assist on all operational and management functions. Recently the SISMIOP system has introduced GIS capabilities to handle the mapping required for property tax purposes. The GIS component is now complete in the four cities of Jakarta, Medan, Denpasar and Surabaya, and is at various stages of completion in 20 other regional tax offices.

The tax administrative process begins with the collection and updating of the property information. Under the PBB Law, taxpayers are legally required to self-declare property information to the tax department for tax assessment purposes. This property information declaration includes such information as location of tax object, taxpayer's name and address, land and building areas and other characteristics needed for determining the value. Third parties (for example notaries, public works, land department) are also required to submit property-related information to the tax department. In 1998, the government introduced a land transaction tax both to generate revenue and to ensure a steady flow of property information. This transaction tax is a central tax also managed by the Directorate of Property Tax – but with revenues shared with the local governments.

The tax department relies on taxpayer and third-party information along with field exercises to maintain the fiscal cadastre information. These field exercises are conducted jointly with local officials using simple, cost-effective survey and measuring methods. The marginal costs for the field exercises are typically covered by the 9 percent of the PBB revenues allocated for collection costs. The basic information is managed through the SISMIOP system.

Except for high-value, unique properties, all property valuation is conducted using mass appraisal. The tax administration determines the land value maps and cost tables that are applied against the property information collected by the tax department. The resulting valuation, assessment and billing are automatically generated through the SISMIOP system. The only exceptions are the individual valuations conducted by the tax department valuers, for which an individual valuation report is produced and included for tax assessment purposes.

The SISMIOP system produces tax bills that are either sent directly to taxpayers or given to the local government for hand delivery. Local governments are involved in the collection process by providing information and follow-up on collection activities. All payments are handled through the banking sector, although local governments sometimes use intermediate revenue collectors who in turn deposit the tax receipts into the banking system. Payments are made through a 'payment point system' (SISTEP) that was introduced as part of the property tax reform in 1988, field tested in 1989 and subsequently replicated throughout Indonesia by 1992 (Kelly, 1993). Under this system, property taxes must be paid at specified bank 'payment points' in the geographic region where the property is located, thus facilitating collection and record-keeping.

In 1999, the tax department introduced a payment on line (POS) system in Jakarta and Surabaya at each property tax payment point within the banking system. This system is now being replicated in several other cities – providing on-line processing, generating timely and complete reports on revenue collections, and improving taxpayer service. The system was implemented through joint cooperation between the PBB tax department, the local authorities and the banking system.

The tax department has also instituted a telephone information system in 37 of the regional offices to improve taxpayer service and the dissemination of PBB-related tax information. The telephone system is an automated information service that allows for information retrieval based on the property identification number.

Property tax reform

In 1986, the government initiated property tax reform as an integral part of a comprehensive tax reform which simplified the tax code, broadened the tax base, minimized equity distortions and increased the efficiency of government revenue collection (Kelly, 1992). The government introduced a revised income tax in January 1984, a value-added tax in April 1995, and the land and building tax in January 1986 (Gillis, 1989).

Before this reform effort, the property tax had evolved into a complex system of seven different land tax ordinances. Each had a slightly different base, with varying tax rates, and was administered by different agencies and levels of government. Property tax collections averaged less than 60 percent, with large variation across property tax sectors (rural, urban, estate, forestry and mining) and across locations. Most property tax information was out of date, much of it having been compiled during the Dutch colonial period. Owing to staff and budget constraints, property data maintenance had been on an *ad hoc* basis, creating major discrepancies in its quality. Property valuations were considerably lower than true market value and inconsistent among properties – one study estimated that appraised values were about a quarter of market value, while effective tax rates ranged from 0.01 percent to 0.4 percent of market value.

Faced with these realities, the government introduced a new land and building tax in 1986 and embarked on a major restructuring of the property tax administration in 1988.

Description of reform

The Indonesian property tax reform began in 1986 with the enactment of the Land and Building Tax Law. This new law introduced a number of changes to the property tax system.

First, the new law significantly simplified the Indonesian property tax system, replacing seven different property-related taxes and introducing a single flat tax rate of 0.5 percent assessed on the capital value of land and improvements. The new law eliminated the previous 50 percent concession to residential property and progressive tax rates on rural land. An assessment ratio ranging from 20 percent to 100 percent was introduced to provide flexibility in adapting property tax implementation to current economic, political and social conditions.

Second, the new law broadened the tax base by reducing tax base exemptions and by switching the tax base from rental to capital value. Shifting to the capital value basis theoretically incorporated the potential development value of property as well as its current use value. Although government property was not explicitly taxed, the law provided an option for its future taxation.

Third, the new law incorporated several provisions to improve equity. A valuation deduction on the building was introduced for all properties which exempted most rural housing and low-value urban structures – making the property tax essentially a land tax in rural and low-value urban areas. The legal structure was simplified to facilitate implementation and reduce ineffective administration.

Fourth, the new law stipulated strict deadlines and penalties to ensure timely and accurate property registration and tax payment. Taxpayers and third-party institutions dealing with property are required to provide property information to the tax department. Failure to provide the information can result in the imposition of penalties. Taxpayers are given six months to pay their tax liabilities, with a 2 percent per month penalty (up to a maximum of 24 months) applied to late payments. Seizure and auction of movable and/or immovable property is permitted in cases of non-compliance.

Fifth, the new law stipulated several fundamental changes in the administrative policies concerned with property information, valuation, revenue collection and enforcement. The major change in revenue collection procedures was the designation of the banking sector as responsible for the tax-receiving and accounting components of the tax collection system. Other revenue collection responsibilities are divided between the regional and central governments. Regional governments are responsible for rural and urban collections while the central government is responsible for the estate, forestry and mining sectors.

Sixth, the new law stipulated a new division of the property tax revenues between levels of government. Sixty-five percent is given to the regional governments (Level II), 16 percent to the provincial governments (Level I), 10 percent to the central government, and 9 percent to cover collection costs. Since 1994, the 10 percent which was originally allocated to the central government has now been given to all Level II regional governments: 35 percent equally and 65 percent as an incentive to reach certain property tax revenue targets. Property tax revenues are considered local-level discretionary revenue and are not earmarked for the routine or development budget.

These legal changes laid the enabling framework for the subsequent reforms in property tax administration policies and procedures. In 1989, the tax administration system was reorganized along functional lines. The number of regional field offices was doubled to 106 and renamed from 'property tax inspection offices' to 'property tax service offices' – reflecting the government's change in emphasis to taxpayer service.

Immediately following the reorganization the government shifted its reform implementation strategy from one narrowly focused on property valuation to a more comprehensive approach that was led by property revenue collections. This 'collection-led' strategy began with the introduction of the payment point collection system (SISTEP) which simplified the collection function, reduced compliance and administration costs and provided a delinquency list for enforcement purposes. Collection efficiency improved and enforcement activities resulted in a historic property seizure for property tax delinquency in October 1991 – the first property seizure since Indonesian Independence in 1945.

The collection-led implementation strategy linked revenue collection and enforcement with the other property tax functions of property information, valuation and assessment in a comprehensive and integrated manner.

Following these initial major reform efforts, the government has subsequently introduced several minor policy and administrative adjustments. On the policy side, the government in 1994 increased the amount of the property valuation deduction and extended it to apply to both land and building value. In addition, as mentioned earlier, the assessment ratio was changed in 1994 from a uniform 20 percent for all properties to a two-rate system where high-value urban properties (luxury houses) over Rp 1 billion began using an assessment ratio of 40 percent. In 2000, the assessment ratio of 40 percent was extended to all rural and urban high-value properties over Rp 1 billion and to all estate and forestry properties. Only mining and urban and rural properties under the Rp 1 billion threshold are currently using the 20 percent assessment ratio. In 2001, in light of the decentralization movement, the government increased the level of the property valuation deduction up to a maximum of Rp 12 million, but gave discretion to each regional government to set the valuation deduction threshold.

In addition to these minor policy changes, the government has continued to introduce further administrative innovations. The SISMIOP system is now gradually incorporating mapping and other GIS components. The government has renamed the basic system i-SISMIOP to signify the change towards a more Internet-friendly and automated taxpayer service environment. In addition, the larger cities have introduced a payment on-line (POS) system to further simplify the collection system – providing on-line information on collections to enable more effective cash flow management and compliance enhancement activities. It is expected that this POS system will be expanded to cover all major local level revenues and can be replicated in additional local governments.

Preconditions for reform
The major precondition for the successful property tax reform in Indonesia was the mobilization of strong political support, made possible through linking the property tax reform to the successful momentum of the broader tax reform. This strong political support enabled the initial enactment of the new law and the successful implementation of the necessary administrative system changes.

The property tax has a long history in Indonesia. Thus, there was a well-established property tax culture both among the citizen–taxpayers and the tax administration. The key to the successful reform was building upon this tradition but simplifying the policy framework, effectively linking policy with administration, and implementing a comprehensive set of administrative reforms in a 'collection-led' – not a 'valuation-pushed' – implementation strategy.

It was necessary to rationalize the tax administration procedures to improve taxpayer service, reduce compliance and administrative costs, improve equity and enhance revenue mobilization. Starting with the payment system rationalization, the reform moved to integrate and improve all tax administration functions through the introduction of the SISMIOP system. The SISMIOP system brought in the use of computerization, which required, among others, a rationalization of procedures, the establishment of a unique parcel identification numbering system, systems development and support, and capacity training on new standard operating procedures and computer use.

These various innovative administrative changes were introduced on a pilot basis that allowed the government to field test procedures, economize on scarce managerial and field staff and gauge possible reactions to the new procedures. Once proven successful, the procedures were gradually adopted and replicated nation-wide. This same approach was used for design and implementation of the payment point system and the SISMIOP information management system.

To facilitate implementation, all methods, procedures and technology were developed to match the available institutional capacity. Training and capacity development initiatives were designed and implemented to ensure that the reforms could be sustained. An agreement was reached with several tertiary educational institutions, which now train about 600 people annually.

It should be noted that an accurate legal cadastre was not necessary for the property tax reform in Indonesia since the property tax system in Indonesia relies on its own separate 'fiscal cadastre.' This PBB fiscal cadastre is more extensive than the legal cadastre under the National Land Agency. In fact, many properties rely on the property tax cadastre and a property tax receipt as proof of 'indicative ownership' (*Hak Girik*). This provides a strong acceptance of the property tax system by taxpayers and a strong incentive to have property recorded in the fiscal cadastre and to pay the property tax itself.

Impact of reform

The property tax reform in Indonesia continues to make remarkable progress – revenues continue to increase each year. Before the reform, the property tax generated Rp 154 billion in 1985–86. Immediately following the reform, property tax revenues increased over sixfold to over Rp 900 billion in 1991–92. In 1999–2000, revenue reached Rp 3200 billion, representing an average annual increase of over 24 percent from 1985–86.

The PBB law enacted in 1986 continues to provide the basic policy and administrative framework for the property tax. Although there have been some minor policy changes, the advantages of simplicity, equity and ease of administration remain. In addition, the basic administration, procedures and systems that were established during the initial reform remain in effect, providing the foundation for continued effective and equitable implementation. The basic payment point system continues to facilitate the tax collection process. The SISMIOP – property tax information management system – is still being used to integrate the data collection, data management, valuation, assessment, billing and collection, enforcement and taxpayer service. Using the SISTEP and SISMIOP as the foundation, the tax department has continued to innovate and improve the administrative system to enhance taxpayer service and revenue collections.

Although there is always room for continued improvement, the property tax reform was and continues to be very successful. Altogether the results of the Indonesian property tax reform have been very rewarding. Revenues have increased substantially, while administrative and compliance costs have decreased. Strong political support has been mobilized to support the needed policy and administrative changes. Taxpayer and bureaucratic resistance have been effectively minimized through a system of positive and negative incentives.

In the long run, sustained and continued growth in property tax revenues will strengthen regional governments and encourage further decentralization. Continued administrative improvements in managing property tax information will improve the efficiency of the tax department and provide important information for broader land policy and administration. Increased accuracy in valuation and systematic enforcement of compliance will ultimately improve the equity of the property tax system.

The key challenge facing Indonesia now is how to channel this success to support the ongoing decentralization effort. Effectively transforming the property tax from a pure central level – shared tax – to one that is more responsive and under the control of the local government will be important. Although the central government may continue to administer the property tax for economies of scale and other reasons, it will be necessary to give local governments some discretion in setting the property tax rates in order to increase local accountability and control over the amount of property taxes collected.

Notes

1. For recent information on property tax reform in Indonesia, see Asher (2003), Kelly (2003), and Lewis (forthcoming).
2. The stated rationale for this tax was as part of a series of land use reform programs to 'design an effective, efficient, and equitable expansion of urban land resources' (*The Jakarta Post*, 27 September 1997, as quoted in Lam, 1999, p. 71). No information on its effectiveness in this respect appears to be available.
3. Since there is no unique taxpayer identifier number, but only a unique property ID number, it is quite difficult to enforce the limit of one deduction per taxpayer, especially if taxpayers have property in more than one local jurisdiction.
4. The original rationale for the deduction was to establish a 'tax threshold' to exempt all improvements below a certain value in order to reduce administrative costs. This argument did not appear to play a role in the 1994 change.

References

Asher, M. (2003), 'The Role of Property Tax in Decentralization of Fiscal System in Indonesia,' paper presented at Seminar on Indonesia's Decentralization Policy: Policy and Programme Directions, Hitotsubashi University, Tokyo, 31 January–1 February (www.icds.co.jp/sympo/pdf/S6(1).pdf)

Gillis, M. (1989), 'Comprehensive Tax Reform: The Indonesian Experience, 1981–1988,' in M. Gillis (ed.), *Tax Reform in Developing Countries*, Durham, NC: Duke University Press.

Kelly, R. (1992), 'Implementing Property Tax Reform in Developing Countries: Lessons from the Property Tax in Indonesia,' *Review of Urban and Regional Development Studies*, 4, 193–208.

Kelly, R. (1993), 'Property Tax Reform in Indonesia: Applying a Collection-Led Implementation Strategy,' *Bulletin for Indonesian Economic Studies*, 29 (1), 85–104.

Kelly, R. (1996), 'The Evolution of a Property Tax Information Management System in Indonesia,' in G. Jenkins (ed.), *Information Technology and Innovation in Tax Administration*, Cambridge, MA: Kluwer, pp. 115–35.

Kelly, R. (2003), 'Property Taxation in Indonesia: Challenges from Decentralization,' Lincoln Institute of Land Policy Working Paper WP03RK1 (www.lincolninst.edu/pubs/pub-detail.asp?id=788

Lam, A.H.S. (1999), 'Real Property Taxation – An Instrument to Restore Asian Economies?' *Asia-Pacific Tax Bulletin*, March, 70–74.

Lewis, B. (forthcoming), 'Property Taxation in Indonesia: Measuring and Explaining Administrative (Under-) Performance,' *Public Administration and Development*, 23 (3).

10 Property taxation in India

Gautam Naresh[1]

India is a federal union of states. Supremacy of the Constitution and division of power between the union and state governments are its prime characteristics. The Union of India is a three-tier polity consisting of a union government, second-tier governments and third-tier governments. There are 28 states and 7 union territories (five of them are without legislature). The union territories are administered by the union government but are not part of it. At the third tier of local level governance there are 101 municipal corporations (larger cities), 1430 municipal councils and 2009 *Nagar Panchayats*[2] for municipal (urban) governance. For rural governance there are 222 108 *Gram Panchayats* (village-level units), 5736 *Gram Samitis* (intermediate-level bodies), and 457 District *Panchayats* (district-level bodies).[3]

The Seventh Schedule to the Constitution of India, 1951, places the levy of taxes on land and buildings in the State List. The states in turn have authorized the local governments to levy, collect and appropriate the tax subject to certain taxes, duties, tolls and fees assigned to them in accordance with procedures and limits. Thus municipal governments do not have powers of taxing properties but derive them from the state governments.[4] Each state has its own Municipal Acts with differing scope, phraseology, tax powers, and so on. The levy of the property tax is obligatory in some Municipal Acts such as those in Haryana, Karnataka and Maharashtra, but optional in others such as Andhra Pradesh, Assam, Delhi, Gujarat, Kerala, Rajasthan, Tamil Nadu and West Bengal. The reasons for this difference are difficult to identify. In any case, in various states some forms of municipal government do not levy property tax: 35 percent of local bodies in Gujarat, 18 percent in Madhya Pradesh, 38 percent in Punjab, 83 percent in Rajasthan and 40 percent in Uttar Pradesh levied no property tax at all.

Property tax base

Essentially, there are three basic forms of assessment: annual rental value (ARV), the improved capital value (CV), or the site value of the land excluding improvement (SV). In addition, hybrid models exist.

In India, the tax base differs not only among states but also among various types of municipal government within a state. Table 10.1 summarizes the interstate variation in terms of tax base and rate. In general, the basis of assessment for the property tax is the ARV or capital value of lands and buildings.

Table 10.1   India: municipal property tax bases and rates, by state

	State	Basis of levy	Rate of levy (%)	Remarks
1	Andhra Pradesh	Annual value	15–19 of annual value	Actual rate to be fixed by each municipality
2	Assam	Annual value	General tax varies from 3–8; water tax 2–8; latrine tax 3–7.5; lighting tax 1.5 + 0.4	In case of government properties 9% construction cost is taken as the annual value
3	Bihar	Annual value	32 including service taxes	Unless specific service is provided, no tax on such service
4	Goa	Annual rental	–	–
5	Gujarat	Rateable value	20 for municipalities	
6	Haryana	Annual value	12.5 for municipalities	The service charges are to be collected as a fee, not tax
7	Himachal Pradesh		12.50	
8	Karnataka	Annual rental value	8–10 + services	
9	Kerala	Annual value	12	
10	Madhya Pradesh	Annual letting value	Rates up to 10	
11	Maharashtra	General annual value	20 for Western Maharashtra and 12.5 for Marathwada	Statutory limit is 30%
12	Orissa	Annual value	10 for Vidarbha, 27 for most other municipalities	
13	Punjab	Annual value	12.5 for municipalities	
14	Rajasthan	Annual rental value	15–19 of annual value	
15	Uttar Pradesh	Annual rental	3.5–15	
16	West Bengal	Annual value	Up to 10	The maximum rate may be extended up to 33% with government's approval

Source: Rao (1989).

Municipal laws have often adopted ARV for assessment of property tax. This form of tax is more than a century old in India. The implementation problem, however, is in determining the rental value of property.[5] The lack of an objective basis on which to determine the base has created enormous administrative problems. The application of rent control laws and various interpretations by the courts in pronouncing judgments in determining the tax base have further confounded matters.

These problems have led some states to adopt new approaches to defining the tax base. For example, the states of Haryana and Gujarat have defined the provision of *reasonable rent* as the actual rent received or the rent receivable in their Municipal Acts. On the other hand, Himachal Pradesh has specified the provision of reasonable rent in terms of the rent received or receivable, whichever is higher. Madhya Pradesh and Andhra Pradesh have tried to insulate the provisions for taxation of land and buildings by inserting a *non-obstante* clause in their municipal laws in the hope that the provisions of the rent control laws will not have any adverse impact on property tax.

In Bihar (Patna Municipal Corporation), Andhra Pradesh, Madhya Pradesh and Uttar Pradesh, the ARV (reasonable rents) has been defined with respect to certain key variables that contribute to the increase in the value of properties, in particular unit value per square meter for particular locations. Andhra Pradesh was the first state to amend municipal laws to redefine the property tax base. The base, however, was still ARV, which is assessed on the basis of certain characteristics of buildings. The provisions in Uttar Pradesh, Madhya Pradesh and Patna (Bihar) are almost the same except for variations in the variables selected to determine the base. Legal authorities have approved this method as non-discriminatory, simple in classification, and good in intention to provide relief to the taxpayers and to reduce the discretionary elements.[6]

Gujarat and Tamil Nadu have avoided the base issue altogether by amending the laws that provide for determination of tax relief. In Gujarat, the tax (not the ARV) is to be determined according to the Bombay Provincial Corporation Act, 1949, at a fixed rate per square meter of the carpet area (coverage) of buildings and the area of lands, as the Corporation may decide. The tax thus levied is lower for residential than for non-residential properties. In Tamil Nadu, the latest Local Bodies Act provides for the levy of the basic property tax and the additional basic tax. The basic property tax is levied on the carpet area of buildings and its uses. Buildings are classified into residential, commercial, industrial or any other classification as prescribed by the rules. The additional basic tax is levied with reference to location and the type of construction of buildings.

The most radical reform has been proposed in Karnataka. It would abandon ARV and replace it by capital value determined by the market. The proposal provides for depreciation according to a prescribed schedule. The capital value of land would be periodically notified in all towns and cities. This is thus a presumptive capital value, not the actual value. Nevertheless, such a system is expected to impart transparency and reduce the discretionary elements of property taxation.

The state government of Maharashtra, which is presently engaged in deliberations to reform property tax, also seems inclined to adopt a capital system. For Delhi, the President of India accorded his consent on 6 June 2003 to a Bill paving the way for adoption of the unit area method of RV determination. The proposal is to determine the unit area value based on the following factors: category factor (CF), structure factor (SF), age factor (AF), occupancy factor (OF), use factor (UF), and size of the street for non-residential properties.

Rate structure

Table 10.1 also summarizes rate structure. There are wide variations in the levels of rates and their structure and composition, as well as in assessment practices among different municipalities. Some Municipal Acts stipulate both maximum and minimum rates of levy while some fix only the maximum rate. Some Acts prescribe only the property tax on the services rendered such as water, drainage, lighting and so on to the property. These rates may be different and are generally higher in municipal corporations.

Not all municipal governments levy all taxes on property as 'property taxes.' Further, rate structure may be graduated in the case of bigger municipal governments, in which slabs of ARV and thus the rates of general tax vary across property classes as well as within the same class. In other systems, a distinction is made between residential and commercial properties, with the rates being higher for the latter category, but there is no graduation or progression in rates. A more simplified rate structure takes the form of a consolidated general tax for all types of properties. The tax rate is generally higher in big cities compared to smaller ones.

Mumbai Municipal Corporation may be used to illustrate the complexities of urban property tax and property-related taxes, and cess and its periodical changes.[7] Table 10.2 shows changes in all the components of property taxes since 1944. Table 10.3 shows how the rate varies depending on whether water supply is metered or unmetered. Table 10.4 compares the rates levied on residential and non-residential properties. Table 10.5 shows the state education cess.

Many taxes and charges are imposed on the rateable value (RV) of the property. The general tax rate is now 26 percent of the RV, but the total municipal taxes imposed on this base are 62 percent, plus another 15 percent of other government taxes on this base. Only some service taxes such as water benefit tax, sewerage tax and sewerage benefit tax vary between resi-

Table 10.2 Mumbai: changes in property tax rate structure since 1944

Year	General tax	Fire tax	Urban immobile property tax	Water tax	Water benefit tax	Sewerage tax	Sewerage benefit tax	Education cess	Tree tax	Street tax	State education cess	Additional state education cess	Employment guarantee cess	Total municipal tax	Other government taxes
1944	11.00	0.50	7.00	0.75		3.00								22.25	
1945	12.00	0.50	7.00	0.75		3.00								23.25	
1946	14.00	0.50	7.00	0.75		3.00								25.25	
1947	14.00	0.80	7.00	0.75		3.00								25.55	
1952	17.00	0.80	5.00	0.75		3.50								27.05	
1958	17.00	0.80	5.00	0.75		3.50		1.50						28.55	
1959	19.00	0.80	5.00	4.50		3.50		1.50						34.30	
1962	19.00	0.80	5.00	4.50		3.50		1.50			2.00			34.30	2.00
1963	24.00	0.80		4.50		3.50		2.50			2.00			35.30	2.00
1967	24.00	0.80		4.50		3.50		2.50			2.50			35.30	2.50
1971	24.00	0.80		7.00		3.50		2.50			2.50	1.50		37.80	4.00
1973	24.00	0.80		7.00	3.00	3.50	2.00	2.50			2.50	1.50		42.80	4.00
1974	24.00	0.80		7.00	3.00	3.50	2.00	4.00			12.00			44.30	12.00
1975	24.00	1.50		7.00	5.00	4.00	3.00	5.00			12.00		3.00	49.50	15.00
1976	24.00	1.50		9.00	6.00	5.00	4.00	5.00			12.00		3.00	54.50	15.00
1983	24.00	1.50		9.00	6.00	5.00	4.00	5.00			12.00		3.00	54.50	15.00
1987	24.00	1.50		9.00	6.00	5.00	4.00	5.00			12.00		3.00	54.50	15.00
1988	24.00	1.50		9.00	6.00	5.00	4.00	5.00	0.50		12.00		3.00	55.00	15.00
1993	26.00	2.00		9.00	6.00	5.00	4.00	5.00	0.50	5.00	12.00		3.00	62.50	15.00

Source: NIPFP (1996).

Table 10.3   Mumbai: metered and unmetered rates for property tax, 1994–95

Tax	Unmetered water supply		Metered water supply	
	Residential percent of RV	Non-residential percent of RV	Residential percent of RV	Non-residential percent of RV
General tax including fire tax (26+2%)	28	28	28	28
Water tax	26	55		
Water benefit tax	10	20	10	20
Sewerage tax	13	20		
Sewerage benefit tax	6	12	6	12
Education cess	5	5	5	5
State education cess	6	12	6	12
Employment guarantee cess		3		3
Tree cess	0.5	0.5	0.5	0.5
Street cess	5	5	5	5
Total	99.5	160.5	60.5	85.5

Source: As for Table 10.2.

dential and non-residential properties. The rate structure includes a so-called 'repair cess' on old properties as well as a state tax called the Maharashtra tax on buildings (MToB) on larger residential buildings. The rate of MToB is 10 percent of the RV. Buildings are classified in three categories depending on the year of construction as well as whether or not the structure has been repaired, the use of the property, and how much of the repair share is paid from public funds.

Both the property tax structure and the rates of the various levies changed significantly in Mumbai in the early 1990s. Under the new system, properties with metered connections do not pay the water and sewerage taxes. Moreover, three state levies – namely, state education cess (see Table 10.5), additional state education cess and employment guarantee cess – were imposed on RV. State education cess started in 1992, at rates varying from 0 to 10 percent of RV.

Another example of a complex rate structure is in Delhi, where a recent study proposed rates of tax of 10 to 12 percent compared to the current rates of 20 percent for residential and 30 percent for non-residential properties. The proposed formula for calculating the tax is illustrated in Table 10.6. Each of the 'multiplicative factors' mentioned in this table is subdivided: for example

Table 10.4 Mumbai: comparison between residential and non-residential rates' 1993 (as percentage of RV)

Tax	Residential rates	Non-residential rates
General tax	26.00	26.00
Fire tax	2.00	2.00
Water tax	20.00	20.00
Water benefit tax	10.00	15.00
Sewerage tax	10.00	5.00
Sewerage benefit tax	6.00	12.00
Education cess	5.00	5.00
Tree tax	0.50	0.50
Street tax	5.00	5.00
State education cess (max)	6.00	12.00
Employment guarantee cess		3.00
Municipal tax on buildings	10.00	
Repair cess	39–1160[a]	

Note: [a] Rates differ for residential and non-residential and are shared between owner and tenant in varying proportions and vary with category of building, level of repairs required, and extent to which public sector contributes to repairs.

Source: As for Table 10.2.

Table 10.5 Mumbai: state education cess since 1962

Period	Rateable value (Rs)	Cess (%)	Rateable value (Rs)	Cess (%)	Rateable value (Rs)	Cess (%)
1.10.1962–3.9.1967	RV<75	0			RV>74	2.0
1.4.1967–31.3.1974	RV<75	0	RV 75–299	2	RV>300	2.5
1.4.1974 onwards						

	Cess (%)	
	Residential	Non-residential
RV<75	0	0
RV=75–150	2	4
RV=150–300	3	6
RV=300–3000	4	8
RV=3000–6000	5	10
RV<6000	6	12

Source: As for Table 10.2.

Table 10.6   Delhi: formula for calculation of tax

Step	Procedure
1	Proposed base unit area value is Rs 30 per ft^2
2	The annual value will be equal to the product of this base unit area value, the multiplicative factors for each parameter (category in which colony falls, occupancy, age, structure and use) and the covered area of the property. *Annual value = base unit area value * multiplicative factor [CF, OF, AF, SF, UF] * covered area*
3	In case where different portions of the property are put to different use or where the other parameters are different, the annual value will be calculated for each such portion separately and the sum of each annual value will be equal to the annual value of the property. *Annual value (AV) = (AV of portion 1) + (AV of portion 2) + ...*
4	Calculate tax by multiplying AV by rate of tax notified. From this deduct any rebates or concessions applicable. *Tax = (AV * tax rate) – (rebates + concessions applicable)*

Source: Municipal Corporation of Delhi (2003).

the 'use factor' is divided into nine categories, with the lowest (category) being the residential and the others ranging from 3 (for education) up to 10 (for 'star' hotels and banks).

Tax administration

The general organizational framework of property tax can be schematized as a functional hierarchy, including authorities at the levels of (1) assessment (or valuation) as shown in Table 10.7, (2) validation (Table 10.8), (3) appeal for valuation (Table 10.9), and (4) appeal against revision (Table 10.10).

In most states, the involvement of elected representatives is noticeable at one or more stages of property tax administration. For instance, in the states of Haryana, Uttar Pradesh, West Bengal, Assam and Rajasthan, the Municipal Acts assign the role of differentiating the tax base to elected representatives either directly (that is, to councils) or indirectly (that is, appointment of authority by the Council). A similar kind of involvement at the stage of validation process is observed in the states of Haryana, Uttar Pradesh, West Bengal, Assam and Rajasthan, Gujarat, Madhya Pradesh and Bihar. Except in Bihar, the role of the elected council is also evident in the task of amendment of valuation. On the other hand, in states like Andhra Pradesh, Orissa and Kerala the Municipal Acts do not prescribe any involvement of elected body

Table 10.7   India: preparation of valuation/assessment list, by state

Activity/authority assigned to	State
1 Council* is entrusted with the task	Haryana, Uttar Pradesh
2 Assessors appointed by the council	Assam, West Bengal, Rajasthan
3 Assessors/valuation officers appointed by the state government	Andhra Pradesh, Orissa**
4 Executive officers***	Bihar, Madhya Pradesh, Maharashtra, Gujarat, Punjab, Kerala

Notes:

   *   The term council is used in some states while in other states it may be called the municipal board or committee, or commissioners at a meeting.

  ** In Orissa, until the valuation officer is appointed, the task is assigned to the executive officer.

*** The municipal executive officer is known as the commissioner in Tamil Nadu, Kerala, Rajasthan, as secretary in Andhra Pradesh and Himachal Pradesh, as chief officer in Maharashtra and Gujarat, chief municipal officer in Madhya Pradesh.

Source: Various state Municipal Acts.

in the property tax administration. Generally, however, property tax administration involves both elected bodies and appointed personnel at its various stages.

Valuation procedures

In most urban local bodies the annual rental value of the property is considered as the base on which the property tax is levied. In order to assess this value, properties are classified into (a) rented properties, (b) owner-occupied properties, (c) central government properties, (d) state government properties, and (e) special category properties belonging to charitable, educational and religious institutions. In most states property tax Acts exempt government properties. However, in some states, such as Gujarat and Maharashtra, compensation is paid in lieu of property tax loss caused on account of exemption of state government owned buildings.

As far as central government property is concerned, it is constitutionally exempt from all taxes imposed by a state or any other authorities within a state. However, such properties are subject to payment of service charges for both direct services such as water and electric supplies, scavenging, and so on and general services such as street lighting, town drainage, and approach roads connecting the central government properties and so on. The rate of service charges ranges from 33.33 percent to 75 percent of the normal rate of

Table 10.8   India: validation of valuation/assessment, by state

	Activity/authority assigned to	State
1.	Public notice to be given by:	
	Municipal council	Assam, Haryana
	Chairman of the council	West Bengal
	Executive officer	Bihar, Madhya Pradesh, Maharashtra, Gujarat, Kerala, Uttar Pradesh
	Valuation officer/assessor	Andhra Pradesh, Rajasthan, Orissa
2.	Objections to be made to:	
	Municipal council	Assam, Haryana
	Executive committee of the council	Gujarat
	Chairman of the council	West Bengal
	Executive officer	Bihar, Madhya Pradesh, Maharashtra, Kerala, Orissa, Uttar Pradesh
	Valuation officer/assessor	Andhra Pradesh, Rajasthan
3.	Objections to be heard by:	
	Municipal council (generally delegated)	Assam, Haryana, Madhya Pradesh, Rajasthan, Uttar Pradesh
	Special committee	Bihar, West Bengal, Gujarat
	Valuation officer/assessor	Andhra Pradesh, Maharashtra, Orissa, Kerala
	Executive officer	Tamil Nadu, Kerala
	Revising authority	Karnataka

property tax applicable to private properties depending upon the quantum of services availed of by the central government properties from the urban local governments.

In India, there are two ways in which state governments directly or indirectly influence the property tax base. The most common is through the Rent Control Act (RCA), which is in operation in almost all states. RCAs have serious implications for the growth of property tax revenue although this restrictive effect is incidental as the legislation's primary concern is the regulation and control of private housing accommodation, occupancy rights and rents chargeable to tenants. The primary objectives of state RCAs are (1) to deter landlords from exploiting tenants and (2) to protect tenants from high rents and harassment. The law is confined to urban townships.

The most important aspect of this Act is that the state rent control authority fixes the rent of dwellings (except for the government and others specified).

Table 10.9   India: appeal against revising authority, by state

Revising authority	Appellate authority	State
Council or its committee whose decision is final	–	Assam, Bihar, West Bengal
Council or its committee or special committee	1. District magistrate/ collector/deputy commissioner	Haryana, Uttar Pradesh, Rajasthan
	2. Civil judge	Madhya Pradesh
	3. Judicial magistrate	Maharashtra, Gujarat
Executive officer	Council/special officer appointed by state government for this purpose	Kerala
Valuation officer	1. Appellate commissioner (appointed by the state government) in consultation with chairman of the council	Andhra Pradesh
	2. District magistrate	Orissa

Table 10.10   India: grant of remission, by state

Authority assigned to	State
Council (may delegate also)	Haryana, Rajasthan, Madhya Pradesh, West Bengal, Maharashtra
Executive committee of the council	Gujarat
Executive officer	Bihar, Kerala, Uttar Pradesh, Andhra Pradesh

The assessment of premises falling under this Act is made on the basis of the criteria laid down by the rent control authority in the individual state. The rent fixed by the rent controller is treated as the most 'reasonable rent' or the 'economic rent' or the 'fair rent'. In other words, unless a revision is made by the rent control authority, rent once fixed for any house is the only rent that is legally recoverable from the tenant. The rent once so fixed becomes station-ary and stagnant over a period of a few years. The existence of RCA also contributes to disparities in the assessed value of rent-controlled compared to non-rent-controlled properties.

Another way in which state governments influence the assessment procedure is by appointing a central valuation authority. In the case of West Bengal and Assam, for instance, in the absence of appropriate assessment staff at the local bodies (except for the Municipal Corporation of Calcutta and Howrah), the state government has created an independent authority known as Central Valua-tion Board (CVB), which has its own staff to undertake assessment of properties in each of the local bodies. In many other states, the state government delegates state officers in municipal offices to carry out the task of assessment.

Tax collections and arrears
The efficiency of tax administration is reflected in smooth collections, fewer disputes, low arrears, and speedy disposal of appeals and pending cases. These outcomes are closely linked to organizational structure, valuation pro-cedures, rate structure, appellate procedures and measures or deterrents against non-compliance. Arrears in India are quite high in general, largely due to the shortcomings in the existing system of property assessment based on ARV. Where ARV is imputed on the basis of historical costs, the assessment of new properties is definitely on the high side on account of inflated land values and costs of construction. Due to this built-in bias against new properties, the property tax levied on such assessed values generally leads to disagreement and litigation from the taxpayers. Consequently, the number of pending court cases and arrears continues to rise as the number of new properties increases in a municipality. Procedural formalities also delay payment. Even after settlement, payments are sometimes phased in easy installments, resulting in the prolonged continuance of arrears. The result of all these problems is that taxpayers, especially large ones, usually think that if a property tax case is taken to the Appellate Authority, some relief of tax liability will generally be achieved on one pretext or another.

Table 10.11 illustrates the arrears for municipal corporations in Tamil Nadu state for the years 1991–92 to 1993–94. On the whole, Tamil Nadu is usually considered to be one of the better-managed states, and the bigger municipal governments are those covered in this table. On average for this period, the arrears were about 50 percent of the demand of property tax. In Madurai, Salem and Trichy, the arrears were in the range of 50 percent to 75 percent. For the corporation of Chennai, the largest city in Tamil Nadu, the range was from 37 to 48 percent during 1995–96 to 2000–2001 (Table 10.12).

Table 10.11   *Tamil Nadu: property tax demands, collections and arrears in municipal corporations, average 1991–94 (Rs lakhs (100 000))*

Corporation	Demand	Collection	Arrears
Coimbatore	5 607.38	2 868.06	2 739.32
(%)	100.00	51.15	48.85
Chennai	18 905.73	12 549.51	6 356.22
(%)	100.00	66.38	33.62
Madurai	8 858.70	2 902.90	5 955.80
(%)	100.00	32.77	67.23
Salem	2 897.60	1 196.60	1 701.00
(%)	100.00	41.30	58.70
Trichy	2 821.85	1 329.37	1 492.48
(%)	100.00	47.11	52.89
Tirunelveli	677.59	379.62	297.97
(%)	100.00	56.03	43.97
All corporations	39 768.85	21 226.06	18 542.79
(%)	100.00	53.37	46.63

Note: Demand includes previous arrears in current year demand.

Source: First State Finance Commission of Tamil Nadu, Chennai.

Table 10.12   *Chennai: property tax performance, 1995–96 to 2000–2001(Rs crores (10 million))*

Year	Demand	Collections	Arrears	
			Actual	% of demand
1995–96	109.14	69.06	40.08	36.72
1996–97	127.74	75.13	52.61	41.19
1997–98	166.48	104.76	61.72	37.07
1998–99	184.67	112.95	71.72	38.84
1999–2000	224.88	129.00	95.88	42.64
2000–2001	262.00	135.60	126.40	48.24

Source: Second State Finance Commission of Tamil Nadu, Chennai, 2001.

Issues of property taxation in India

Property tax systems in India are inefficient for many reasons:[8]

- absence of an open market in rental and sale transactions;
- non-availability of professionally trained valuers;
- subjective assessments in a corruption-prone administrative environment;
- scope for excessive use of discretionary powers for individual assessments;
- other lacunae such as subletting of premises or subdivision of units of assessments;
- absence of records on landownership absence of tax-mapping initiatives;
- defective rate structures whereby higher valuation properties get away with lower tax burdens;
- ever-decreasing per capita incidence of local taxes in high-priced inner-city areas due to pegging the annual values to fair rent; and
- proportionately more cases involving appeals and litigation.

The cumulative impact of all these factors is an inequitable distribution of tax burdens between individual assessees (old versus new tenants in the same premises), different apartments in the same buildings (some of the same floors, for identical uses), old and new constructions (for identical uses, in the same vicinities), and between assessees in different geographic areas in the city (high-priced inner-city area versus the new area developments and the urbanized fringes).

Fiscal significance of property tax

Despite these problems, as a source of municipal revenues property tax plays a major role in India. In municipalities that levy *octroi*,[9] this tax is of secondary importance. Otherwise, however, it is the mainstay of local own revenues. No comprehensive data are available, but Table 10.13 depicts the fiscal significance of this tax in terms of compound growth rate, percentage share of property tax in tax revenues, own-source receipts, and total ordinary revenues for selected municipal corporations for the period of 1990–91 to 1999–2000. No perceptible consistency or trend behavior is evident in these data.

Conclusion

Property taxation in India mirrors the diversities across the states and local governments of this vast country. Sometimes property tax is an obligatory levy at the local level; sometimes it is optional. Nevertheless, on the whole it is a significant source of revenue for Indian local governments. This source of

Table 10.13 Property tax: significance and growth in selected municipal corporations in India, 1990–91 to 1999–2000

Municipal corporation (state)		Fiscal year										ACGR (%)	
		1990–91	1991–92	1992–93	1993–94	1994–95	1995–96	1996–97	1997–98	1998–99	1999–2000	10-yrly	Last 5-yrly
		Octroi-levying corporations (states)											
Baroda (Gujarat)	Property tax	107.72	64.37	118.65	115.71	107.19	88.91	107.26	159.43	194.49	216.86	9.58	26.85
	As % of TR	19.63	15.40	19.80	15.81	13.43	9.05	10.27	13.52	14.78	14.78		
	OSR	17.78	14.11	18.14	14.55	12.61	8.78	9.74	12.78	13.15	13.48		
	OY	15.48	12.31	15.67	12.84	10.69	7.66	8.50	10.89	11.24	11.11		
Ahmedabad (Gujarat)	Property tax	161.77	214.91	215.60	242.00	731.37	800.28	920.88	1009.89	1190.08	1166.53	28.66	10.63
	As % of TR	14.58	16.16	13.51	13.93	31.36	27.31	28.19	28.41	29.64	26.12		
	OSR	12.82	14.41	12.57	12.84	29.30	25.89	26.89	27.03	28.39	24.97		
	OY	10.88	12.31	10.84	11.01	25.62	22.59	23.78	24.00	25.05	20.61		
Surat (Gujarat)	Property tax	103.25	122.19	141.13	186.31	270.31	404.02	466.69	591.96	566.74	610.63	25.18	10.74
	As % of TR	13.88	14.77	15.50	15.22	18.72	21.54	21.92	24.22	21.16	18.83		
	OSR	13.11	13.91	14.55	14.32	17.32	19.94	19.25	22.12	19.82	17.57		
	OY	12.41	13.16	13.77	13.39	16.41	18.57	17.74	20.82	18.08	16.26		
Brihan Mumbai (Maharashtra)	Property tax	882.16	950.56	1079.00	1329.76	1234.48	3867.76	5102.81	1691.38	–	–	22.02	20.93
	As % of TR	15.79	15.10	15.61	14.17	8.99	30.77	35.22	11.20	–	–		
	OSR	10.07	9.78	10.51	9.68	7.81	21.81	24.04	5.59	–	–		
	OY	9.97	9.47	10.12	9.37	7.61	21.27	23.02	5.46	–	–		
Nagpur (Maharashtra)	Property tax	882.16	950.56	1079.00	1329.76	1234.48	3867.76	5102.81	1691.38	–	–	22.02	20.93
	As % of TR	15.79	15.10	15.61	14.17	8.99	30.77	35.22	11.20	–	–		
	OSR	10.07	9.78	10.51	9.68	7.81	21.81	24.04	5.59	–	–		
	OY	9.97	9.47	10.12	9.37	7.61	21.27	23.02	5.46	–	–		
Nashik (Maharashtra)	Property tax	39.53	47.24	57.26	72.24	70.14	75.08	88.71	104.24	115.66	125.70	13.13	13.84
	As % of TR	9.21	7.80	9.50	10.82	9.00	7.71	7.37	6.64	7.74	6.77		
	OSR	8.22	7.20	8.42	9.63	8.08	6.51	6.66	6.02	6.85	5.98		
	OY	7.12	6.68	7.70	9.27	7.81	6.19	6.52	5.85	6.60	5.78		
Pimpri – Chinchwad (Maharashtra)	Property tax	33.40	35.01	45.99	52.77	59.55	55.28	107.34	83.94	134.58	118.07	16.96	19.05
	As % of TR	5.88	5.20	6.18	6.74	7.26	5.24	7.43	5.25	8.70	7.40		
	OSR	5.35	4.84	5.83	6.30	6.72	4.90	7.00	4.72	7.08	6.28		
	OY	5.28	4.69	5.78	6.12	6.41	4.79	6.88	4.62	7.01	6.17		

Table 10.13 continued

Municipal corporation (state)		1990–91	1991–92	1992–93	1993–94	1994–95	1995–96	1996–97	1997–98	1998–99	1999–2000	ACGR (%) 10-yrly	Last 5-yrly
Sholapur	Property tax	27.35	22.77	21.74	22.27	32.28	41.69	38.98	44.15	48.05	54.13	10.75	7.59
(Maharashtra)	As % of TR	14.99	11.59	8.98	7.88	9.93	10.09	9.42	9.89	10.23	9.63		
	OSR	12.26	9.69	7.47	6.19	7.86	8.28	7.00	7.11	8.01	7.17		
	OY	10.60	8.14	6.72	6.08	7.60	8.17	6.85	6.96	7.86	7.07		
Jalandhar	Property tax	15.25	–	–	22.49	30.37	32.46	38.26	31.98	41.20	–	–	6.13
(Punjab)	As % of TR	11.52	–	–	8.46	11.47	9.57	10.10	8.70	9.80	–		
	OSR	9.44	–	–	7.65	9.60	8.13	8.39	7.24	7.92	–		
	OY	9.05	–	–	6.73	9.03	8.07	8.11	7.21	7.41	–		
Ludhiana	Property tax	36.96	39.04	44.30	72.03	90.14	112.90	128.33	140.59	169.43	221.32	22.97	17.63
(Punjab)	As % of TR	14.87	12.55	14.81	17.25	16.29	17.40	18.17	18.21	17.55	16.43		
	OSR	12.88	12.09	11.74	13.26	12.93	13.34	14.19	15.21	14.00	13.34		
	OY	12.88	12.09	11.74	13.26	12.93	13.34	14.19	15.21	14.00	13.34		
				Non-octroi-levying corporations (States)									
Belgaon	Property tax	–	4.62	–	10.02	15.25	15.69	23.31	18.40	18.90	–	–	6.07
(Karnataka)	As % of TR	–	8.10	–	12.02	16.45	12.33	15.84	10.36	9.20	–		
	OSR	–	6.48	–	9.91	14.02	11.43	15.11	9.65	8.73	–		
	OY	–	6.43	–	9.91	14.01	10.60	14.10	9.11	8.69	–		
Hubli-	Property tax	14.68	21.50	33.75	34.24	30.45	30.93	35.15	41.17	49.98	55.04	12.13	16.24
Dharwad	As % of TR	57.94	61.40	67.52	70.76	70.59	66.70	76.23	57.19	57.38	40.05		
(Karnataka)	OSR	36.74	42.02	50.26	47.77	47.09	44.97	46.63	40.27	42.52	39.05		
	OY	12.60	15.16	23.62	18.58	15.85	18.91	17.79	16.54	11.27	13.53		
Indore	Property tax	23.98	27.96	–	–	–	64.97	67.86	77.63	144.04	154.49	–	28.21
(Madhya	As % of TR	14.31	13.61	–	–	–	17.37	18.23	16.36	28.93	20.21		
Pradesh)	OSR	13.14	12.43	–	–	–	16.21	11.15	15.66	26.60	18.35		
	OY	12.90	12.28	–	–	–	14.12	9.96	13.38	23.34	16.85		
Ujjain	Property tax	6.12	7.41	–	8.65	7.47	11.09	10.69	23.54	14.98	–	–	23.92
(Madhya	As % of TR	43.56	52.59	–	40.78	28.55	72.07	82.75	88.06	81.88	–		
Pradesh)	OSR	36.17	31.02	–	32.08	22.88	51.18	55.65	65.64	51.53	–		
	OY	14.57	11.79	–	14.99	9.65	14.68	11.29	19.91	16.00	–		

City	Metric											ACGR
Pondicherry (Pondicherry)	Property tax	5.59	–	–	–	8.75	8.98	8.46	9.07	11.11	11.61	8.17
	As % of TR	21.34	–	–	–	24.08	17.93	20.99	13.53	18.73	15.78	–
	OSR	17.81	–	–	–	19.28	14.89	15.62	10.75	13.99	11.76	–
	OY	16.15	–	–	–	15.25	12.49	11.16	8.20	10.15	7.81	–
Shillong (Meghalaya)	Property tax	3.08	–	–	–	4.41	5.88	3.87	6.65	8.27	9.04	17.59
	As % of TR	30.71	–	–	–	36.37	52.55	25.16	39.78	33.32	41.40	–
	OSR	26.82	–	–	–	30.28	41.71	21.29	34.64	29.83	36.46	–
	OY	10.28	–	–	–	13.01	17.98	9.21	18.56	12.24	18.61	–
Udaipur (Rajasthan)	Property tax	6.74	–	–	12.11	15.20	21.31	30.24	30.81	27.07	–	16.45
	As % of TR	1.48	–	–	1.31	1.38	1.56	1.90	1.74	1.37	–	–
	OSR	1.25	–	–	1.08	1.06	1.26	1.50	1.35	1.02	–	–
	OY	1.20	–	–	1.06	1.04	1.24	1.46	1.32	0.99	–	–
Tiruchirapalli (Tamil Nadu)	Property tax	24.86	–	–	37.81	48.57	74.64	78.58	86.58	90.67	–	14.99
	As % of TR	60.83	–	–	66.56	54.10	58.69	30.23	56.39	43.41	–	–
	OSR	35.91	–	–	36.89	35.65	55.75	28.23	36.26	27.38	–	–
	OY	34.51	–	–	35.67	34.06	32.47	27.42	24.65	19.36	–	–
Coimbatore (Tamil Nadu)	Property tax	19.84	23.86	37.23	69.19	86.36	95.54	106.18	127.69	117.84	27.50	9.54
	As % of TR	74.01	72.09	70.56	89.59	89.59	86.22	59.87	51.87	25.40	–	–
	OSR	21.23	18.26	21.50	31.89	38.57	28.71	25.92	28.98	17.06	–	–
	OY	20.79	17.79	19.32	31.03	35.68	28.40	24.79	23.70	16.67	–	–
Chennai (Tamil Nadu)	Property tax	280.20	–	–	–	591.20	690.70	751.30	1047.60	1129.50	1150.00	15.34
	As % of TR	43.36	–	–	–	44.81	38.86	40.56	44.40	43.37	40.84	–
	OSR	37.37	–	–	–	37.30	33.29	35.19	38.61	37.88	36.01	–
	OY	35.67	–	–	–	35.25	32.00	34.49	38.02	37.09	35.29	–
Kozikode (Calicut-Kerala)	Property tax	21.66	–	–	–	17.27	33.64	40.42	40.06	44.43	44.81	6.91
	As % of TR	46.06	–	–	–	16.45	28.30	32.83	34.88	33.68	32.15	–
	OSR	36.72	–	–	–	13.88	24.27	27.64	28.55	28.40	26.58	–
	OY	36.24	–	–	–	13.79	24.13	20.15	26.97	28.13	26.28	–

Note: Property tax collections are in Rs million. TR – Tax revenue; OSR – Own-source revenue; OY – Ordinary income of the municipal corporations, ACGR – Annual compound growth rate computed by using regression method, and (–) information not reported in the source of information.

Source: Government of India (various issues): Statistical Abstract India, Central Statistical Organization, Statistics and Programme Implementation.

local revenue may be made more buoyant if adequate reforms are introduced. A new wave of reform is intended to remove subjectivity of assessment and to reduce malpractices and loss of potential revenue. States are moving to a simpler unit area method of determining the tax base. More transparent administrative processes, supported by computerization of the system, are also gathering momentum.

Major urban reforms seem likely in the near future at state level in part because the union government is contemplating linking grants with state-level urban sector reforms.[10] States would have to reform the property tax system so that it could become a major source of revenue for urban local governments. States would also have to streamline the approval process for the construction of buildings and development of sites, simplify the legal and procedural framework for conversion of agricultural land for non-agricultural purposes, and introduce property title certification systems.

Notes

1. The author is grateful to Dr M.G. Rao for useful and critical comments on an earlier draft.
2. Categorized basically on the basis of population size, characteristics of population, and level of non-primary sector economic activities.
3. All India Institute of Local Self-Government (2000) and Government of India (1996).
4. This chapter deals only with property taxes. Real property may be subject to wealth tax (union tax), stamp and registration duty imposed on transfer of property (state government levy), property tax and property-related service taxes (local taxes). Properties in rural areas are generally subjected to similar taxes but at lower rates and with some exemptions. When rural areas are converted into urban, the state Municipal Acts apply. The study in the Annex on Maharashtra State illustrates the case of conversion from small to larger urban areas. The taxation of agriculture and especially agricultural land in India has, over the years, been the subject of many studies, which have not been reviewed here.
5. Gross annual rent value of land and building at which they might reasonably be expected to let from year to year with reference to their location, type of construction, plinth area, age of buildings, and the nature of use.
6. The Government of India has recently circulated to state governments a *Guideline for Property Tax Reforms*, which is based mainly on experience in the Patna Municipal Corporation and is essentially an area-based system.
7. Some further illustrations of the complexity of property taxes in India are provided in the Annex of this chapter with respect to Maharashtra state. In this state, there is no provision to levy a property tax on open lands. Layouts of many of such plots are sanctioned, but there are no clear provisions in the rules as to how rateable value should be determined in respect of vacant plots.
8. Based on Municipal Corporation of Delhi (2003).
9. A local levy on the entry of goods into the local jurisdiction for use, consumption or sale.
10. Although not discussed in this chapter, property transfers in India are generally subject to state stamp duties. Another required reform would be to rationalize these stamp duties in phases to bring the rate down to no more than 5 percent by FY 2006/07.

References

All India Institute of Local Self-Government (2000), *Nagarplalika Network Newsletter*, July, Vol. 3, No. 4.

Government of India (1996), *Basic Rural Statistics*, Ministry of Rural Areas and Employment, Krishi Bhawan, New Delhi.

Municipal Corporation of Delhi (2003), *Report of the Expert Committee on Property Tax Reforms*.

National Institute of Public Finance and Policy (1996), *Potential of Property Tax in Major Indian Cities*, New Delhi.

Rao, N.R. (1989), *Municipal Property Tax in India*, Delhi: Renaissance Publishing House.

Annex: property taxation in Maharashtra state

This section covers a case of variations in the levy of property tax within a state among various types of local government unit. It is based on various state Municipal Acts enacted in the state of Maharashtra. However, it may be noted that due to the provisions of the Rent Control Act that has been in force since the Second World War, rents of old buildings have remained frozen and thus the property tax income of the urban bodies from such buildings is very small. The property tax on new buildings is comparatively high as it is based on the current annual rateable value (ARV). Due to disparities in the rateable values, different properties have to pay different rates of property tax even though the civic services available to them are at the same level. Such disparities from the point of view of citizens are highly undesirable. Revaluation of ARV of buildings and lands are not provided for in the Act unless the character of the building changes.

Various types of municipal governments are covered by separate state Municipal Acts. The Brihan Mumbai is governed by the Mumbai Municipal Corporation Act 1888; the City of Nagpur is governed by the City of Nagpur Corporation Act 1948; and the remaining corporations are governed by Mumbai Provincial Municipal Corporation Act 1949. The municipal councils are governed by the Maharashtra Municipal Councils and the Industrial Townships Act, 1985, and the smaller urban areas (SUA) are governed by the Maharashtra Municipal Corporation and Municipal Councils (Amendment) Act 1994. The state government classifies every SUA with a population of more than 100 000 as Class A. Class B have a population of more than 40 000 but not more than 100 000, and Class C a population of 40 000 or less.

Brihan Mumbai Municipal Corporation
The following taxes are levied on buildings and lands in Greater Bombay. All or any of the property taxes may be imposed on a graduated scale.

1.   General tax at a rate of 8 percent to 26 percent of their ARV, together with not less than 0.125 percent and 2 percent of their ARV added thereto in order to provide for the expense necessary for fulfilling the specified duties of the Corporation.
2.   Water tax based on their ARV for providing water supply.
3.   Water benefit tax based on their ARV for meeting the whole or part of the expenditure incurred in capital works for making and improving the facilities of water supply and for maintaining and operating such works.
4.   Sewerage tax based on their ARV for collection, removal and disposal of human waste and other wastes.
5.   Sewerage benefit tax based on their ARV for meeting the whole or part of the expenditure incurred in capital works for making and improving

the facilities for collection, removal and disposal of human waste and other wastes and for maintaining and operating such works.
6. Education cess not to exceed 5 percent of their ARV except on buildings and lands exempted from the general tax.
7. The street tax.
8. Betterment charges.

Nagpur Municipal Corporation
The Corporation may impose all or any of the following property taxes on a graduated scale:

1. Property tax.
2. Latrine or conservancy tax payable by the occupier or owner upon private latrines, privies or cesspools or upon premises or compounds cleansed by the corporation agency.
3. Tax for the construction and maintenance of public latrines.
4. Water rate where water is supplied by the Corporation.
5. Education cess not exceeding 5 percent of ARV, if the buildings and lands were not exempted from levy of general tax.

Other city corporations
The following taxes shall be levied on buildings and lands in the city. All or any of the property taxes may be imposed on a graduated scale.

1. General tax not less than 12 percent of ARV together with 0.125 percent to 0.75 percent of ARV added to the general tax in order to provide for the expenses necessary for fulfilling the specified duties of the Corporation.
2. Water tax based on ARV for providing water supply for the city.
3. Water benefit tax based on ARV for meeting the whole or part of the expenditure incurred on capital works for making and improving the facilities of water supply.
4. Conservancy tax or sewerage tax based on ARV for collection, removal and disposal of human waste and other wastes.
5. Sewerage benefit tax based on ARV for meeting the whole or part of the expenditure incurred in capital works for making and improving the facilities for collection, removal and disposal of human waste and other wastes.
6. Education cess not to exceed 5 percent of ARV except on all buildings and lands vested in the central government or all other buildings and lands exempted from the general tax.
7. Street tax not to exceed 10 percent of ARV.

8.   Betterment charges.

Municipal councils
The following taxes shall be levied on buildings and lands or both situated within municipal area, based on ARV. The consolidated property tax may be imposed on a graduated scale. The consolidated property tax includes (a) general tax; (b) general water tax; (c) lighting tax; (d) general sanitary tax; (e) special latrine tax; (f) fire tax; and (g) environment tax. In addition, provision is made for:

1.   A special sanitary tax upon private latrines, premises or compounds cleansed by municipal agency provided that no special sanitary tax in respect of private latrines, premises or compounds shall be levied, unless and until the council has made provision for the cleansing thereof by manual labour, or for conducting or receiving the sewage thereof into municipal sewers, and issued either severally to the persons to be charged, or generally to the inhabitants of the municipal area or part thereof to be charged with such tax, one month's notice of the intention of the council to perform such cleansing and to levy such tax.
2.   A drainage tax.
3.   A special water tax for water supplied by the council in individual cases charges for such supply being fixed in such mode or modes as shall be best suited to the varying circumstances of any class of cases or of any individual case.
4.   A special education tax.

Smaller urban area: temporary provision for levying general tax at reduced rate in an area of a Zilla Parishad
If a new SUA is declared wholly or partly, of an area of a *Zilla Parishad* (district board); or the limits of a SUA are altered so as to include any area of a *Zilla Parishad*, then the general tax shall be levied on buildings and lands in the former *Zilla Parishad* Area (ZPA) during the period specified in column 2 of Table 10A.1 at the amounts specified against them in column 3 thereof, and such amounts shall not be liable to be increased during the said periods.

The council shall spend at least one-third of the per capita expenditure incurred in the municipal area for the year immediately preceding the year of inclusion of the ZPA or any such higher amount as may be convenient on development works in the newly included area for the period mentioned in entries 1 to 5 in Table 10A.1.

Table 10A.1

(1)	Period (2)	Amount of general tax (3)
1	Period from the date of inclusion of the area in the SUA up to and including 31 March of the second year in which the area is included in the SUA	The amount calculated at the rate for tax on buildings and lands payable in the area immediately before the inclusion in the SUA under clauses of various Acts as the case may be (hereinafter in this scheme referred to as 'the amount of tax payable in the ZPA')
2	Period of one year following the period referred to in entry 1	20% of the amount of general tax payable in the SUA or the amount of tax payable in the ZPA, whichever is more
3	Period of one year following the period referred to in entry 2	40% of the amount of general tax payable in the SUA or the amount of tax payable in the ZPA, whichever is more
4	Period of one year following the period referred to in entry 3	60% of the amount of general tax payable in the SUA or the amount of tax payable in the ZPA, whichever is more
5	Period of one year following the period referred to in entry 4	80% of the amount of general tax payable in the SUA or the amount of tax payable in the ZPA, whichever is more
6	Any period after the expiry of the period referred to in entry 5	The same amount of general tax as in force and payable in the remaining area of the SUA

11 Real property taxation in the Philippines

Milwida Guevara

The political subdivisions of government in the Philippines are the provinces, cities, municipalities and *barangay* (villages). There are currently 113 cities, 80 provinces, 1386 municipalities, and 42 000 *barangay*.

The *barangay* serves as the basic political unit of government and the primary planning and implementing unit of public policies and programs. The *barangay* is also the forum where views of the community are crystallized and articulated. It is tasked with the provision of simple services such as the maintenance of day-care centers for children and the administration of the village justice system. It is a mechanism through which disputes between community members are arbitrated or settled through informal means.

A municipality consists of a group or clusters of *barangay*. The municipal government is primarily responsible for primary health-care, social welfare services, the solid waste disposal system, and agricultural extension services.

A province comprises a cluster of municipalities and component cities. The maintenance of provincial hospitals, provision of provincial infrastructure, the enforcement of laws on environment and social welfare services, and the provision of tertiary health services have been devolved to the provincial government. In addition, provincial governments are responsible for relief operations and population development services.

A city is an urbanized and developed municipality. The Philippine Congress can convert a municipality into a city given certain benchmarks in terms of population and income. The city government is charged with the provision of services that provinces and municipalities provide, as well as support for education, police, and fire prevention services.

Local governments in the Philippines are vested with the power to create their own revenue sources within the limitations set by law. The Local Government Code of 1991 allocated taxing powers among local government units to prevent double and multiple taxation. A ceiling on the tax rates is also provided under the law. National policy thus sets the tax base (and the valuation rules) as well as the limits for tax rates.

Tax base and rates

The power to impose the real property tax has been given to provinces, cities and municipal governments within the Metropolitan Manila area. The tax applies to all forms of real property such as land, buildings, improvements and machinery. Exemption is given to real properties owned by government, charitable institutions, churches, cooperatives, and those that are used in the supply of water and generation of electric power. Equipment for pollution control and environmental protection is not subject to tax.

The base of the tax, or the assessment level, is a fraction or a percentage of the market value of the land. The undertaxation of land is therefore built into the tax structure. This is compounded by assessment levels that are differentiated depending on land use, as follows:

Land use	Assessment levels
Residential	20%
Agricultural	40%
Commercial, industrial and mineral	50%
Timberland	20%
Special classes: cultural, scientific	15%
Hospital, and water districts	10%

The assessment levels for improvements are also differentiated on the basis of land use and market value, as shown in Table 11.1. For example, residential houses with a market value of P 175 000 (Philippine pesos) ($3271) are exempt. Residential buildings with a market value of P 10.0 million ($186 915) and above are taxed at 60 percent of market value. Similar buildings are taxed at 80 percent of market value if they are used for commercial or

Table 11.1   Philippines: assessment levels for improvements (%)

Market Value ('000 pesos)	Residential	Agricultural	Commercial or industrial	Timberland
<175	0	0	0	0
176–300	10	25	30	45
301–500	20	30	35	50
501–750	25	35	40	55
751–1000	30	40	50	60
1001–2000	30	45	60	65
2001–5000	40	50	70	70
5001–10 000	50	50	75	70
>10 001	60	50	80	70

Note: Machinery is assessed at the following levels: 40% for agriculture, 50% for residential, and 80% for commercial and industrial.

industrial purposes. The different assessment levels can distort decisions on resource allocation. For example, since farmlands are taxed more heavily than residential lands, there is an incentive rather than a disincentive to convert farmlands into residential subdivisions.

The local legislative councils are mandated to legislate the assessment levels to be used in their localities. However, the levels set cannot exceed the maximum levels authorized under the Code.

The Code also sets a minimum tax rate of 0.25 percent (0.5 percent for cities) as well as maximum rates that can be imposed on real properties of 1 percent for provinces and 2 percent for cities and municipalities in Metro Manila.

Under the principle of fiscal autonomy, assessment levels and tax rates can vary among different local government units (LGUs) as long as they are within the ceilings that are prescribed under the law. In Quezon City in 2002, for example, the basic real property tax rate was set at 2 percent for commercial and industrial property and 1.5 percent for residential property. Generally, the maximum rate is imposed by LGUs and a uniform tax rate is maintained on land and improvements. Of course, with the differential assessment ratios noted earlier, the 'effective' rates vary by property class, up to a maximum of 1.6 percent (80 percent of 2 percent).

Property valuation

As in the case of many internal revenue taxes in the Philippines, real property taxation relies heavily on self-declaration of landowners, particularly in rural areas.[1] The Code requires every owner and administrator of property to declare properties before the office of the provincial assessor once every three years. The local assessor then prepares the assessment roll that contains a list of all properties in the LGU and their current market value. Property values are in accordance with a schedule that the assessor prepares for different classes of real properties. In theory, the process should be guided by principles of equity and uniformity. The provincial legislative council then enacts the schedule of values into an ordinance, although practice varies in this respect. Provinces thus establish both valuations and rates, and provincial legislatures determine revaluations.

Lands are valued by provincial assessors following rules and regulations issued by the central government's Department of Finance. Land is generally valued using the comparative sales approach, although apparently often for current uses. Assessors use information on recent sales of similar properties, with adjustments to compensate for differences in location or topography. Buildings on the other hand are valued using the replacement cost method. An estimate of the costs of replacing the property with similar materials is made with an allowance for depreciation. Machinery is valued using the original invoice value with an allowance for depreciation. The market value of the produce is used as a basis for the valuation of agricultural improvements.

Properties are classified in accordance with their actual use. In cases where there are mixed land uses, the predominance rule is applied.

Since revaluation of properties is done only once in three years, values are generally behind current values. Other factors pull down the values. The mean or average value of properties in a locality is used in preparing the schedule. Comparative sales data are also sparse and inaccurate. Property-owners tend to undervalue properties to escape paying a high tax on 'capital gains' (actually on transfer value – see below). There are also chronic inadequacies in tax administration such as lack of assessment tools and absence of technically qualified personnel. There have been investments in tax maps and computerization in select LGUs, but these programs have been heavily reliant on support from foreign donors.

The system for monitoring and recording of land transfers needs significant improvements. Although the Code requires the register of deeds, notaries public and building officials to submit documents on property transfers to the assessor, this is easier said than done. Thus assessors generally rely on the volition of taxpayers to present instances of land transfers.

Property valuation has also become political because assessment levels and the schedule of market values are legislated by local councils. Taxpayers may appeal within 60 days to local boards of appeals and further to the central board of Appeals, and there are reportedly many court challenges. In addition, it is common to have public protests against revaluation and extensive lobbying for preferential tax treatment accompanying legislation.

Collection of the real property tax

The tax starts to accrue on 1 January every year and can be paid to the local treasurer in four installments on or before the end of each quarter. A discount (10 percent or sometimes 20 percent) is available to taxpayers who pay the tax in advance while late payments are subject to a 2 percent surcharge per month, up to a maximum of 36 percent. Provinces collect the tax, although they often delegate this function to local treasurers.

In more developed LGUs, tax payments are computerized. In many LGUs, however, recording of tax payments is done manually. Treasurers maintain alphabetical records of taxpayers and their payments. These are supposed to be reviewed quarterly so that letters of demand can be sent to delinquent taxpayers. The Code vests LGUs with the power to sell delinquent properties through public auction. Although the exercise of this power has produced positive results, its use has still to gain wide acceptance. Treasurers are more disposed to use traditional methods of collection such as demand letters. This attitude is similar to the relatively soft approach of the national government with respect to the prosecution of tax evaders.

As a result, the low revenue performance of the real property tax does not come as a surprise. The effective tax rate (ETR – the ratio of the actual collection to the tax base) on the assessed value was estimated at 0.75 percent compared to a statutory rate of 1 percent for provinces and 2 percent for cities. If tax collection were related to market values, the ETR dips to 0.067 percent, implying that the realty tax paid by taxpayers is only P 0.07 for every P 100.00 of market value (Guevara et al., 1994).

The ratio of actual collection to collectibles is an average of 47.0 percent for cities, 54.0 percent for provinces and 77.0 percent for municipalities. In total, LGUs were only able to collect one-half of the real property tax that is due to them.

Importance of the real property tax as a revenue source

The real property tax is the most important tax revenue of local governments. In the 1980s, the property tax accounted for 23 percent of total revenues of local governments. Its relative importance started to decline in 1990 to 18 percent and dropped in 1994 to 11 percent. Thereafter, it picked up strength and now accounts for 13.4 percent of total revenues of LGUs.

The decline in the revenue importance of the real property tax largely resulted from the increase in grants to LGUs from the central government. Before the devolution program in 1991, the share of LGU from internal revenue taxes was only 20 percent. The contribution of grants had since gone up to 40 percent.

Property tax collection grows at an average of 18 percent annually. Since revaluation is only done once every three years, the normal increase is brought about by collections from improvements on land and collection from delinquencies.

The real property tax effort of LGUs – the ratio of the real property tax (including the SEF – special education tax – described below) to GDP – in 1999 was 0.48 percent. The rate elasticity or the ratio of the growth in revenues to the growth in tax base is almost unitary, implying a constant or very marginal increase in collection efficiency among LGUs. Base elasticity or the degree of responsiveness of the base to changes in national income is less than unity, which indicates that the tax base lags behind the growth of national income.

Collections from the real property tax are shared with smaller local government units that compose the province or the city. In the case of a province, 40 percent goes to the municipality; 25 percent goes to the village where the property is located, and the province retains 35 percent. Collections of city governments are divided, with the village getting one-third and the city retaining two-thirds.

The political underpinnings of the devolution program have yet to be empirically analysed. The 1991 Code essentially stripped municipal governments of the power to impose the real property tax. Provincial governments now determine property values and tax rates.

Other land-based taxes

A special education tax (SEF) of 1 percent is imposed on the same base, that is, assessed values of real properties. The proceeds are earmarked for public education. (The yield of this tax is included in the revenue figures reported earlier.)

Local governments are also empowered to impose an idle land tax and a special levy on real properties. The tax on idle lands is intended to optimize land utilization and discourage land speculation. It is an additional levy of 5 percent on: (1) agricultural lands with an area of more than one hectare on one-half of the land remaining; (2) non-agricultural lands with an area of 1000 m^2 which remain unimproved; and (3) unimproved residential lots in subdivisions.

The special levy on land may be imposed on lands benefited by public work projects that are financed by national or local governments. The levy should not exceed 60 percent of the actual costs of the project and should be apportioned among concerned landowners based on a formula to be established by the local legislative council.[2] The idle land tax and the special levy remain largely unutilized. The definition of idle lands is structurally infirm since the average size of idle lands in urban areas is less than 1000 m^2. The non-utilization of the special levy is mainly due to the lack of technical expertise of LGUs on its implementation.

Finally, a so-called 'capital gains' tax is imposed by the central government at 6 percent on the market or zonal value of real property transfers. In addition, provincial and city governments can impose a tax on the transfer of real property ownership at 1 percent of the market value.

Notes

1. This reliance on self-assessment remains despite earlier major reform efforts to introduce accurate official valuation methods which at the time were considered 'quite successful' (Kelly, 1995, p. 64). Although the USAID-funded Real Property Tax Administration Project from 1981 to 1991 resulted in a substantial increase in the tax base – interestingly, mainly by revaluing property already on the rolls rather than adding new properties – in the end it had relatively little effect on yields. Moreover, as noted in the text, it seems to have had little lasting effect on valuation practices.
2. There is an additional tax on real property in Metro Manila, at a rate of 0.25 percent, for the Flood Control and Drainage Fund.

References

Guevara, Milwida, Joyce P. Gracia and Ma. Victoria C. Espano (1994), 'A Study of the Performance and Cost Effectiveness of the Real Property Tax,' July.

International Bureau for Fiscal Documentation (2000), *Asia-Pacific Taxation*, Supplement No. 194, October.

Kelly, Roy (1995), 'Property Tax Reform in Southeast Asia: A Comparative Analysis of Indonesia, the Philippines, and Thailand,' *Journal of Property Tax Assessment and Administration*, **1** (2), 60–81.

12 Property tax in Thailand

Sakon Varanyuwatana[1]

Thailand is organized in 75 provinces and 795 districts. Each province is administered by an appointed governor, except for Bangkok, in which the governor is elected. In addition, there are 7950 local governments, including provincial administrative organizations (PAO), municipalities, sub-district (*tambon*) administrative organizations (TAO), Bangkok Metropolitan Administration, and Pattaya City. PAOs consist of elected councils, which in turn choose executive committees. Apart from Bangkok and Pattaya City, most urban areas are organized in municipalities. There are 20 metropolitan areas with a population of 50 000 or over, 85 cities which either have a population of 10 000 or over or are provincial capitals, and 1024 towns. Finally, there are 6744 *tambons* (TAOs) organized in five categories. Most tambons are small rural communities, but some are larger than some municipalities. Both municipalities and TAOs have elected councils.[2]

Despite this complex local government structure, local revenues and local property taxes in Thailand are not very important. Two local taxes can be considered as property taxes: the buildings and land tax and the land development tax. In addition to these two taxes, there is also a property transfer registration fee based on the market value of transferred property.

As can be seen from Table 12.1, these taxes are important as revenue sources for local self-government units. The buildings and land tax accounted for around 80 percent of total locally raised tax revenue in 1997, but its significance subsequently declined due to the introduction of new local revenue sources for PAOs. The land development tax accounted for about 9.7 percent in 1997 and similarly declined in relative terms subsequently. These taxes were much less important relative to total local revenues, however.

Buildings and land tax

Under the buildings and land tax, taxable property consists of houses not occupied by the owner, industrial and commercial buildings and the land appurtenant thereto. Structural additions to taxable property are also subject to taxation.

Owners of buildings and other structures and land appurtenant thereto are liable to pay the buildings and land tax. The owner of the buildings is liable for the whole amount of the tax. Royal palaces, property of government and state enterprises that are used for public activities and religious property are exempted, as are buildings unoccupied for 12 months or longer.

Table 12.1 Thailand: revenue importance of property taxes, 199–2001

	Buildings and land tax					Land development tax					Property registration fees				
	1997	1998	1999	2000	2001	1997	1998	1999	2000	2001	1997	1998	1999	2000	2001
Amount (million baht)	7209.6	7314.6	7696.1	8326.7	9067.6	868.7	712.6	752.1	766.8	705.4	5688.0	3444.0	2517.7	3908.0	7427.5
% locally levied taxes	80.32	82.18	80.3	73.3	73.8	9.7	8.0	7.9	6.8	5.7	63.4	38.7	26.5	34.4	60.5
% local tax revenues	12.79	12.59	14.2	14.8	11.9	1.5	1.2	1.4	1.4	0.9	10.1	5.9	4.6	6.9	9.8
% local revenues	1.54	1.23	1.4	1.4	0.9	0.9	0.7	0.7	0.8	0.5	5.6	3.4	2.4	4.1	5.7

Source: Local Fiscal Policy Division, Fiscal Policy Office, Ministry of Finance.

Tax base
Local authorities are responsible for calculating the tax base on annual rental value, actual or imputed, of the taxable property. These values are to be declared annually by owners. The actual or imputed rental income from buildings and land utilized for all purposes, except for owner-occupied residences, is taxable under the buildings and land tax. However, when properties are not rented, the Ministry of Interior establishes the annual value as a prescribed percentage of the capital value of the property. That is, to assist the local authorities in tax collection, 'annual value,' defined as the sum for which the property might be expected to lease from year to year, is prescribed. This annual value is then used as the tax base. Owners can appeal to local authorities if dissatisfied with assessments of the rental rate. If property-owners continue to disagree with the local authority decision, they can submit a petition to civil court to investigate the correctness of the assessments. The court ruling is final.

Tax rates and reductions
The buildings and land tax is a proportional tax, specified at the flat rate of 12.5 percent of the annual value. In addition, to encourage manufacturing investment, the tax code also provides a reduction to one-third of annual values for factories and dwellings to which machinery has been attached.

Similar reductions apply where buildings become unoccupied during the year. One of the main weaknesses of this tax is its exemption of owner-occupied residential buildings. This exemption not only encourages the wealthy to build larger houses, but it also creates serious administrative problems in determining whether or not buildings are really used for residential purposes. Similarly, the exemption for vacant buildings is difficult to verify, as is, more generally, the veracity of the self-declared rental values for taxable property.

Land development tax
Taxable property for the land development tax comprises all land, including mountains and water basins. However, government and religious land is excluded, as is land used for personal residences and land used for cultivation, subject to certain maximum areas. If land is located within municipal jurisdiction it can receive maximum exemption of areas up to 5 rai.[3] In densely populated areas in Bangkok, this exemption is only up to a 0.25 rai, though in less populated areas of Bangkok the exemption is again up to 5 rai. Landowners in Pattaya City can be exempted up to 0.25 rai.

Tax base and taxpayer
All persons or groups of persons, individual or corporate, who own or are in possession of land are liable to pay the tax. The tax is assessed on the value of

the land. No account is taken of any improvements thereon or of any crops. The land value is the product of the area of the land and the 'medium value' of land within the tax district (or part of the tax district) in which the particular land is situated.

The medium value is computed by a local committee from at least three recent sale values of land located in the district, without accounting for the value of improvements, structures or crops that may be included in such sale values. Once determined, the medium value of land for a given district is used for a period of four years. This medium value must be announced to the general public. If dissatisfied, landowners can appeal for its revision to the provincial governor.

If no transactions of lands occurred in the area, the medium value is calculated by reference to the closest neighboring areas that have similar land conditions and usage.

The provincial governor has authority to appoint appraisal committees for each jurisdiction. Members of the committees vary with different types of local government.

Tax rates

The Ministry of Interior sets the tax rate schedule for use by all local governments. The rate of this tax is progressive with the size of land holding but the rate itself is low when compared to the medium value of land on which the tax rate is based. The assessed value once determined is used for a period of four years. The tax is imposed as a fixed amount per rai on a progressive scale, increasing with the 'medium value' of the land, with many brackets. The implicit rates, however, are regressive, ranging from about 0.25 percent to 0.5 percent. Idle land is supposed to be charged at twice the normal rate and land used for annual crops at half the rate, with landowners doing their own farming being subject to a low maximum rate.

Tax administration

Under current laws, Bangkok Metropolitan Administration, Pattaya City, municipalities and sub-district (*tambon*) administrative organizations are in charge of the buildings and land tax and the land development tax in their respective jurisdictions. The civil engineering department of the local governments is responsible for identifying the property subject to taxation by conducting a survey of every statutory taxpayer within their district to obtain data needed to administer the tax. When the survey has been compiled, it is submitted to the district local revenue department to assess tax collection and enforcement. However, it is too expensive for local governments to maintain a good record and to update property identification data. Consequently, not all properties within a jurisdiction are taken into account for tax collection.

The tax collection process begins by self-declaration of property-owners to the relevant local authority. That authority then determines whether the self-declared values and identifications of the property match its own data. Local authorities seem comfortable with an *ad hoc* approach in assessing property values. A great weakness in administering this tax is the highly manual nature of the administrative system: listing, filing, assessing and billing. As a result of taxpayer complaints and government policy intended to ease tax burdens, the present tax base for both the buildings and land tax and the land development tax is still restricted to 1977 levels as a base for calculating for tax revenue. The result is that tax revenue from the two property taxes has not increased substantially with the level of economic development.

Property transfer registration fee
In addition to the two main property taxes there is a property transfer registration fee that can also be considered a property tax. The land department of the Ministry of Interior levies a 2 percent fee on the value of the property transaction. The revenue collected is then transferred to the local government in which the property is situated. After the economic crisis in 1997, however, as part of an economic stimulus package, the government lowered the rate of this fee to just 0.01 percent.[4]

Recent developments
An attempt to alter the structure of the property taxes described above took place in 1995 when the government proposed to abolish both the buildings and land tax and the land development tax and to replace them by a new tax called the land and building tax. It was expected that merging the existing property taxes would enhance administration and taxpayer compliance. An additional proposed change was to remove many of the exemptions such as those for owner-occupied housing that have been major revenue loopholes. The assessment base would be the market value of property (including both buildings and land) instead of rental value. The proposed tax code set only the maximum tax rate that local government can collect, allowing local governments discretionary autonomy in determining rates for their jurisdiction. Local revenue departments were to be responsible for tax assessments instead of relying on self-assessment by property-owners as under the existing system. Provincial committees were to be established to scrutinize the rates set by the local governments. These committees would be composed of representative chief executives from each type of local government as well as provincial officers. A threshold exempting low-income property-owners was proposed to ease burdens on the poor. For the most part, however, the collection organizations, penalties, relief and concessions would remain as in the present system. As of 2003, however, the property tax reform proposed in

1995 is still under consideration by the government.[5] Since such a reform encounters stiff resistance from property-owners, the government must develop sufficient popular consensus for property tax reform.

Notes

1. An earlier version of much of this material may be found in Varanyuwatana (1999).
2. Data are drawn from Department of Local Administration (2002), p. 1.
3. A rai is equivalent to 1600 m².
4. The Finance Ministry also proposed an increase in the tax on vacant land to discourage speculators, to be phased in over five years, but it appears this change was not implemented (Lam, 1999).
5. Thailand has yet to develop a politically acceptable consensus on the property tax reform objective, which partially explains the lack of systematic reform effort (Kelly, 1995, p. 76).

References

Bahl, Roy W. and Johannes Linn (1992), *Urban Public Finance in Developing Countries*, New York: Oxford University Press.

Chayabutra, Choowong (1997), *Local Government in Thailand*, Bangkok: Local Affairs Department Press.

Department of Local Administration (2002), *Annual Report on Local Government Administration*, Ministry of Interior, December.

Kelly, Roy (1995), 'Property Tax Reform in Southeast Asia: A Comparative Analysis of Indonesia, the Philippines, and Thailand,' *Journal of Property Tax Assessment and Administration*, **1** (2), 60–81.

Lam, A.H.S. (1999), 'Real Property Taxation – An Instrument to Restore Asian Economies?' *Asia-Pacific Tax Bulletin*, March, p. 72.

Varanyuwatana, Sakon (1999), 'Property Tax in Thailand,' in William McCluskey (ed.), *Property Tax: An International Comparative Review*, Aldershot, UK: Ashgate, pp. 148–62.

Laws and regulations

The Land Development Tax Act of 1954

The Buildings and Land Tax Act of 1932

Royal Decree for Medium Land Value Assessment for 1986, 1988, 1989, 1990–1993

Royal Decree for Exempting Royal Property of 1943

Royal Decree for Using House and Buildings Act of 1932 inside and outside Municipal Jurisdiction of 1973

13 Land and property tax in China

Xu Shanda and Wang Daoshu

China has four levels of government: the central government, the provinces (a term used throughout this chapter to include not only provincial governments but also several large municipalities directly under the state council as well as autonomous regions), county governments and town governments. There are in total 31 provinces. Each level of government has its own budget, with some fiscal revenue from its own tax/fee revenue and some from the grants of higher-level governments.

The central government is exclusively entitled to impose taxes, and only the provincial level of government can make decisions with respect to tax rates, within the limits set by the central government. According to the current tax-sharing system, all land and property tax revenue belongs to subnational governments.

At the central level, the State Administration of Taxation (SAT) is responsible for taxation. There are two kinds of tax administrative system at the subnational level: one is the state tax office, which is directly controlled by SAT; the other is the local tax office, which is under the control of provincial governments.

Taxes on land and property in China

There are seven kinds of taxes on land and property in China, as depicted in Table 13.1.

Tax bases

Business tax
All units and individuals engaged in the provision of taxable services, the transfer of intangible assets or the sale of immovable properties within the territory of the People's Republic of China are liable to business tax. With respect to land and property tax, the regulations stipulate that the business tax shall be based on the total proceeds and all other charges receivable from the buyers for the transfer of intangible assets or sales of immovable properties by the taxpayers. However, from 2003, the tax base has been narrowed to the price spread between the buying price and sale price for the buildings that were not built by the taxpayers themselves.

Table 13.1   Taxes on land and property in China

Tax category	Effective date	Scope
Business tax	1 Jan. 1994	All
Urban and township land use tax	1 Nov. 1988	Domestic enterprises and individuals
House property tax	1 Oct. 1986	Domestic enterprises and individuals
Urban real estate tax	8 Aug. 1951	Enterprises with foreign investment, foreign enterprises and foreigners
Farm land occupation tax	1 Apr. 1987	Domestic enterprises and individuals and those enterprises with foreign investment, foreign enterprises and foreigners who do business in the field of real estate
Land appreciation tax	1 Jan. 1994	All
Deed tax	3 Apr. 1950; revised 1 Oct. 1997	All

Urban and township land use tax
Those utilizing land within cities, counties, townships and mining districts are liable to this tax. The tax is based on the area of land actually occupied and the specified rate (see below). The area occupied shall be determined by the provinces according to practical circumstances.

House property tax
The house property tax is levied in cities, county towns, state-designated townships and industrial and mining areas. The owner of the property rights pays the house property tax. The tax is calculated on the residual value after subtraction of between 10 percent and 30 percent of the original value of the property. Provinces determine the details of the scope of the subtraction. Should the property's original value not be available as a basis, the local tax offices examine and decide on an amount with reference to the value of other real estate of a similar nature. Where the property is leased, the rental income

from the property is used as a basis for the computation of the house property tax.

Urban real estate tax

The owner of the property is liable for the payment of the urban real estate tax. Where the property is subject to a mortgage, the mortgagee shall be liable for payment. Where the owner and the mortgagee are not present at the locality in which the property is situated, where ownership of the property has not been established, or where disputes in connection with tenancy and mortgage of the property have not been resolved, the tax is to be paid by the custodian or the user of the property on behalf of the owner or mortgagee.

The urban real estate tax is assessed as follows:

1. The tax on buildings is assessed annually on the standard value of buildings.
2. The tax on land is assessed annually on the standard value of land.
3. If it is difficult to determine separately the standard value of land and the standard value of buildings, the tax is to be assessed on the consolidated standard value of land and buildings.
4. If it is difficult to determine the standard value of land and buildings, the tax is to be assessed on the basis of the standard rental value of real estate.

The standard values mentioned above are determined as follows:

1. The standard value of buildings is appraised in terms of different categories and grades according to the general local market value and with reference to the current price of local building construction.
2. The standard value of land is appraised in terms of different districts and grades according to such conditions as the location of the land, the degree of prosperity of the locality and communication facilities, and with reference to the general local market value of the land.
3. The standard value of real estate is appraised according to the location of the real estate and building construction circumstances, taking into account the local general market value of real estate for different districts and categories and grades of real estate.
4. The standard rental of real estate is appraised in terms of different districts, categories and grades and, in general, according to the local general rental value of the land and its affixed buildings.

A committee for real estate assessment is to be established in all cities in which the real estate tax is imposed. Real estate is to be assessed once a year.

Where, on examination of the original assessed value, the committee for real estate assessment determines that reassessment is not necessary, the assessment of the previous year is extended, subject to approval by the local government. The results of assessments or the extension of the validity of the assessment of a previous year are subject to examination, approval and notification by the local government.

Farmland occupation tax

The taxpayers of the farmland occupation tax are enterprises, units, individual household businesses and other individuals (except enterprises with foreign investment, foreign enterprises and foreigners) who occupy farmland for building construction or for other non-farm purposes. This tax is imposed on all state-owned and collectively owned crop-planting land, and also on newly developed wasteland, fallow land, land for rotation of crops, and land for rotation of grass and crops.

The tax is based on the area of farmland actually occupied by taxpayers by applying the specific applicable tax per unit (see below). It is paid as a lump sum.

Land appreciation tax

The land appreciation tax is computed according to the 'appreciation amount' derived by the taxpayer on the transfer of real estate and the tax rates specified.

The appreciation amount shall be the balance of proceeds received by the taxpayer on the transfer of real estate, after deducting the sum of deductible items specified below. Proceeds received by the taxpayer on the transfer of real estate include monetary proceeds, proceeds in kind and other proceeds. The deductible items are as follows:

1. The sum paid for the acquisition of land use rights
2. Costs and expenses for the development of land
3. Costs and expenses for the construction of new buildings and facilities, or assessed value for used properties and buildings
4. Taxes related to the transfer of real estate
5. Other deductible items as stipulated by the Ministry of Finance.

Deed tax

The taxpayers of the deed tax are those who transfer land and house property within the territory of China. The deed tax is normally based on one of the following:

1. The transaction price in case of sale/purchase of houses, or sale of use right of state-owned land

2. Assessment made by tax collection offices in reference to the market price of sale of land use rights or house sale when transferring land use right or house as a gift
3. The difference of the land use right price and the house price in case of an exchange of land use right or house.

Tax rates

Business tax
The rate of business tax concerning land and property is 5 percent for both transfer of intangible assets (includes transfer of land use rights among several items) and for the sale of immovable properties (that is, sale of buildings and other attachment to land).

Urban and township land use tax
The annual amount of urban and township land use tax per square meter is as follows:

1. RMBY 0.5–10 in large cities
2. RMBY 0.4–8 in medium-sized cities
3. RMBY 0.3–6 in small cities
4. RMBY 0.2–4 in counties, townships and mining districts.

The annual ranges are set by the central government. The governments of provinces determine the applicable ranges of tax for their own jurisdictions within the ranges listed above, taking into account city construction conditions and the extent of economic prosperity.

Based on practical conditions, municipal and county governments classify the land in their jurisdictions into different grades, and formulate the applicable amount of tax in accordance with the range stipulated by the provinces. This classification is then submitted to the provinces for approval. Upon approval, the applicable range of tax in economically backward areas may be reduced. However, the reduction shall not exceed 30 percent of the minimum amount of tax as stipulated by 'Provisional Regulations of the People's Republic of China on Urban and Township Land Use Tax.' The range of tax in economically developed areas may be raised subject to approval of the Ministry of Finance.

House property tax
The house property tax shall be calculated on the residual value of the property at a rate of 1.2 percent, or on the rental income from the property at a rate of 12 percent.

Urban real estate tax
The urban real estate tax shall be calculated at the following rates:

1. The tax on buildings shall be calculated at the rate of 1 percent of the standard value of buildings.
2. The tax on land shall be calculated at the rate of 1.5 percent of the standard value of land.
3. If it is difficult to determine separately the standard value of land and the standard value of buildings, the tax shall be calculated at the rate of 1.5 percent of the consolidated standard value of the land and buildings.
4. If it is difficult to determine the standard value of land and buildings, the tax shall be calculated at the rate of 15 percent of the standard rental value of the real estate.

Farmland occupation tax
Different ranges of the farmland occupation tax per unit are specified for different regions in consideration of the average size of farmland occupied per person and the local economic situation. The annual amount of tax payable per square meter is, taking the county as the administrative region for calculation, 2–10 yuan for a county with one mu (one hectare equals 15 mu) or less of farmland per person; 1.6–8 yuan for a county with 1–2 mu farmland per person; 1.3–6.5 yuan for a county with 2–3 mu farmland per person; and 1–5 yuan for a county with more than 3 mu farmland per person. The land occupied by residents within the countryside for the construction of new houses is subject to half these rates.

The amount of tax payable per unit may be raised for special economic zones, economic and technological department areas, and regions of developed economy and small average size of farmland per person.

In order to avoid big discrepancies between neighboring regions, the Ministry of Finance has assessed the average tax per unit for provinces, autonomous regions and municipalities at provincial level, which ranges from 2.5 to 9 yuan.

Land appreciation tax
The land appreciation tax has four progressive rates, as follows:

1. For that part of appreciation not exceeding 50 percent of the sum of deductible items, the tax rate is 30 percent.
2. For that part of the appreciation amount exceeding 50 percent, but not exceeding 100 percent, of the sum of deductible items, the tax rate is 40 percent.
3. For that part of the appreciation amount exceeding 100 percent, but not

exceeding 200 percent of the sum of deductible items, the tax rate is 50 percent.

4. For that part of the appreciation amount exceeding 200 percent of the sum of deductible items, the tax rate is 60 percent.

Deed tax

The deed tax has a flat rate within the range of 3–5 percent. The rate applicable in jurisdictions at provincial level shall be determined within the above range by the provinces.

Tax administration

Local tax bureaux are responsible for collecting and enforcing these seven taxes. Their collection and administration shall be in accordance with the relevant regulations of the 'Law of the People's Republic of China Concerning Tax Administration and Collection.'

The revenue of these taxes belongs to local governments. There are differences, however, among the provinces regarding the revenue-sharing system of these taxes among different level governments.

Business tax

The time at which a liability to business tax arises shall be the date on which the business proceeds are received or documented evidence of the right to collect business proceeds is obtained by the taxpayer. Taxpayers transferring land use rights shall report and pay tax to the competent local tax authorities where the land is located. Taxpayers selling immovable properties shall report and pay tax to the competent local tax authorities where the immovable properties are located.

Urban and township land use tax

The urban and township land use tax shall be computed on an annual basis and paid in installments. The provinces determine the time limits for tax payment.

The local tax bureau in the region where the land is located collects the urban and township land use tax. The land administration departments are obliged to provide tax bureaux with the documents related to the ownership of land use rights.

House property tax

The local tax office in the region where the property is located shall collect the house property tax. The tax shall be collected annually with payment in installments. The provinces determine payment deadlines.

Urban real estate tax

Taxpayers of the urban real estate tax shall, within one month following the notification of the real estate assessment, file a return with the local tax authorities of the location in which the real estate is situated as to the condition of the buildings, the number of rooms, the floor space and other such information. Changes in the addresses of the owners, transfers of ownership or the expansion or renovation of buildings which result in changes in the value of the property must be reported to the local authorities within ten days following such changes.

Tax authorities must establish a register in respect of the investigation and imposition of real estate tax and shall prepare detailed maps showing the different grades of land. On the basis of the results of assessment made by the committee and the returns filed by taxpayers, the tax authorities proceed with the investigation, registration and verification of the tax and issue a notice for payment of the tax to the Treasury within the time limit. If the taxpayer disagrees with the result of the assessment of the real estate, the taxpayer shall both pay the tax and apply to the committee for reconsideration.

The local tax authorities determine whether the urban real estate tax must be paid in quarterly or semi-annual installments. The provincial (municipal) tax authorities shall, in accordance with these provisions, formulate measures for the investigation and collection of the urban real estate tax and submit the measures to the provincial (municipal) government for approval and implementation and also to the State Administration of Taxation for the record.

Farmland occupation tax

Currently, the local financial department or local tax bureau in the region where the land is located is responsible for the collection of this tax. The department of land administration is obliged to inform the local financial department or local tax bureau when the units or individuals are approved to occupy the land. The taxpayers of the farmland occupation tax shall pay the tax to the local competent tax authorities within 30 days after getting permission for land occupation from the department of land administration. The department of land administration transfers the use right of the land to units or individuals on receipt of tax payment.

Land appreciation tax

Taxpayers are to report the tax to the competent local tax bureaux in the regions where the real estate is located within seven days of signing a real estate transfer agreement, and pay the tax within the period specified by the tax bureau. The local tax bureau in the region where the real estate is located also collects the land appreciation tax. The departments of land administration and real estate administration must provide the tax bureaux with relevant information, and assist them in the collection of the land appreciation tax pursuant to the law. For taxpayers who have not paid the land appreciation tax according to the regulations, the departments for land administration and departments for real estate administration shall not process the relevant title change.

Deed tax

The financial authorities or tax authorities in the regions where the land or house property is located are in charge of collecting the deed tax. Provinces determine the responsible authorities. The department of land administration and the department of real estate administration are obliged to provide the documents related to the deed tax to the responsible authorities and to assist the responsible authorities in the collection of the deed tax pursuant to the law.

Taxpayers must report to the tax authorities within ten days from the day on which the contract of transferring land and houses is signed and must pay the tax within the time limit stipulated by the responsible authorities. With the tax return form, taxpayers can apply to the department of land administration and the department of real estate (house properties) administration to transfer the rights pursuant to laws and regulations.

Table 13.2 China: revenue from taxes on land and property, 1986–2002 (in 100 million yuan)

Year	Business tax	Urban and township land use tax	House property tax and urban real estate tax[1]	Farmland occupation tax	Land appreciation tax	Deed tax	Sub-total revenue of all but business tax[2] (1)	Total revenue of all taxes (2)	Total fiscal revenue[3]	Percentage [(1)/(2)*%]	Local government fiscal revenue[4] (3)	Percentage [(1)/(3)*%]
1986	n.a.	n.a.	2.46	n.a.	n.a.	0.30	2.76	1877.94	2122.01	0.15	1343.59	0.21
1987	n.a.	n.a.	18.58	6.12	n.a.	0.44	25.14	1975.61	2199.35	1.27	1463.06	1.72
1988	n.a.	0.51	21.76	21.84	n.a.	0.68	44.79	2333.76	2357.24	1.92	1582.48	2.83
1989	n.a.	25.64	25.79	18.06	n.a.	0.93	70.42	2661.84	2664.90	2.65	1842.38	3.82
1990	n.a.	31.37	31.71	15.46	n.a.	1.34	79.88	2740.22	2937.10	2.92	1944.68	4.11
1991	n.a.	31.68	37.22	18.89	n.a.	2.14	89.93	2987.12	3149.48	3.01	2211.23	4.07
1992	n.a.	30.52	41.78	30.85	n.a.	4.07	107.22	3300.87	3483.37	3.25	2503.86	4.28
1993	n.a.	30.32	49.15	30.95	n.a.	7.00	117.42	4261.83	4348.95	2.76	3391.44	3.46
1994	680.23	32.53	60.26	36.90	0.01	12.94	142.64	5331.53	5218.10	2.68	2311.60	6.17
1995	869.38	33.65	81.67	36.21	0.27	20.19	171.99	6288.48	6242.20	2.74	2985.58	5.76
1996	1065.35	39.42	102.18	32.79	1.12	27.68	203.19	7463.84	7407.99	2.72	3746.92	5.42
1997	1353.42	43.99	123.93	33.94	2.53	36.00	240.39	8649.39	8651.14	2.78	4424.22	5.43
1998	1608.03	54.21	159.85	35.62	4.27	65.35	319.30	9539.87	9875.95	3.35	4983.95	6.41
1999	1696.53	59.07	185.53	35.14	6.81	105.93	392.48	10784.96	11444.08	3.64	5594.87	7.01
2000	1885.70	64.94	209.58	37.30	8.39	142.86	463.07	13180.81	13395.23	3.51	6406.06	7.23
2001	2084.45	66.18	228.59	40.28	10.33	177.89	523.27	15413.89	16386	3.39	7803.3	6.71
2002	2467.63	76.84	282.40	58.33	20.51	243.00	681.08	18422.52	18913.9	3.70	8523.9	7.99

Notes:
1 The revenue from house property tax and urban and township land use tax are given together.
2 Figure is the sum of the revenue of the six taxes, excluding business tax, because business tax revenue derived from transferring the use right of land and sale of immovable property cannot be separated from that derived from other taxable items.
3 Total fiscal revenue includes not only central government revenue but also subnational government revenue.
4 Local government fiscal revenue does not include the revenue granted from the central government.

PART III

AFRICA

14 Property taxation in Kenya

Roy Kelly

The Republic of Kenya, which gained independence in 1963, serves as the regional hub for trade and finance in East Africa. With a population of close to 31 million, Kenya has an estimated per capita GDP of about US$1020.[1] Kenya is structured as a unitary government, with the central government administered through eight provinces and 47 districts which operate under the Office of the President. The local government system consists of 175 local authorities, including the capital city of Nairobi, 43 municipalities, 63 towns and 68 counties.

Role of property taxes within local authorities in Kenya[2]

The central government in Kenya is responsible for over 95 percent of all public revenue and expenditure decisions, leaving less than 5 percent of public expenditures decided upon by local authorities. Total annual public sector expenditures are approximately Ksh 230 billion, with the local authorities accounting for about Ksh 10 billion in FY 2001–2002.

As Table 14.1 indicates, local authorities (LAs) receive 26 percent of their revenues from central government transfers and raise the remaining 74 percent from a variety of taxes, fees and charges. The major source of LA revenue is water and sewerage fees (17 percent), followed by property taxes (known as rates) (15 percent) and the single business permit (11 percent). Property rates in FY 2001–2002 provided Ksh 1.6 billion (US$21.4 million): Ksh 1.5 billion to the municipal councils and Ksh 88 million to town and county councils. Property rates account for 21 percent of total revenues in the municipalities and only 6 percent in the town and county councils. While the municipal councils rely on water and sewerage fees and property rates, the town and county councils tend to rely on business permit fees, market fees, game park fees and an agricultural output tax known as a cess.

In inflation-adjusted real terms, rates revenues have been declining since 1991. As a percentage of local authority revenues, rates have declined in relative importance from 26 percent in 1990–91 to 22 percent in 1994–95 and to 20 percent in 2000–2001, while revenue from rates has fallen from 0.37 percent of GDP in 1990–91 to 0.30 percent of GDP in 1995–96 to 0.25 percent of GDP in 2000–2001. Rates revenues in Kenya are declining (1) in real terms over time, (2) in relative contribution to total LA revenues and (3) as a percentage of GDP. Reversing this decline

Table 14.1   Revenue structure for local authorities in Kenya, 2001–2002

Revenue source	Ksh amounts	%
Central government grants	2 808 644 554	26
Local authority own revenues		
Water and sewerage fees	1 857 076 404	17
Property rates	1 605 774 799	15
Single business permit	1 204 351 994	11
Market fees	566 091 032	5
House rents	436 893 898	4
Game park fees	433 360 127	4
Vehicle parking	391 956 015	4
Cess receipts (agricultural output tax)	303 044 179	3
Plot rents	114 473 606	1
Others	997 314 624	9
Subtotal LA own revenues	7 910 336 677	74
Total local authority revenues	10 718 981 231	100

Source: Ministry of Local Government, 2002.

will require an effective mix of policy and administrative reform, along with stronger political will.

Property tax base

In Kenya, the Rating Act allows local authorities to tax either land or land and improvements. Although the first application of 'rating' in Mombasa in 1921 was based on land and improvements (that is, the annual rental value of occupied premises), all property rates in Kenya are currently levied only on land.[3] Improvements (for example buildings and structures) are not taxed. In addition, most local authorities exclude 'freehold' land, agricultural land less than 12 acres, and indeed most private land in the area rating rolls.[4] Public land (both central government land and council trust land) which is not yet 'registered' is also excluded from the private valuation roll – although technically this land should be listed on the public valuation roll and be liable for contributions in lieu of rates.[5] In addition, allocated council trust land not yet registered is not liable for either rates or contributions in lieu of rates.

Although the Rating Act allows LA(s) to choose various assessment approaches, in practice, all local authorities are using either area rating or valuation rating. Out of the 175 local authorities in Kenya, 102 levy a property tax. Of these 102 rating authorities, 75 use valuation rating and 55 use

Table 14.2   Breakdown of property rating in Kenya, 2001

Type of local authority councils	Number of rating authorities	Number using valuation rating	Number using area rating	Number using both area and valuation rating
Municipalities	36	36	8	9
Towns	27	24	12	9
Counties	39	15	35	11
Total	102	75	55	29

Source: Ministry of Local Authorities, 2001.

area rating, while 29 use a combination of both area and valuation rating. As Table 14.2 indicates, municipalities and towns tend to rely on valuation rating, while counties tend to use area rating or a combination of area and valuation rating. Area rating tends to be used for rural or agricultural properties, while valuation rating tends to be used for more urbanized properties.

Fiscal cadastre information in Kenya has two components. First, there is a valuation roll that contains land and value information for properties taxed under an *ad valorem* rate. This valuation roll is broken down into the private valuation roll and the public valuation roll, and typically covers only land located in the established, gazetted area of local councils. Second, there is an area rating roll which is used primarily for government forests and large farms. Rural agricultural land (if even included in the tax roll) is typically taxed on an area basis, while urban land (or built-up areas) is typically taxed on an *ad valorem* basis.

Local authorities are responsible for property tax assessment. LAs must identify a valuer who is responsible for gathering the necessary land information, ascertaining values, and producing the valuation roll for the local council. The council then tables the valuation roll, informs the public, and handles any objections. The valuation roll is then certified by the council and used for taxation purposes.

Local authorities typically do not have the capacity to systematically maintain and coordinate their fiscal cadastre information.[6] With the exception of Nairobi, Mombasa, Nakuru and Kisumu, LAs depend on the Ministry of Lands rating department to create and update their valuation rolls. All fiscal cadastre information is maintained manually: computers are not used for fiscal cadastre maintenance. Officially, valuation rolls must be prepared every ten years, while supplementary rolls must be prepared on an annual basis. In practice, however, valuation rolls are out of date. Most valuation rolls date back to the early 1980s, with few *ad hoc* and incomplete supplementary valuation rolls. Nairobi Municipal Council, for example, uses a valuation roll from 1982, adjusted by sporadically issued annual supplemental rolls.[7] There are at least 18 local authorities using valuation rolls over ten years old.

Property tax rates

The Rating Act gives LAs the power to set tax rates, either as a per unit rate or as a per value rate. These tax rates can be structured as either a uniform rate on all property, or proportional or graduated based on the property land use, value, or size. LAs are allowed to choose an *ad valorem* tax rate of up to 4 percent, before requiring approval from the Minister for Local Government.

LAs tend to use a uniform tax rate structure. As Table 14.3 indicates, tax rates range from 2 to 22 percent, with median tax rates at 6 percent for municipalities and towns and 5 percent for counties, respectively. Only a few local authorities use a classified tax rate structure. The most notable is Mombasa, which differentiates tax rates by location: properties on Mombasa Island are taxed higher than properties on the mainland. Nairobi City Council also differentiates rates based on land use, taxing residential, commercial and industrial properties at different rates.

Table 14.3   Kenya: range of tax rates by type of local authority, 2000

Type of local authority	Range of tax rates (%)	Median tax rates (%)
Nairobi City Council	14	14
Municipality	2–10	6
Towns	2–8	6
Counties	2–22	5

Source: Ministry of Local Government, 2001.

Councils with higher tax rates tend to be those with the oldest valuation rolls. Since valuation rolls tend to be out of date, the Minister for Local Government has allowed councils to increase nominal tax rates to compensate for the lag in revaluations. For example, Nairobi has been allowed to increase its tax rates on residential property from 2.25 percent in 1982 to 5 percent in 1991 and to 14 percent in 2000. These increases in tax rates have almost equaled the rate of inflation, thereby holding the average real tax burden per residential property almost constant since 1982.[8]

Tax administration

Local authorities are responsible for all aspects of property tax administration, including the construction and maintenance of the tax roll, valuation, assessment, tax billing, collection, enforcement, appeals and taxpayer service. While most LAs rely on the Ministry of Lands for producing the valuation rolls, all other administrative functions tend to be carried out by the local councils. The only major exception is for revenue collections in some of the larger municipal councils, which have given contracts to private sector lawyers – typically with disappointing results.

Although the basic legal structure and policy guidelines provide an appropriate framework for an effective property tax system, the primary obstacle to successful local revenue mobilization seems to be ineffective administration. In general, property information and property valuations are incomplete and out of date, collections are low, and enforcement is virtually non-existent.

The weakest component in tax administration is collection. Collection rates range from 10 to 60 percent of assessed liabilities depending on the local authority due to such factors as (1) lack of taxpayer confidence or understanding in how the tax is levied, collected, enforced and used, (2) lack of legal and administrative collection and enforcement mechanisms, and – perhaps most importantly – (3) lack of strong political will.

Despite the options available under the Rating Act, councils have taken a largely passive role in enforcement, depending almost exclusively on rate clearance certificates, which rely on taxpayer initiative to clear outstanding debt and are thus only effective when the property is being transferred or when a local business permit is being requested from the local authority. Active enforcement (through fines, tax liens and foreclosures) by the government is virtually non-existent. Several local authorities, such as Nairobi and Mombasa, occasionally publish the names of delinquent taxpayers in the newspaper. Other local authorities initiate court cases against delinquent taxpayers, with mixed results. To date, however, no local authority has applied the legal option of tax caveats to titles, or used property foreclosures as a means to enforce tax payment.

In general, property information and values are out of date or incomplete, only capturing between 20 and 70 percent of the total taxable land. This situation is not because of the lack of trained valuers but because of perverse incentives and reliance on individual 'single parcel' valuation. Valuers tend to focus on non-rating valuation activities because there is little remuneration for producing valuation rolls. In addition, reliance on single parcel appraisal makes the valuation process costly in terms of time and resources. Mass valuation techniques have not been employed. All property records are maintained manually. Once again, although the legal basis for maintaining up-to-date and complete valuation rolls is adequate, the major obstacle is ineffective administration.

Experience confirms that the key to increasing property tax revenue in Kenya is improved administration. LAs must ensure that revenue is collected and enforcement undertaken against non-compliance, that all properties are captured and properly valued, and that the tax levy is assessed accurately. The collection ratio (that is, the extent to which the liabilities are collected and enforced), coverage ratio (that is, the extent to which the tax objects are captured on the tax rolls), and the valuation ratio (that is, the extent to which the tax objects are valued accurately) are the critical administrative variables that ultimately determine effective tax rates, the tax burden for each property, total revenue yield, economic efficiency and overall fairness. Priority must be given to strengthening the LAs' capacity and willingness to manage and administer all aspects of the property rates as necessary in order to increase these collection, coverage and valuation ratios.[9]

The context and rationale for property tax reform[10]

The government of Kenya is currently implementing a series of local government reform initiatives through its Kenya Local Government Reform Program (KLGRP). The ultimate KLGRP objective is to enable local authorities to improve service delivery, enhance governance and alleviate poverty. It is expected that better functioning local authorities will create an enabling environment for improved economic and social development, ultimately leading to increases in incomes and a reduction in poverty.

The KLGRP was initially conceptualized in the early 1990s and became effectively operational in 1998. From its beginning, the local government reform has focused on (a) rationalizing the central–local fiscal relationship, (b) enhancing local financial management and revenue mobilization and (c) improving local service delivery through greater citizen participation.

The KLGRP strategy recognizes that successful local government reform must focus both on the internal operating environment within LAs themselves and on the external intergovernmental environment – strong LAs can only function well internally within a strong enabling external intergovernmental fiscal environment. Priority has been strategically placed on establishing a rational external environment and then linking these intergovernmental fiscal reforms to provide resources and incentives to strengthen the ability of LAs to perform effectively.

In 1998, the government established the Local Authorities Transfer Fund (LATF), which was the first intergovernmental grant system in Kenya in 30 years. The LATF annually transfers 5 percent of the personal income tax to all 175 LAs on a formula basis, providing about 26 percent of all LA revenue resources. The LATF now serves as the flagship of the KLGRP effort, providing both a mechanism to transfer additional resources, and incentives to encourage improved local service delivery, financial management, debt resolution and revenue mobilization.

Improved local financial management and revenue mobilization are critical components of the KLGRP initiative. In 1999, the government introduced the single business permit (SBP) system to rationalize the previous system of multiple local licensing.[11] Prompted by the establishment of the SBP, the government initiated the development of a prototype local authority integrated financial operations management system (LAIFOMS) that would assist in the management, operation and control of all council financial operations, including revenue mobilization.

A key KLGRP objective is the establishment of a sustainable local revenue mobilization capacity in order to provide the financial foundation for sustaining improved local service delivery, governance and poverty alleviation. Along with the revenue improvements brought about by the single business permit reform, the government recognizes the need to rationalize the property rates system.

Description of reform
A careful evaluation of the Rating Acts and related regulations confirms that there are virtually no legal constraints to improving property rates collections. The law itself provides sufficient flexibility in tax base definitions, tax rate structures, valuation techniques, assessment, billing, collection and enforcement procedures. The primary constraint has been ineffective administration and the lack of political will.

The property tax reform strategy proposed under the KLGRP has therefore been designed to focus on improving basic tax administration and generating the necessary political will. As previously indicated, property tax revenue collections are extremely low, with virtually no enforcement against noncompliance. Priority has therefore been placed on rationalizing the overall administration system, focusing on improving tax assessment, billing, collection and enforcement.

To introduce improvements in property tax administration, the government has designed and incorporated a comprehensive property tax administrative management system within the LAIFOMS to manage all operations related to property tax base maintenance, valuation, assessment, billing, collection, enforcement and taxpayer service. The proposed strategy is to integrate the basic revenue administrative components for all local revenues into the LAIFOMS – including rates, business permits, housing and plot rents, and user charges – in order to standardize procedures, provide consistency and maintain simplicity to facilitate the implementation of the financial management reforms within the LAs.

The LAIFOMS – which includes the property rates administrative components – was first introduced and field tested in 1999 in two local authorities.
By August 2003, LAIFOMS has been made operational in eight LAs, including five municipal and three rural county councils. LAIFOMS will be
strategically replicated to additional LAs in accordance with the Ministry of
Local Government's reform strategy.

In addition to incorporating the property rates administrative improvements into the LAIFOMS, the KLGRP conducted several pilot projects to
test a simple and cost-effective field methodology for collecting property
information required to extend the tax base, ensure a more complete coverage
and allow for mass valuation. The first pilot project focused on developing
and testing field data collection procedures to construct the property rates roll
in Mavoko Municipal Council. The pilot exercise refined field data collection
procedures and confirmed that the existing tax roll was incomplete, with
many missing properties and inaccurate information (that is, the property
coverage ratio was low). The second set of pilot projects was conducted in
Mavoko Municipal Council and Nyeri Municipal Council to test the feasibility of introducing mass valuation. These two pilot projects confirmed the
practicality of shifting from the current, single parcel appraisal approach to a
simpler, more cost-effective mass appraisal system.

Preconditions for reform

The Kenya Local Government Reform Program – and its property rates
reform component – is at a very early stage of implementation. The focus has
been on strengthening revenue collection and enforcement components, rec-
ognizing that the primary obstacle to enhancing revenues is weak
administration and the lack of political will.

Mobilizing political will requires education and incentives to those involved in the revenue mobilization effort. The taxpayer, for example, must be
persuaded to pay the tax through receiving improved local services and
perceiving that the taxes and fees are being administered fairly. Priority must
therefore be on improving service delivery – since people are always more
willing to pay taxes if in return they receive some tangible benefits or services. Improved service delivery is therefore one of the government's reform
priorities.

As with all taxes, attention must also be given to educating the taxpayer
on the rationale, procedures, obligations and responsibilities for the property tax. Linking revenue collections to improved service delivery and a
better-educated taxpayer population is expected to enhance compliance.
Through its reform program, the Ministry of Local Government introduced
a participatory planning process called the local authorities service delivery
action plan (LASDAP) in February 2002, a process designed to enhance

citizen participation in governance, which should also encourage tax compliance.

In addition, the government must strictly follow the laws, regulations and procedures to earn and maintain the reputation for consistently administering taxes and fees in a transparent, accountable and fair manner. Management and operational staff must be motivated to assist in the revenue mobilization effort – to ensure that the property tax rolls are complete and kept up to date, assessments are calculated properly, tax demand notices are distributed, taxpayers are made aware of their obligations and the procedures to pay, and taxes and fees are collected systematically and fairly from all ratepayers. Close supervision and improved management of revenue collectors can improve the revenue yield and equity of the rating system. Consistent and transparent enforcement against non-compliance is also essential.

Local authorities need to improve service delivery to show effective use of taxpayers' money, while at the same time taxpayers need to be educated on the rationale, procedures and responsibilities related to the property tax. In addition, the property tax needs to be administered fairly and effectively to gain the confidence of the taxpayers in its equity. This requires the development and implementation of an improved revenue administrative system that will include property identification and management, valuation and assessment, billing and collection, enforcement and taxpayer service. As part of taxpayer/customer service, it is essential to improve public relations efforts to ensure acceptance by future taxpayers.

In short, the major constraint to improved property rates is not technical (that is, the ability to administer the property tax) but rather political (that is, the willingness to administer the property tax). Current discussions about expanding the tax base to include improvements are irrelevant since the problem is not the size or the value of the tax base but rather the inability to collect and enforce the tax that is currently due. The focus must be on mobilizing the necessary political will to administer the tax in a comprehensive and equitable manner. Until this lack of political will can be overcome, it is hard to justify investing significant resources into further improving tax administration by expanding the tax base and improving property valuation.

Impact of reform
As stated previously, the KLGRP components – including the property rates reform – are at their very early stages of implementation. Many of the new policies and procedures have only been operational for four years. Thus, although laws and regulations have been enacted and there has been some initial success in reform implementation, the reforms are still quite fragile, needing time to mature and to be further institutionalized within the central and local governments before massive replication and acceleration.

Given the fragility of the reforms to date, the government must carefully and systematically monitor the implementation experience, refining the policies and procedures, providing training and technical assistance, and effectively managing the reform process. This requires time and a major infusion of personnel and financial resources, capacity development and improved reform management. Ultimately it is essential that LAs can both initially implement and sustain the various reforms and that the central government can effectively manage, support and monitor the reform process. This is especially true as reforms such as the LA integrated financial operations management system (LAIFOMS) – and ultimately the other property rates reform components – are replicated in other LAs.

Reform requires the transformation of the existing local government system – its policies, procedures and administrative structure – into a more accountable, transparent and efficient service delivery institution, one that can promote increased economic and social development to assist poverty alleviation. This institutional and cultural transformation is a dynamic process and it will take time for all stakeholders to absorb, internalize and institutionalize the new policies and procedures.

To date, the KLGRP components have begun to make progress. The Local Authorities Transfer Fund (LATF) is now annually distributing additional resources to LAs. LAs are now beginning systematically to prepare and submit annual financial statements, revenue enhancement plans, and participatory service delivery plans. The LAIFOMS is now being implemented. Local authority budgets will begin to become more realistic – it is hoped with a harder budget constraint. Revenue enhancement plans will also begin to become more realistic and useful as a means of encouraging increased and more accountable local revenue mobilization.

As the momentum of these reforms begins yielding more substantial results, it will be increasingly possible to mobilize sufficient political will to further enhance property tax revenues in Kenya. Before this, however, any resource investment in improving the quality of the fiscal cadastre information and the valuations will not easily generate the needed property taxes for improved local services.

Notes

1. See UN Human Development Indicators 2002 (www.undp.org/hdr2003/pdf/hdr03_HDI.pdf) and World Fact Book 2003 (www.cia.gov/cia/publications/factbook).
2. For further information on property taxation in Kenya, see Gachuru and Olima (1998), Kelly (2000), Olima (2001), and Franzsen and Olima (2003).
3. The Government of Kenya, The Rating Act (cap 267), 1972 and the Valuation for Rating Act (cap 268), 1972 provides for three types of rates: area rate based on the size and use of the land; unimproved site value rate based upon the capital value of the bare land and the site value; and improvement rate based on the land and improvements separately. The Rating Act 1972 provides extreme flexibility in defining the tax base. Rating authorities

may use an area rating, an agricultural rental value rate, a site value rate or a site value rate in combination with an improvement rate. For area rating, the Rating Act (Section 5) again provides flexibility to use one of five options, including the use of a flat rate or a graduated rate upon the area of land, differentiated flat or graduated rates according to land use or any other method of rating upon land or buildings that the rating authority may resolve.

4. Most local authorities do not tax freehold land. This is especially true for agricultural freehold land. The arguments given are (a) that these properties are already taxed through the agricultural cess, (2) that these properties do not receive local authority services, and (3) that these properties are not legally obligated to pay property taxes. Much of the peri-urban land is not included in the tax base because the Agricultural Act exempts farms less than 12 acres. The only exception is when an agricultural plot is subdivided into residential use, at which time the local authority will include the property on the valuation roll.

5. The Rating Act (Section 23) stipulates that the government must pay an annual 'contributions in lieu of rates' (CILOR) to the local authority. This CILOR is, in essence, the property rates owed by the government for its property. Although the government owes Ksh 396 million (US$5 million) on an annual basis, it has historically allocated only a portion of the liability. In FY 2000–2001, the government paid Ksh 110 million (less than a third of what was owed). CILOR arrears are estimated to be Ksh 2.55 billion.

6. At one time, Kenya was considered a 'model' with respect to its land titling and cadastre (Dale, 1976, p. 234). More recent studies, however, agree with the position taken in this chapter: see, for example, Olima (1999) and Aherne (2000).

7. Nairobi City Council issued a revised valuation roll in November 2001, which was strongly opposed by the public, forcing its withdrawal pending resolution of appeals.

8. Although changes in tax rates can maintain revenues, it should be remembered that only regular property revaluations ensure equity across properties since relative property values change by location over time.

9. For more detailed discussion of the various administrative ratios for property taxation, see Kelly (2000) and Kelly et al. (2001).

10. For details on the local government reform process in Kenya, see World Bank (2002) and Ngugi and Kelly (2002).

11. For further information on the SBP reform effort, see Devas and Kelly (2001).

References

Aherne, R.A. (2000), 'Nations of Eastern Africa,' in R.V. Andelson (ed.), *Land-Value Taxation Around the World*, 3rd edn, Malden, MA: Blackwell.

Dale, P.F. (1976), *Cadastral Surveys within the Commonwealth*, London: HMSO.

Devas, N. and R. Kelly (2001), 'Regulation or Revenues? An Analysis of Local Business Licensing, with a Case Study of the Single Business Permit Reform in Kenya,' *Public Administration and Development*, **21**, 381–91.

Franzsen, R. and W. Olima (2003), 'Property Tax Issues in Southern and East Africa: Lessons from South Africa and Kenya,' paper presented at the 4th International Conference of the African Real Estate Society, Nairobi, Kenya, 12–13 March.

Gachuru, M. and W. Olima (1998), 'Real Property Taxation – A Dwindling Revenue Source for Local Authorities in Kenya,' *Journal of Property Tax Assessment & Administration*, **3** (2), 12–18.

Kelly, R. (2000), 'Designing a Property Tax Reform for Sub-Saharan Africa: An Analytical Framework applied to Kenya,' *Public Finance and Budgeting*, **20** (4), 36–51.

Kelly, R. et al. (2001), 'Improving Revenue Mobilization In Malawi: Study On Business Licensing And Property Rates (Final Report)' (October) (www.uncdf.org/malawi/lg_reports/revenue_mobilization.html).

Ngugi, J.P. and R. Kelly (2002), 'Decentralization and Local Authority Empowerment for Development: The Kenyan Experience,' Paper presented at UNCHS HABITAT World Urban Forum, Nairobi, Kenya, 29 April–3 May.

Olima, W. (1999), 'Real property taxation in Kenya,' in W. McCluskey (ed.), *Property Tax: An International Comparative Review*, Aldershot, UK: Ashgate.

Olima, W. (2001), 'Property Tax Issues in Kenya,' *Journal of Property Tax Assessment & Administration*, **6** (2), 45–56.

World Bank (2002), 'Kenya: An Assessment of Local Service Delivery and Local Government in Kenya,' World Bank Report No. 24383.

15 Property rates in Tanzania

Roy Kelly

The United Republic of Tanzania was formed in 1964 through the merger of Tanganyika and the island of Zanzibar. Located in East Africa, Tanzania is one of the poorest countries in the world, with an estimated per capita GDP of $523. Its economy is heavily dependent on agriculture, which accounts for almost half of GDP, provides 85 percent of exports, and employs 80 percent of the workforce. Tanzania has a land area of 945 087 km² and a population of 35.9 million.[1]

Tanzania is organized as a unitary government, divided into 25 administrative regions, each headed by a regional commissioner appointed by the President. Its local government system consists of 114 local government councils, comprising eight town councils, two city councils, 12 municipal councils (including the three that make up Dar es Salaam), which govern urban areas, and 92 district councils which are established in rural areas, and have the same basic responsibilities as municipalities. There are a total of 2538 ward development councils. The lowest structures are *Kitongoji* (village neighborhood) and *Mtaa* (street/township neighborhood), which operate more as forums to mobilize community participation than as administrative units.

Role of property taxes within Tanzania[2]

In Tanzania property-related taxes and charges in 1998 yielded about Tsh 7.1 billion (US$8.9 million) – Tsh 3.8 billion (US$4.8 million) from national land rents and Tsh 3.3 billion (US$4.1 million) from the local building taxes. This represents about 0.2 percent of GDP, 1.1 percent of total government taxes and about 18 percent of local government own-source revenues.

Although disaggregated national-level information on local government revenues is not easily available, it is estimated that local governments in Tanzania receive about 70 percent of their resources through block grants, 8 percent from shared taxes and 23 percent from own-source revenues. Local government expenditures represent 4 percent of GDP and roughly 25 percent of total government expenditures.

The major own-source revenues for district councils are the development levy, agricultural cess,[3] business licenses and market fees, which together account for about two-thirds of local council own revenues. The development levy accounts for 30 percent, agricultural cess for 22 percent, business licenses for 9 percent and market fees for 5 percent. Urban councils' revenues, on the other hand, are largely from business licenses (33 percent), property tax (21 percent) and development levy (19 percent). Except for the urban property tax, all other local own revenues are administered through local by-laws issued under the Local Government Finances Act of 1982, which has generated a complex system of over 60 different local taxes, fees, charges and surcharges – many with varying rates applied to slightly different bases, and often administered by different local offices.

The property tax itself is narrowly applied only to buildings in Tanzania.[4] Land charges are collected through a system of annual land rents administered through the Ministry of Lands. The level of land rents is set by the central government, with the land rent-sharing rate in 1999 giving 80 percent to the central government and 20 percent to the local government.[5]

Under the property tax rural property is essentially not taxed. In fact, non-surveyed rural land is not even required to pay land rent. This means that a large portion of rural wealth is left untapped by the government. Rural districts continue to rely on the agriculture cess as a means of taxing their agricultural bases. The rating law only applies to urban areas, and there are only a few district governments that are applying a flat rating approach as allowed under the Local Government Finance Act of 1982.

Tax base
The Local Government Finance Act of 1982 authorizes all local authorities to impose a flat rate property tax through enacting local by-laws subject to central government approval. These flat rate property taxes can be levied on buildings, adjusted by such factors as size, location and use. Tanzanian urban and township authorities also have the option to impose an *ad valorem* property tax on buildings through the Urban Authorities (Rating) Act of 1983. Since the Rating Act only applies to urban and township councils, district and village councils are only authorized to adopt the flat rate tax under the Local Government Finance Act of 1982. To date, very few districts are using the available by-law provisions to begin taxing buildings in the built-up areas.

Under both Acts, the property tax base is narrowly limited to buildings, structures or similar developments. Land is not taxed under property rating since all land (rural and urban) belongs to the state and is therefore liable for land rent collected by the central government. These land rents are extremely low compared to market values – for example, rural land was typically paying a uniform land rent of less US$0.68 per acre up to FY 2000–2001.

Property tax base exemptions under the Rating Act are granted to property personally occupied by the President, properties used for public utilities or public worship, public libraries and museums, cemeteries and crematoria, civil and military aerodomes, sporting facilities, railway properties and any such property as the Minister responsible for Local Authorities shall prescribe.

In principle, until 1999, the Rating Act provided power for the responsible minister to authorize the government to pay local authorities a payment in lieu of rates, 'such amount as may be considered expedient.' In practice, however, the central government never paid this property tax equivalent. In 1997, the government issued a circular that explicitly exempted government buildings, government residential properties used exclusively by government officers and employees, property used by educational institutions, and property owned by religious institutions not used for commercial purposes. Then in 1999 the Urban Rating Act was modified to repeal the payment in lieu of rates provision.

The Rating Act stipulates that property should be valued based on the capital market value of the premises or, where the market value cannot be ascertained, the replacement cost of the buildings, structures and other developments, adjusted for depreciation. Although never used, the law does provide the minister power to prescribe a system other than market value or the cost replacement approach for assessment purposes. The flat rate property tax system, as allowed under the Local Government Act, also provides for extreme flexibility in the factors used to adjust the rates applied to buildings if the minister approves. In fact, the flat rate property tax system has been creatively used to implement a simple mass valuation system in Dar es Salaam and other urban areas.

To date, due to the perceived lack of market information, all valuation for rating is done on a cost replacement approach. The rating law provides for a maximum allowable depreciation rate of 25 percent and stipulates that the property tax roll be revalued every five years or for such longer period as the responsible minister may approve.

The property tax law provides for a centralized Appeals Tribunal that can only be appointed by the minister responsible for local authorities. It is reported that the high level at which this Tribunal must be appointed has often caused considerable delay in the hearing of appeal cases. Since valuation rolls for taxation cannot be used until they are certified, and certification cannot be given until the appeals are heard and resolved, this then postpones the use of the valuation rolls for taxation.

Until recently, property valuations in Tanzania were conducted on a sporadic basis funded by the central government – usually without proper maps and without a systematic property ID system. The property tax roll preparation (including the valuation) is the responsibility of the local authority. However, due to the lack of in-house valuation expertise, valuations were traditionally carried out by the Ardhi Institute on behalf of the local authorities.[6]

As with all sub-Saharan African countries, property valuations under the Rating Act are carried out through single parcel appraisals where each property must be visited by a registered valuer. Mass appraisal techniques are not utilized except under the simple flat rating system being implemented under the Local Government Finance Act.[7] To date, no empirical studies have been undertaken to estimate the accuracy of property valuations in Tanzania.

Property tax rates
The flat rate property tax system enacted through local by-laws used to be levied as a uniform flat amount per building. However, local authorities are now increasingly making adjustments for size, use and location in an attempt to improve equity and revenues. For example, Dar es Salaam reinstated the property tax in 1987 based on a simple flat rate system which applied a flat amount per building according to location. Under this initial system, Dar es Salaam divided the city into eight distinct zones with a specific unit amount applied to each building located within a particular zone. In 1996, Dar es Salaam modified this flat rate system by expanding the number of flat rates categories from eight to 52, with adjustments made for size and building use. Other municipalities, such as Tanga and Tabora, also use a similar 52 category flat rating system in their jurisdictions. This flat rate property tax system is still used on all buildings not yet taxed through the *ad valorem* system provided under the Rating Act.

For those properties that are valued, local councils are entitled to use any tax rate passed by a council resolution supported by a two-thirds majority and approved by the responsible minister. Although local governments can choose either a uniform or a classified rate structure, most local authorities use uniform rates. For example, Dar es Salaam and Tabora apply a uniform rate of 0.15 percent, while Mbeya and Arusha use a 0.5 percent rate. Very few local governments use differential rates. For example, Iringa differentiates by property use, levying 0.1 percent on residential properties and 0.4 percent on commercial/industrial properties. Mwanza, on the other hand, differentiates by height of the buildings, levying 0.15 percent on single-story properties and 0.6 percent on multi-storied properties.

In addition to the general rate, councils (with the responsible minister's approval) may levy a special rate to cover the costs of special capital works schemes which only benefit the owners of a portion of the rateable area. To date, this special betterment assessment (known as a 'special rate') option has not been used in Tanzania.

Property tax administration
Property tax administration is the responsibility of the local authority. The local authority is responsible for the construction and maintenance of the

fiscal cadastre, billing and revenue collection, enforcement and taxpayer service. The central government is responsible for the establishment of the valuation tribunal.

Within the local authorities, the responsibility for the property tax cadastre and property valuation lies with the valuation department (or valuer), while revenue collection and enforcement come under the local treasurer's department. Historically the property valuation rolls were often outsourced to the Ardhi Institute and are now being outsourced to the private sector under the World Bank funded property tax reform (see below).

Buildings are identified through periodic field surveys. The tax roll coverage has historically been incomplete. Until recently, property tax base identification was done mostly on an *ad hoc* basis. Property cards were created and updated periodically, with considerable lag in the building market information, especially in the fast-growing unplanned areas. There was a lack of systematic administrative procedures, proper tax maps or a consistent property identification numbering system. All this led to tax roll information that was usually incomplete and out of date. There was no use of computerization, further complicating the maintenance of the property tax rolls.

To begin addressing some of these deficiencies, the government, with funding assistance from the Norwegian Agency for Development (NORAD), undertook an aerial photographic survey of the major urban centers in 1992. Base maps were generated from this survey and were used to update the property tax rolls in Dar es Salaam (DSM) from 1993 to 1998 and are now being used to update the property tax rolls in eight other major urban centers.

Billing, collection and enforcement are the responsibility of the Town Treasurer's office. With the exception of Dar es Salaam, which introduced computerized billing for about 30 000 parcels in 1996, all tax demand notices are produced manually, creating problems of delay and transcription errors.[8] Demand notices are delivered either manually or through the postal system – often with difficulty due to incomplete or out-of-date addresses and names. In Dar es Salaam, for example, 15.7 percent of the demand notices were returned as undeliverable in 1996.

The rating law is silent on the due dates and the number of installments for the property taxes, leaving these to the by-laws of each local authority. Under the by-laws issued by Dar es Salaam, for example, the tax deadline is defined as 30 days 'after receipt of the property tax bill.' In practice, tax payments in DSM are made in one installment, although large taxpayers are allowed more than one installment.

For those taxpayers who do not pay the tax, the DSM by-laws provide for a 25 percent penalty per year or imprisonment for a term not to exceed one month, or both fine and imprisonment, or any other penalty as contained in the Urban Rating Act. The Urban Rating Act itself provides for a 1 percent per month interest penalty on all outstanding tax amounts.

The Urban Rating Act also provides for a warrant to be issued to seize the personal goods and chattels of defaulters up to the value of the outstanding rates. The rating authority may, at its discretion, recover any amount due, by civil action without further notice or demand. In addition, all outstanding rates are to be a charge on the premises, having priority over other claims, and the law allows for the premises to be auctioned to recover the rates outstanding.

Despite the various legal provisions to enforce payment, collection rates appear to be quite low (for example, less than 30–50 percent in Dar es Salaam). There are various possible explanations for this low collection rate, ranging from a lack of taxpayer education/understanding to outright resistance, due to lack of local services. Some attribute the low collections largely to lack of political will and administrative efficiency. Therefore, effectively applying the legal provisions available for improving the collection and compliance rate would dramatically improve the revenue, equity and efficiency of the entire property tax system.

The property tax reform experience
Tanzania began its property tax reform in 1993. Under Phase One, completed in 1996, the government developed a property tax reform strategy that introduced a valuation-based property tax system in Dar es Salaam to replace the flat rating system, which had been used previously. Under Phase One, the government produced a valuation roll of about 30 000 properties in Dar es Salaam, established a valuation office in Dar es Salaam, and began preparatory work on the property tax in eight other municipalities. The property tax reform was essentially a 'valuation-pushed' strategy in which priority was narrowly placed on improving property valuation rather than on a broader comprehensive systems approach beginning with collection.[9]

A priority for the property tax reform was the development of a systematic procedure for both conducting the property tax base identification and providing building valuations. Thus the government, using the maps produced in 1992, developed a system to identify the buildings, enumerate them, assign a property identification number and collect the relevant physical information on each building. In addition, the government developed a consistent set of rating assessment guidelines to establish a uniform valuation basis for the revaluation process. Due to the lack of perceived market values, the government decided to use the cost replacement approach as provided for in the law. These guidelines categorized all buildings into four basic groups (residential, commercial, industrial and hotels). Within each of these categories were three sub-categories of building types, each with an established range of values per square meter. In addition, a separate category was established for site works, with a percentage adjustment to be applied to the basic cost figure. There were three percentage adjustments, namely 0, 5 and 10 percent, depending on the quality of the site works. Finally, four categories for depreciation adjustment were established, depending on the physical condition, functional obsolescence, and remaining economic life of the property.

Using these fieldwork and valuation guidelines, the government's reform strategy was to outsource the valuation work to private valuation companies due to the lack of in-house valuation capacity within the local governments. Six valuation firms were contracted under Phase One to value approximately 30 000 buildings at a total cost of about US$1 million (approximately $33 per property).

This exercise produced a valuation roll in 1995 of 30 000 buildings, with a total estimated value of Tsh 800 686 920 000 (roughly US$100 million). In 1996, Dar es Salaam adopted a 0.1 percent tax rate which generated a tax potential of Tsh 800 million. This tax revenue potential, combined with the potential for buildings under the flat rate system (that is, Tsh 400 million), produced a revenue potential of over Tsh 1.2 billion (US$1.5 million).

In 1996, the new valuation tax roll was used for tax purposes. At the same time, the central government appointed a new City Commission to replace the DSM City Council in 1996 due to severe financial mismanagement. These actions jointly contributed to a major increase in local revenues. As Table 15.1 indicates, Dar es Salaam local own-source revenues rose by an

Table 15.1   Revenue collection in Dar es Salaam, 1993–96 (Tsh millions)

Revenue source	1993	1994	1995	1996	Annual average change (%) (1993–96)
Property rates	128.1	111.9	60.1	559.7	112
Development levy	143.8	116.8	140.5	506.9	84
Hotel levy	76.5	68.7	80.5	118.9	18
Industrial cess	28.0	78.6	191.4	304.2	329
Taxi fees	22.9	9.0	27.7	82.7	87
Licenses	167.9	107.5	137.5	413.4	49
Market dues	36.8	29.8	26.2	37.3	0
Total revenue	604	522.3	663.9	2023.1	78

Note: The exchange rate is approximately Tsh 800/US$1.

Source: USRP (1999).

average annual rate of 81 percent over the three-year period from 1993 to 1996, with above-average increase in property rates, development levy, the industrial cess, and taxi/bus park fees. Although the new property valuation roll may have provided some assistance, the major cause for the overall revenue increase was the strong political will and overall revenue mobilization efficiency under the new City Commission.[10]

Phase Two of the property tax reform began in January 1999 following the same basic valuation-pushed strategy. Private sector valuation companies were hired to value an additional 17 000 properties in Dar es Salaam and 26 000 properties in eight other municipalities. The total cost of the second phase was slightly over US$1 million to value approximately 44 000 properties, for an average cost of about US$23 per parcel.

Before finalizing Phase Three of the reform, the government funded an independent evaluation of the property tax reform experience in 2002, which suggested that the current strategy focused on private sector contract valuations was not sustainable (McCluskey et al., 2003). The study estimated that the current approach would require about US$105 to $135 million and about 18 years to value the entire country, even if all of the 109 certified valuers in Tanzania were to work full-time. The conclusion was that an alternative, more cost-effective valuation approach should be adopted and that the strategy be broadened to include billing, collection and enforcement. Several valuation alternatives were identified, all leaning towards introducing mass valuation rather than continuing to rely on individual, single parcel valuation. In addition, recommendations were made to rationalize the property tax administration system, strengthen in-house capacity, and introduce appropriate computerization to effectively manage the entire property tax administration process.

As with other sub-Saharan African countries, the challenge for the Tanzanian property tax reform is how to design and strategically implement policy and administrative procedures that can improve the property tax base coverage, property valuations and the tax collection and enforcement in an equitable, cost-effective and politically acceptable manner (Kelly, 2000).

Notes

1. See UN Human Development Indicators 2002 (www.undp.org/hdr2003/pdf/hdr03_HDI.pdf) and World Fact Book 2003 (www.cia.gov/cia/publications/factbook).
2. For further information on property taxation in Tanzania, see Masunu and Rwechungura (1995), Kelly and Musunu (2000), Ahene (2000), McCluskey et al. (2003), and Geho (2003).
3. This cess (essentially a tax paid on marketed sales of specified produce in a district) has long been more important in Tanzania than in neighboring countries. An early report (Lee, 1965) noted considerable variation in the rates, coverage and administration of this cess from district to district.
4. This chapter focuses exclusively on the building taxes as implemented under the Local

Government Finance Act of 1982 or the Urban Authorities (Rating) Act of 1983. See Kelly (1999) for a comparative analysis of the Tanzania, Uganda and Kenya property tax systems.

5. Tanzania shares three major taxes between the central and local governments. The fuel tax is shared 70:30, game fees are shared 84:16 and the land rents are shared 80:20. The 20 percent share of the land rents is allocated to local authorities by the Ministry of Lands based on the land rents actually collected by the LAs – not the amount collected within the local authority. This distinction is important since Dar es Salaam does not receive any land rents since the actual collection is done by the Ministry of Lands. This is significant since 70 percent of all land rents are collected in Dar es Salaam.

6. The Ardhi Institute was an educational institute offering an advanced Diploma in Land Management and Valuation that served as the training ground for valuers throughout East Africa. In 1996, this Institute became the University College of Land and Architectural Studies (UCLAS) within the University of Dar es Salaam system.

7. For further information on mass valuation options for Tanzania, see Geho (2003) and McCluskey et al. (2003). See also Kelly et al. (2001) for pilot application of simple, cost-effective mass valuation in Malawi.

8. Dar es Salaam is the only municipality that uses computers in its tax administration, having a property tax billing system introduced in 1995–96 as part of the World Bank project.

9. See Kelly (1993) for more information on the difference between a collection-led strategy versus a valuation-pushed strategy.

10. As Table 15.1 indicates, the average annual increase for all DSM own-source revenues between 1993 and 1996 was 78 percent. There were substantial above-average increases in industrial cess (329 percent) and property rates (112 percent), close to average increases in development levy and taxi parks, and less than average growth in licenses and hotel levies. The table shows a general decline from 1993 to 1996 in all revenue sources except the industrial cess. The sharpest decline was in 1995, just before the replacement of the City Council with a City Commission. A portion of the revenue increase in 1996 was no doubt from arrears – not current liabilities. For example, it is estimated that approximately 40 percent of the property tax collections in 1996 were from arrears from previous years.

References

Ahene, R.A. (2000), 'Nations of Eastern Africa,' in R.V. Andelson (ed.), *Land-Value Taxation around the World*, Malden, MA: Blackwell.

Geho, M.L. (2003), 'Prospects of Applying Computer Assisted Mass Valuation in Tanzania,' paper presented at the FIG Working Week 2003, Paris, France, 13–17 April (www.fig.net/figtree/pub/fig_2003/TS_21/TS21_3_Geho.pdf).

Kelly, R. (1993), 'Property Tax Reform in Indonesia: Applying a Collection-Led Strategy,' *Bulletin of Indonesian Economic Studies*, **29** (1), 1–21.

Kelly, R. (1999), 'Property Taxation in East Africa: The Tale of Three Reforms,' in Daphne E. Kenyon (ed.), *Proceedings 92nd Annual Conference on Taxation*, Washington, DC: National Tax Association, pp. 443–540.

Kelly, R. (2000), 'Designing Effective Property Tax Reforms in Sub-Saharan Africa: Theory and International Experience,' *Journal of Property Tax Assessment and Administration*, **5** (3), 31–52.

Kelly, R. and Z. Musunu (2000), 'Property Tax Reform in Tanzania,' *Journal of Property Tax Assessment and Administration*, **5** (1), 5–25.

Kelly, R. et al. (2001),'Improving Revenue Mobilization in Malawi: Study on Business Licensing and Property Rates (Final Report)' (October) (www.uncdf.org/malawi/lg_reports/revenue_mobilization.html)

Lee, E.C. (1965), *Local Taxation in Tanzania*, Dar es Salaam: Institute of Public Administration, University College.

Masunu, Z.J. and T.C. Rwechungura (1995), 'Property Tax in Tanzania: An Examination,' in

World Bank, *Major Property Tax Issues in Africa*, papers from regional seminar organized by Municipal Development Programme for Eastern and Southern Africa.

McCluskey, W. et al. (2003), 'Property tax reform: the experience of Tanzania,' Working Paper for the RICS Foundation (http://www.rics-foundation.org/publish/document.aspx?did=3171)

Urban Sector Rehabilitation Project (USRP) (1999), 'Revenue Collections: Dar es Salaam,' mimeo.

16 Property taxation in South Africa

Enid Slack[1]

The population of South Africa is 44 million. The country is organized into nine provinces, six single-tier metropolitan municipalities, 47 district municipalities, and 231 municipalities (within the district municipalities). This new municipal structure came into effect in December 2000 as a result of a major re-demarcation of municipalities and the rationalization and amalgamation of primary-tier urban and rural municipalities into new local municipalities.

The property tax (known as 'rates on property') is a local tax (provinces are constitutionally prohibited from levying property tax). In metropolitan areas, the metropolitan councils levy and collect property rates; in non-metropolitan areas, local municipalities levy property taxes. District municipalities may only levy property rates in areas where no local municipality exists (so-called district management areas). Presently, national and provincial governments regulate how the property tax is charged, assessed and collected, however.

Within the former white local authorities (before 1993), the property tax was an important tax. Generous rebates were granted to residential taxpayers, shifting much of the burden onto commercial and industrial properties. In contrast, the former black municipalities did not levy property taxes and relied largely on grants from the central government. The absence of a property tax reflected apartheid policies that prohibited black landownership outside of the homelands. In 1993, the property tax bases of the former white local authorities were extended to former black local authorities to achieve a uniform structure throughout the jurisdiction of newly established non-racial local government structures. In some black township areas the property tax is still being phased in.[2]

The Local Government Property Rates Bill (published in March 2003), if implemented, would create a nationwide legal and regulatory framework for valuing property and levying property rates. Although this bill is still under revision, some of its specific provisions are mentioned under the tax base and tax rates sections below.

Revenue importance

As Table 16.1 shows, the property tax is an important source of revenue for local governments (metropolitan, district and local councils), accounting for approximately 21 percent of their revenues. Property taxes are used for

*Table 16.1   Consolidated operating income budgets, South Africa, 2001–02
and 2002–03*

Operating income	2001–02		2002–03		% change
	R billion	%	R billion	%	
RSC levies	3.9	7.2	4.4	7.1	12.8
Property tax	11.5	21.2	12.5	20.3	8.6
Bulk services	25.0	46.0	28.0	45.5	12.0
Government grants	3.6	6.6	6.7	10.9	86.1
Other	10.3	19.0	10.0	16.2	–0.1
Total	54.3	100.0	61.6	100.0	13.4

Source: Republic of South Africa, *Intergovernmental Fiscal Review 2003*.

funding those services that are not fully supported by fees, for example, general government, recreation, street lighting and libraries.

Non-property tax revenues include gross utility fees from trading services (surcharges on specific municipal services such as electricity, water, sewerage and refuse removal, with electricity making up the largest share). Historically, these fees have been the largest source of municipal revenue. It is anticipated, however, that the introduction of new directions for the provision of water and electricity will affect the profits of these services and the municipal revenues. This means that property taxes will likely become more significant in the future.

Transfers include conditional and unconditional grants. Regional services council levies (RSC levies) are taxes on businesses. Although, on average, they account for only 7 percent of municipal revenues, they represent the primary source of revenue for district municipalities and also constitute a significant source of revenue for the six metropolitan municipalities. The regional establishment levy accounts for two-thirds of the revenue from these levies and is based on turnover. The remaining one-third is a regional services levy on the annual value of the payroll. Other municipal revenues include interest on investment, non-trading services, fees and charges, and fines.

The tax base
The property tax is levied on owners of immovable property. All land (residential, commercial, industrial, agricultural and government) and any improvements to the land are rateable. The property tax base also includes land owned by local government and vacant land. Although rural properties (land outside the boundaries of urban centres) are in principle included in the

tax base, many local municipalities are not yet properly geared to levy and collect property rates in the rural areas within their jurisdictions.

Capital value (that is, market value) is used as the basis for valuation. Currently, municipalities may choose between at least two of the following tax bases:

- site rating (rating on unimproved land only);
- flat rating (rating the improved value of the land); and
- composite or differential rating (rating both land and improvements but at different rate levels).

The use of these three tax bases is evenly split among local councils at the present time. No matter which base is used, the valuation roll must include the value of the land, the improvements and the total property value. Under the proposed legislation, however, all municipalities would be required to use only total improved value of property as the tax base.[3] It would also require comprehensive revaluations, which would mean that taxes would be at a value that is closer to market value for those properties that have appreciated or depreciated significantly.

'Site value' is defined as 'the amount which such land or right in the land would have realized if sold on the date of valuation in the open market by a willing seller to a willing buyer assuming that the improvements had not been made.' The value of improvements is determined by subtracting the site value of land from the improved value.

The comparable sales method is used to value rateable property. This method attempts to estimate the price that would be paid by a willing buyer to a willing seller in an arm's-length transaction. To value the improvements, two methods are used: subtract site value from the improved land value (the most commonly used method) or value buildings at replacement cost less depreciation.

Some exemptions and other tax relief measures are provided in all nine provinces but they are few in number. Exemptions include religious institutions (but only those used exclusively for religious purposes). Unlike in many other countries, state-owned properties are not exempt from the property tax, but they currently receive a 20 percent rebate.

Tax relief is granted through grants-in-aid, rebates, differential tax rates, or remission of some or all of the tax payable. Rebates are used most widely for residential properties, for which rebates of 40 percent are not uncommon. Additional rebates may be granted to disabled persons, pensioners, or low-income taxpayers.

Tax rates

The rate is set to make up the shortfall between expenditure requirements and revenue from other sources. Municipalities are not presently permitted to levy differential rates on different classes of property. Rather, uniform or flat rates are used. In lieu of differential property tax rates, local councils can grant rebates or relief measures to different property types. Differential rates are only available for land held for specific uses such as agriculture or mining. In some provinces, a maximum rate is set by the provincial government. Where the tax base constitutes both land and improvements as separate taxable objects (that is, composite rating), the rate on land is higher than the rate on improvements.

Under the proposed legislation, decisions about differential rating of different categories of property, as well as exemptions and rebates, would be left to municipal councils. Each council would be required to adopt a property rates policy and to reflect the implicit cost of all exemptions and rebates as budget expenditures.

Tax administration

Valuers are employed by local governments and must be registered under the Property Valuers Profession Act, 2000. Valuers are supervised by the South African Council of Valuers, a statutory body established under the same Act. Most of the larger municipalities use their own in-house valuers; smaller municipalities contract the valuation function to the private sector.

A general valuation must be undertaken at least once in a four-year period in most provinces; in two provinces, the period is five years. The system is poorly administered in many municipalities and, in some cases, comprehensive revaluations have not been undertaken for ten years or longer (Republic of South Africa, 2001, p. 150). An important reason for this, however, is that until 1993 the statutory period between revaluations was ten years in the former Cape of Good Hope province.

At the present time, provincial ordinances do not provide for computer-assisted mass appraisal (CAMA). Full inspection of each property is required. As an interim measure until the new rating legislation is passed, however, national legislation was enacted to ensure that CAMA may be used. The City of Cape Town has recently completed a revaluation using CAMA.

The valuation roll contains information on the valuation or revaluation. The roll shows the name of the owner, a description of the property, the size of the property, the value of the land, and the value of the improvements. There is no informal inquiry stage but taxpayers can submit written objections within a specified time period. The valuation board hears objections and takes a decision before certifying the roll. There is also a valuation appeal board to hear appeals.

In terms of enforcement, local governments may collect interest on arrears. A clearance certificate is required before any formal transfer can take place. Finally, seizure and public sale by the municipal council can take place after three years. In the City of Tshwane (Pretoria), for example, collection is high but there is disparity among the different parts of the metropolitan area (Franzsen, 2001, p. 39). Small discounts are applied to early payment.

Other taxes on land and buildings

A transfer duty is payable to the central government when immovable property is acquired.[4] The duty is payable by the person who acquires the property. Persons other than natural persons (for example, companies) pay the transfer duty at a flat rate of 10 percent. Natural persons pay on a progressive scale at rates of 0 percent on the first R 140 000 of value, 5 percent on the value between R 140 000 and R 320 000, and 8 percent on the value over R 320 000. A transfer duty is not payable when property is inherited. An estate duty or donations tax (both at a flat rate of 20 percent) may be payable with regard to the transfer of immovable property. Since 1 October 2001, a capital gains tax may also be payable where a capital gain is made on a transaction pertaining to immovable property unless an exemption is allowed.

Some minor taxes may also be levied by local governments on the property tax base. Such levies include: an extraordinary rate; health rate; water rate; sewerage rate; sanitary rate; and a special rate.

Notes

1. We are grateful to Riël Franzsen for assistance with updating the information in this chapter.
2. Property taxes are at present not yet charged and collected in most rural areas, particularly on tribal land, for many reasons, for instance because properties have not yet been assessed and because there are few services provided in these areas (Franzsen, 2000, p. 5). For discussion of the potential for land taxation in rural South Africa, see van Zyl and Vink (1995).
3. An interesting comment on this prospect appears in a recent paper by an advocate of site-value taxation: 'Despite the fact that site-value rating has proved to be so successful ... it is unlikely to be legislated as the preferred system. The idea of a tax so broadly based as to include everybody in its net seems to weigh more heavily than do traditional concepts of equity as proportionate to either benefits received or ability to pay' (Dunkley, 2000, p. 309).
4. VAT is charged by registered vendors making taxable supplies of fixed property. Transactions attracting VAT are exempt from transfer duty. Residential properties are not exempt from VAT (in other words, where a dwelling is bought by a natural person from a VAT vendor, VAT is payable).

References

Dunkley, G.R.A. (2000), 'Republic of South Africa,' in R.V. Andelson (ed.), *Land-Value Taxation around the World*, 3rd edn, Malden, MA: Blackwell.

Franzsen, Riël (1999), 'Property taxation in South Africa,' in William McCluskey (ed.), *Property Tax: An International Comparative Review*, Aldershot, UK: Ashgate, pp. 337–57.

Franzsen, Riël (2000), 'Local Government and Property Tax Reform in South Africa,' *Land Lines*, Cambridge, MA: Lincoln Institute of Land Policy.

Franzsen, Riël (2001), 'The Current Status and Future Prospects of Land Value Tax and/or Other Property Taxes in Botswana, Lesotho, Namibia, South Africa, and Swaziland,' mimeograph.

McCluskey, William J. and Riël C.D. Franzsen (2001), 'Land Value Taxation: A Case Study Approach,' Cambridge, MA: Lincoln Institute of Land Policy, Working Paper.

Republic of South Africa (2001), *Intergovernmental Fiscal Review 2001*, National Treasury.

Republic of South Africa (2003), *Intergovernmental Fiscal Review 2003*, National Treasury.

van Zyl, Johan and Nick Vink (1995), 'An Agricultural Economic View on Land Taxation in South Africa,' *Journal of Property Tax Assessment and Administration*, **1** (2), 101–21.

17 Land and property taxation in Guinea

François Vaillancourt[1]

There are two levels of local administration in Guinea. The 33 prefectures plus Conakry (the capital) comprise one level. The second level consists of 38 'communes urbaines' (CU) or urban municipalities – one per prefecture (their capital) plus five in metropolitan Conakry – and 303 rural municipalities (CRD, Commune Rurale de Développement). Prefectures, which are grouped in seven regions, are deconcentrated units administered by an appointed official, the prefect. In contrast, the second level (CU and CRD) is administered by an elected council (with direct elections of councilors at the district level and indirect elections at the city council level) and a mayor (except for Conakry, where the mayor is appointed).

The population of Guinea is about 7.6 million, of whom 30 percent live in urban areas ranging in size from over one million in Conakry to fewer than 50 000 in remote areas. Land and property taxes, while applied in both CU and CRD, raise significant revenues only in CU since housing units in CRD have a low value and agricultural land is not taxed. Tax rates and valuation rules are set centrally with no local discretion.

Tax revenues

There are no official statistics on the revenues of local governments (CU and CRD) in Guinea. Little information is available at the central government level. In 1999, only 256 out of 336 local public accounts for 1998 had been received at the central level. More fundamentally, there is a serious lack of human and computing resources. Such a situation is not unusual in Francophone Africa; it also occurs in Cameroon, for example. The only data available at the time of writing are unofficial figures for the first nine months of 1998. These figures yield the following breakdown of local (that is, either fully local taxes or the local share of shared taxes) revenues:

1. Poll tax (IMDL, impôt minimum sur le dévelopement local) – 62 percent
2. Business taxes (TPU, taxe professionnelle unique, and patente) – 25 percent
3. Other taxes (including the taxes on stuctures, the CFU, contribution foncière unique and its predecessor) – 7 percent
4. Other taxes, fees and fines – 6 percent.

Total revenue was 3.9 billion Franc Guinéen (FG) or about US$2 million. Assuming a total of 5 billion FG for the full year, an amount not too different from amounts mentioned in various studies on Guinea for 1995–96, local government revenues would be equal to no more than 1 percent of central government revenues in 1998. (To show how approximate most data are in Guinea, central government spending is estimated to be of the order of 5–10 percent of GDP in 2000.) In 1998, the TPU replaced three business taxes: the IBIC (impôt sur les bénéfices industriels et commercial), the TCA (taxe sur le chiffre d'affaires) and the patente for small businesses. In the same year, the CFU replaced four taxes: the CFPB (contribution foncière sur la propriété bâtie), the CFPNB (contribution foncière sur la propriété non bâtie), the taxe d'habitation and the impôt sur le revenue foncier.

Finally, one should note that the revenues of these various taxes are shared as shown in Table 17.1 between the various levels of governments.

Table 17.1   Shares of local taxes, Guinea, 2002

Tax	Central government (%)	CU/CRD districts (%)
IMDL	0	100
TPU	30	70
Patente	0	100
CFU	20	80

Tax base

We shall discuss briefly four taxes that have some bearing on property taxation: the poll tax – IMDL, the rental value tax on housing – CFU, and the two local business taxes – TPU and patente.

IMDL

Taxpayers are Guineans aged 14–60 years who are not students, civil servants, military personnel or very poor (*indigents*).

TPU

Taxpayers are professional establishments not specifically enumerated as excluded in the budget law (Loi de Finances 1996 et 1998, Article 71/27). Such exclusions include VAT taxpayers, pharmacies, medical laboratories and clinics, gas stations, hotels, photo labs, vehicle rental agencies, gold and diamond merchants, financial agencies, import–export businesses, liberal professions, cinemas and video stores, manufacturers, modern bakeries and brick-makers, restaurants, bars, dancing and incorporated businesses.

Given this list, and the fact that VAT is collected when taxable sales exceed 60 million FG annually (about US$30 000), obviously only small businesses and the informal sector are subject to the TPU.

Patente
Patente taxpayers are those excluded from the TPU; in other words, large individual businesses and corporations.

CFU
This tax, the contribution Foncière unique, is the only tax in Guinea specifically on real property. Owners are taxpayers unless covered by investment exemptions (le Code d'investissement) or exonerated by the Ministry of Finance. Schools, religious buildings and diplomatic quarters are exempt. In effect, businesses pay either the TPU or the patente (according to the exclusion list of the TPU) and the owner of the business premises pays the CFU. Housing is also subject to this tax. If the owners of a building cannot be identified, then the tenants are liable for the CFU.

Tax rates

IMDL
The poll tax rate is 2000 FG per year (or about US$1).

TPU
Rates for this tax are set not by law or decree but by a table produced internally by the Ministry of Finance to establish taxable income and thus tax due from each taxpayer. Essentially, this system replicates for small businesses what is done for large businesses with the patente (see below). The taxable income established varies by the size and nature of the business, from 500 000 FG to 30 million FG in 1999. The tax rate is 5 percent on the income of the previous year

Patente
The amount of this tax is established by a set of tables formally approved by a governmental decree that enumerates economic activities. Each business must pay, depending upon its classification in a specific table, both a fixed and a variable tax, with the latter proportional to the rental value of the facilities it uses. The fixed amount varies from 60 000 FG to 5 million FG. The variable rate is 10, 12, or 15 percent. For example, patente table A is divided in two parts, of which the first is further divided into seven classes which in turn cover 124 types of businesses such as medical laboratories (fixed tax of 500 000 FG and variable rate of 15 percent), cinemas in Conakry

(400 000 and 12 percent), cinemas outside Conakry (300 000 and 10 percent), urban butchers (200 000 and 10 percent), market butchers (150 000 and 0 percent), and watchmakers without a display window (100 000 and 0 percent).

CFU

The rates are 10 percent for owner-occupied housing units and 15 percent for leased housing, commercial, or industrial units. This rate is applied in all cases to rental value (similar to the patente) as set by leases, by comparables or by calculations (0.7 × purchase price) × rate, in decreasing order of preferred method. Business lessees must retain 15 percent of lease payments and pay this amount to the tax collection offices, thus retaining at source the CFU.

Tax administration

IMDL

An annual census of the population is carried out by the local sector (village in the countryside) chief, and controlled by the district elected officials. Collection of the tax is carried out by the same person.

TPU and patente

The tax roll is produced annually by an employee of the taxation branch of the Ministry of Finance. This branch is also responsible for tax collection.

CFU

Again, the tax roll is produced annually by an employee of the taxation branch of the Ministry of Finance. Agents use administratively set values that refer to building materials and number of rooms to establish values when there is no rental contract or comparison available. This branch is also responsible for tax collection.

In general, tax agents have very few means available to carry out their work; their offices are poorly equipped and they have no vehicles or gasoline to go out into the field. As a result, the annual censuses for the TPU and CFU appear to have a low coverage rate and mainly include businesses located in the core of urban centers. Discussions in November 1999 with tax officials in two tax offices, one urban and one rural, indicated that they estimated that their tax roll for that year covered only one-third of the taxable base. The patente census is of better quality since it targets larger and less numerous taxpayers. In addition, informal practices such as adjusting the tax roll to reflect lower past (pre-CFU, for example) levels of taxation were described by central government tax officials as common and accepted. Thus the quality of the tax roll is low.

Table 17.2   Administration of the CFU, Conakry, 2000–2002

Indicator/year	2000	2001	2002
Units enrolled (1)	3021	4045	6150
Tax roll ('000 FG)(2)	3410	4031	5241
Tax collected ('000 FG)(3)	2134	2536	3872
Tax collection rate (3/2) (%)	62.6	62.9	73.9

Source: Balde (2002).

A recent study (Balde, 2002) confirms that this was still an issue in 2002, with the lack of a cadastre the main problem. That said, some recent improvements in the management of the CFU in the capital, Conakry, may be noted, as shown in Table 17.2. Note, however, that with a population of about 1 500 000 in 2002, these data show 245 individuals per enrolled unit, indicating that under-enrollment remains a serious problem.

Note
1. We thank Zogbelemou Cece, Ministère des Finances, Guinée for his comments and help in updating this information.

Reference
Balde, B. Ibrahima (2002), *Gestion des Impôts financiers en milieu urbain à Conakry*, mimeo, Ministère des Finances, Guinée.

18 Land and property taxation in Tunisia

François Vaillancourt[1]

There are two levels of local administration in Tunisia – the 24 'conseils régionaux' (CR or regional councils) and the 262 'communes urbaines' (CU, or urban municipalities). CR, which cover the entire territory of Tunisia, are deconcentrated units administered by an appointed council reporting to a governor. In contrast, CU are administered by elected councils and mayors. CU accounted for 61 percent of the population (8 785 000) of Tunisia in 1994 (last census). They range in size from Tunis (638 600) to small communes (about 1000). Land and property taxes, while applied in both CU and CR, raise significant revenues only in CU since housing units in CR have a low value and agricultural land is not taxed. In 1996, 94 percent of the autonomous revenues (direct taxes, indirect tax, and sales and fee revenues) collected by both levels of local administration were collected by CU.

Land and property taxation was reformed in Tunisia in February 1997 (retroactive to 1 January 1997). This reform pursued three goals:

- to increase the importance, absolute and relative, of tax revenues in the total revenues of local governments in Tunisia;
- to make more uniform and simplify taxation of housing units;
- to improve the distribution of business tax collections (TCL, originally taxe des collectivités locales, now Taxes sur les établissements à caractère industriel, commercial ou professionnel) across CU.

The second goal was pursued by switching from taxing housing units using a rental value approach (legally based on rental amounts and comparables and referred to as the TL, taxe locative) to using administrative values to assign values per square meter (referred to as the TIB, taxe sur les immeubles bâtis). This decision was inspired by the success of local tax administration in Sfax, a large Tunisian city, which used a similar method to establish the TL payable. This procedure was not legal but was tolerated for years. Other cities also used other non-legal methods such as the number of rooms (Tunis).

The third goal of the reform was pursued by collecting better information on the area (m^2) of business establishments. Before the reform, TCL collections were concentrated in cities in which head offices were located since they paid the tax for the entire business. The central government collectors

did not redistribute revenues according to the location of the various establishments across Tunisia.

Tax revenues

Three taxes are of interest here: the rental value tax on housing (TIB), the tax
on unbuilt land (TTNB), and the local business tax (TCL). The role of these
taxes in CU revenues is presented in Table 18.1. This table covers 1995,
before the current system of property and land taxation was introduced, 1998,
the first year after the reform of 1997, and 2000, the most recent year for
which data are available.[2] The data show a decrease in the reliance on transfers from 34 percent in 1995 to 27 percent in 2000. This was one of the goals
of the reform of 1997. In addition, there was a slight decrease in the importance of housing taxation revenues (TL/TIB) from 1995 to 2000 and an
increase in the importance of TCL revenues over the same period. The decrease in TL/TIB revenues shows that difficulties in collection associated
with the TL have not been overcome by switching to the TIB.[3] The increase
in TCL revenues is not surprising as the reform was designed in part to make
CU more interested in collecting the TCL. Finally, Table 18.1 shows the
small size of the local sector in government in Tunisia, which decreased over
1995 to 2000.

Tax base

TIB

CU are responsible for establishing the tax roll, using national values for
covered square meters (m^2) (that is, the surface of buildings, including out-
buildings) to calculate the TIB. The range of values set by presidential decree
is shown in Table 18.2; specific values are set by each communal council.
The tax roll is based on a decennial census (first carried out in 1997) with
annual updates. The values are based on an analysis by the Ministry of
Finance staff, carried out using a 10 percent sample of the tax rolls of large
Tunisian cities. They are, however, set by the Tunisian government (in a
cabinet decree).

For each size category (column 1 of Table 18.2), a price range (column 2
of Table 18.2) is specified by decree of the central government for the whole
of Tunisia. The CU council chooses the exact price used for computing the
rental value in a specific area of a CU. It should reflect the quality of the
houses in the neighborhood. Given that most CU chose the minimum price
(73 percent), very few the maximum (5 percent), and the remainder 22
percent), a price within the range (often the mid-point), it is likely that
political considerations played a role in setting these reference prices. Rental
value (column 3 of Table 18.2) is then obtained by multiplying the price per

Table 18.1   Tunisian CU revenues, 1995, 1998 and 2000

Tax or ratio/year	1995	1998	2000
Revenues of CUs, '000 Dinars (1)	205 175	253 998	285 900
% revenues from TL (1995) and TIB (1998 and 2000) (housing tax) (2)	10.4	9.6	9.1
% revenues from TTNB (unbuilt land tax) (3)	0.9	1.0	1.6
% revenues from TCL (business tax) (4)	12.7	16.4	16.5
% revenues, all direct taxes (5)	28.1	31.6	32.4
% revenues, indirect taxes, fees and others (6)	37.6	40.0	40.6
% revenues from FCCL, transfers (7)	34.3	28.4	27.0
Revenues as % of central government revenues (8)	4.0	3.5	3.6
Revenues as % of GDP (9)	1.2	1.1	1.1

Notes:
CU: Urban municipalities (communes urbaines).
TL: Rental value tax on housing (taxe locative) before 1997.
TIB: Rental value tax on housing (taxe sur les immeubles bâtis) after 1996.
TCL: Tax on business levied on gross business income (taxes sur les établissements à caractère industriel, commercial ou professionnel; originally taxe des collectivités locales).
FCCL: The source of central government transfers to CU (fonds commun des collectivités locales).

Sources: Rows (1)–(7): CPSCL data, Tunisian government, courtesy of the World Bank. Rows (2)–(7) have (1) as their denominator and (5) is the sum of (2), (3) and (4) and of hotel taxes (TH).
Row (8): (1)/ Item 1, summary table, consolidated central government, Tunisia, *Government Finance Statistics Yearbook*, IMF, 2000, p. 420.
Row (9): (1)/ Item 99b (GDP), Tunisia, *International Financial Statistics*, IMF, July 2001, p. 838.

m^2 by 2 percent (depreciation rate). The tax rate is then applied to this rental value.

TTNB

This tax roll is also the responsibility of the CU, but establishing the owner-ship of land is a significant problem in Tunisia. Indeed, TTNB is often paid

Table 18.2   Tunisia: values used to calculate rental values of owner-occupied buildings

m² (1)	Reference price per m² (Dinars) (2)	Rental value per m² (3)
0 < 100	100–150	2–3
101–200	151–200	3–4
201–400	201–250	4–5
401 +	251–300	5–6

Source: Décret 97-431. JORT 7/03/1997 and DGEFL.

only when a building permit is requested, with little penalty. Thus it is advantageous to withhold payment of the TTNB. Agricultural land, land in no-building zones or land reserves, land subdivided in lots until ceded by the developer, and state–communal land are not taxable.

TCL

The minimum (see below) can be collected only if the CU has prepared the relevant tax roll, using the rental values found in Table 18.3 and TIB rates. These rental values are set by central government decree: they depend on the type of non-residential building (the four rows of Table 18.3) and on the number of services offered by the CU in the area where the building is located. Thus the rental value per m² depends in this case on both the size and nature of structure and on services. This is done to integrate this aspect of the TIB in the TCL calculations, since TCL tax rates do not vary by number of services offered. This roll is an indicative one, used by the collector as a check on the TCL paid by businesses when paying central government taxes and on TCL amounts transferred by tax collectors from other jurisdictions, which collected TCL from head offices paid for both head offices buildings in their CU and buildings in other CU. The TCL is deductible from the corporate income tax.

Businesses are required to indicate the area (in m²) of each establishment as an attachment to their tax return to the central government. CU are sent a copy of these returns. If the area in their territory was not indicated, then they impose a penalty tax. The TCL collected by the central government from one business entity is distributed between CU according to these areas.

Table 18.3   Tunisia: values used to calculate rental values of industrial and commercial buildings

Type of building	Tax per m² (in dinars) by applicable TIB tax rate			
	8%	10%	12%	14%
Administrative or commercial	0.760	0.950	1.140	1.330
Industrial				
light structure	0.520	0.650	0.780	0.910
heavy structure, ≥ 5000 m²	0.640	0.800	0.960	1.120
heavy structure, > 5000 m²	0.840	1.050	1.260	1.470

Notes:
A light building will have a wooden structure, and a medium or heavy one a concrete structure, with the latter larger than 5000 m².
Prices by m² are 20 times higher, as the depreciation rate is 5%.

Source: Décret 97-433. JORT 7/03/1997 and DGELF.

Tax rates

TIB

There are four tax rates set by the central government by law; CU have no say in the matter. These tax rates are applied by the CU on an area basis. Areas are classified according to the availability of six services: garbage collection, street lighting, covered (paved, cobblestone, and so on) roadway, covered sidewalk, sanitary sewers, and rainwater sewers. The tax rates are set according to the number of services, not taking into account which are offered, as follows:

1–2 services	8%
3–4 service	10%
5–6 services	12%
5–6 services + other services	14%

Using a tax rate of 10 percent per m² for an apartment of 75 m² , the proposed tax rate is 0.2 of 1 percent of the value of the property ('valeur vénale'). State, communal, religious, welfare organizations and foreign government buildings are exempt, as well as low-income housing units. Empty units obtain a 25 percent abatement if empty for one year. Note that unserviced housing units pay no taxes. Thus the marginal tax cost of the first service is 8 percent; the second, 0 percent, the third and fifth, 2 percent, and the fourth and sixth 0 percent.

TTNB

This tax is set at 0.3 of 1 percent of the value of the land, since its rate is 10 percent of rental value determined as 3 percent of the land value. When market value is not available, which is often the case, a tax amount per m^2 is used, as set by decree. This amount varies across cities according to the urban plan (set by the Ministry of Urban Affairs), distinguishing the high (0.3 D per m^2), the medium (0.09 D per m^2), and the low (0.03 D per m^2) urbanization zones.

TCL

This tax is payable by individuals who pay income tax on profits or professional income, as well as by partnerships and corporations (except those paying the TH, hotel tax). It can be collected at three different rates on one of three bases:

- 0.2 of 1 percent on local (that is, export income is excluded) gross business income;
- 0.1 of 1 percent on the above for businesses whose gross profit margin may not exceed 4 percent (by regulation);
- 25 percent of either the lump-sum income tax (which ranges from 15 to 700 D) or the minimum income tax on individuals or corporations (0.5 of 1 percent of business income with a maximum of 5 D for individuals and 1000 D for corporations).

The tax is subject to a maximum of 50 000 D (Decree 97–435) per business and to a minimum (which overrides the maximum) of the notional TIB that would have been collected if these establishments had been subject to the TIB, which they are not. It is this last provision that explains why Table 18.3 is needed.

Tax administration

Employees of the Ministry of Finance collect all taxes. Some are assigned to local taxation offices, while others carry out their work from regional offices responsible for collecting national taxes. CU can choose to assist them with their own employees; most do. In 1996–97, local tax officials in both the Ministry of Finance and in municipalities were equipped with computers and specialized software to facilitate implementation of the TIB reform. Overall, the housing roll is reported to be of good quality, ranging from very good in smaller municipalities with little growth in their housing stock to poor in larger municipalities, especially those experiencing faster growth.

TIB

The following steps were carried out in preparing the TIB roll in 1997 (for the first time). Following publication of the official notice of the tax roll preparation, CU distributed the self-declaration form called for in the 1997 TIB. Municipal employees, going from door to door, did this in March and received from some housing units a completed form indicating the area (in m^2) of the unit. CU then established the tax bill for each housing unit. This was done using the following information:

- m^2: this was obtained from the self-declaration form. When the information was not available, the housing unit was by law supposed to be classified as having 400 m^2. This was done in some CU, while others used existing m^2 information (from the previous TL roll) or a formula to transform the number of rooms from the previous TL roll into m^2 with a gross-up factor then added. Some CU verified the declared m^2 against existing information (TL roll) but most did not.
- Reference prices (column 2 of Table 18.2): these were set by CUs.
- Tax rates: these depend on the number of services, which was established using both information from technical services and from tax office employees who gathered information visually.[4] In most cases, the operation was completed in late 1997 or early 1998.

CU then sent out the tax bill informing each household of its presumptive tax bill. The household then had until the end of the month following the month of receipt of this notice to appeal it. Appeals often attempted to move the m^2 from one price category to a lower one (105 m^2 to 95 m^2, for example).

Notes

1. We thank Nejib Belaid, director, Institut Supérieur de Finances et de Fiscalité Université du Centre, Sousse, Tunisia for his comments and for information ensuring that all rates and values were up to date as of 1 January 2003.
2. At the time of writing in 2002.
3. Although the collection rate for the TL in recent years (1990–95) of (year t receipts/year t tax roll) was only 35–40 percent, the rate for (all years receipts/year t tax roll) was 55 percent, reflecting collection of arrears. The main difficulty is that the threat of sanctions such as seizing household goods or housing itself is not credible as they are very rarely, if ever, applied since they are seen as being in conflict with social norms.
4. This raised the issue of the level of services offered. One Tunis resident pointed out to the author that while there may well be street lights, some of them were 'very tired'!

PART IV

CENTRAL AND EASTERN EUROPE

19 Land-based taxes in Hungary

Almos Tassonyi[1]

In 1990, the Hungarian system of local governance was substantially changed, with a recognition of the principles of local autonomy and the reassertion of historical local rights. The Act on Local Self Government (1990) eliminated 1523 local councils that had acted as agents for the central government in a system of 19 county councils. Further, local governments were given responsibilities on an exceptional scale (Davey and Peteri, 1998), ranging from traditional local services such as the provision of water, sewerage, roads, fire protection and local recreational and cultural services to the provision of primary education.

Hungary's municipal tax system has also experienced radical changes since 1992. The previous system was replaced by one that made it possible for the majority of local taxes to be imposed on non-residents. The use of the business turnover tax by local governments became widespread (Bird et al., 1995). At the same time, most municipalities terminated taxes on residential properties, with the aim of enhancing the political popularity of local officials. Since then, the need for local revenue as more restraints on transfers imposed by the national government has driven many to reinstate the building tax, plot tax or the communal tax. Towards the end of the 1990s, property taxation has been pushed into the spotlight again, as local governments continued to search for more revenue. Many municipalities continue levying size-based taxes (the building tax) on business properties and the communal tax (the most widespread land-based tax in Hungary) on residential properties to generate revenue. However, there is no statutory requirement to levy local taxes; consequently, tax policy and administrative practice vary widely from one municipality to the next.

The structure of local government

Hungary is a unitary state and a parliamentary republic. There are 3156 local governments, 2844 of which have a population of under 5000 inhabitants. There are 19 counties and four types of communal entity in Hungary. These are: 2920 less populated communities (36.8 percent of the population; 173 cities (24.2 percent); 20 large cities with county rights (19.5 percent); and Budapest, the capital, with nearly 2 000 000 inhabitants, which is divided into 23 districts with special status (19.5 percent).[2]

The Act on Local Self-Government (1990) sets out provisions for county and local government and determines the basic principles of the separation of central and local affairs.

Local governments constitute a system in which there are no hierarchical relations. Their decisions are subject to revision only by the Constitutional Court or, if there is a breach of the law, by the local courts. Generally state bodies have only normative control over local governments, for example, setting standards of service delivery. Parliament regulates the legal status, exclusive tasks and functions, mandatory organs, guarantees of operation, financial means and basic rules of the economic management of local governments. It also regulates the legal status of the representatives of the local government, the order of the elections, and their rights and duties.

Local governments are legal entities and may pass by-laws. Their tasks and functions are the responsibility of the representative body headed by the mayor. Local governments may voluntarily undertake any local matter not covered by legal provisions and not within the responsibility of another authority. There is also a widely held view that limitations on the power to make local decisions on either the revenue or expenditure side of the municipal budget would be an improper intervention in local affairs on the part of the national government.

With respect to taxation, county governments are not entitled to levy local taxes. Their fiscal resources are based on revenues other than direct local taxes. Local governments dispose of their own property and manage their budgetary revenues and expenses independently. Between 1991 and 1997, the revenues of local governments grew significantly (in nominal terms) and the share of local own-source taxes went from 2.45 percent to 9.31 percent of the total revenues of local governments. Estimates for 2002 were that local own-source taxes would reach 13.6 percent of total local government revenues (see Table 19.1).

The current tax system
With the exception of the business tax, local taxes essentially extend the pre-existing tax system of the old regime. The new localities were given the power to levy any or all of these taxes. Bird and Wallich (1992) describe the transitional arrangements for 1991, noting the expectation that municipalities would choose to maintain nominal revenues.

An obstacle to the wider implementation of property taxation in Hungary is that municipal taxation is not mandatory. The number of local governments levying taxes has, however, steadily increased from approximately 80 percent in the mid-1990s to 93 percent by 2000. Table 19.2 shows the extent of the differences in local tax policies.

Table 19.1   Hungary: revenues of local governments in 1991, 1997 and 2002

	1991 revenues		1997 revenues		2002 revenues	
	Million HUF	%	Million HUF	%	Million HUF	%
Own revenues	61 156	15.82	305 764	25.47	627 300	28.76
of which own taxes	9 478	2.45	111 162	9.26	296 772	13.61
other own revenues	51 678	13.37	194 602	16.21	330 528	15.15
Shared revenues	47 019	12.16	143 562	11.96	350 141	16.05
Governmental grants	190 672	49.33	348 724	29.05	620 487	28.45
of which normative grants	148 528	38.43	257 722	21.47	329 539	15.11
Transfer from other public authorities	68 722	17.78	201 170	16.76	345 152	15.82
of which social security fund transfers	67 087	17.36	167 748	13.97	305 136	14.00
Capital revenues	15 095	3.91	185 356	15.44	208 595	9.56
Debt	1 064	0.28	20 727	1.73	135 096	6.19
Other revenues	2 792	0.72	15 764	1.31	29 279	1.34
Total	386 520	100.00	1 200 340	100.00	2 180 955	100.00

Sources: Hogye (2000), Ministry of the Interior Statistical DataBase (1991–2001), Szalai (2002).

Table 19.2   Local taxes collected by Hungarian local governments, 2001

Tax type	Number of local governments	Tax revenue	
		Amount (billion HUF)	Proportion (%)
Property tax			
Residential	337		
Non-residential	697	26 138*	9.8
Plot	380	3 221	1.2
Communal tax			
Private	1 981	4 933	1.9
Corporate	746	1 174	0.4
Tourism tax	410	4 157	1.6
Business tax	2 354	226 084	85.1
Total	3 027	265 707	100.0

Note: * The two types of taxes on structures taken together. The Act on Local Taxes provides the authority for the six types of tax that can be levied by local governments.

Source: Szalai (2002) p. 26.

Legal framework of local taxation

The general framework of local taxes is contained in the Act on Local Taxes (1990). Municipal governments are empowered to decide which of the available local tax types to introduce and also to determine the rates within legal limits.

Local governments are entitled to introduce taxes on property, communal taxes and local business taxes. Within local government jurisdiction, tax liability applies to real property and related rights of financial value, to employment, to temporary residency, and to the pursuit of an entrepreneurial activity defined in the Act.

The right of taxation of local governments includes the right to:

- introduce any or all of the taxes set in the Act, and to repeal or amend taxes already in effect. However, any amendment instituted during the year may not increase the tax obligations of taxpayers arising during the same calendar year;
- establish the date of introduction and the period for levying a tax (for a definite or indefinite period);
- define the tax rates with due consideration for local characteristics, the

financial requirements of the local government, and the capacity of taxpayers, in observation of the upper limits (maximum tax) prescribed by the Act.

The following restrictions apply, however:

- in respect of any particular taxable item, taxpayers may only be ordered to pay one type of tax as selected by the local government;
- within the sphere of taxes levied on property, the taxes should be assessed in a consolidated form, either as an itemized sum, or on the basis of the adjusted market value;
- no tax rate may be introduced above the maximum tax;
- district governments may not utilize taxes introduced by the City Council of Budapest until the repeal of such taxes (Hogye, 2000, p. 231).

Local business turnover tax
This tax is levied by most local governments and is not a land-based tax. The tax base for business activities is the net sales revenue of products sold or services provided, less the purchase value of the goods sold, and the value of services provided by subcontractors, less material costs. The taxable base is the net value of goods sold and services rendered (excluding VAT), less consumption tax paid. The tax rate may not exceed 0.014 (1.4 percent) times the business entity's taxable base. In 2001, this tax raised over 85 percent of the total local taxes levied.[3] Generally, the largest cities (for example the cities with county status in Table 19.3) levy this tax, but many small municipalities try to avoid using it.

Communal tax on private individuals (poll tax)
Communal taxes may be levied on individuals owning dwellings or plots of land. The tax may not exceed HUF 12 000 per dwelling or plot per year. Garzon (1998) comments that from a revenue perspective, the communal tax on dwellings partially substitutes for taxes on real estate. Over 60 percent of the local taxing jurisdictions used this tax but it accounts for less than 2 percent of total local taxes levied.

Communal tax on entrepreneurs (payroll tax)
Communal taxes may be levied on entrepreneurs who have a seat or permanent establishment within a municipality. The tax base is the average number of people employed. The annual maximum rate of tax is HUF 2000 per employee.

Table 19.3   Hungary: local taxation in cities with county status, 1998

	Number of taxpayers				Revenue ('000 HUF)			
	Business tax	Building tax	Plot tax	Communal tax	Business tax	Building tax	Plot tax	Communal tax
Békéscsaba	5 921	1 246		Bus. 4 501	931 000	121 000		40 000
Debrecen	20 828	22 226	984	15 601	2 506 000	290 000	15 000	100 000
Dunaújváros	2 085				2 409 042			
Eger	3 686	7 901	487	22 090	827 038	65 892	2 398	43 835
Győr	2 772	12 540			2 381 965	190 581		
Hódmezővásárhely	2 514	238	76	12 240 Bus. 3 008	526 132	78 351	9 995	15 885 Bus. 23 689
Kaposvár	7 368	2 161	310	23 812	781 349	95 572	97 649	62 330
Kecskemét	4 000	5 900		8 300	1 255 298	170 000		60 000
Miskolc	4 112	15 915		Bus. 2 220	2 330 928	216 080		Bus. 3 334
Nagykanizsa (1997)	2 718	2 835			422 779	137 385		
Nyíregyháza	4 097	1 222		Bus. 3 596	1 468 309	140 596		22 000
Salgótarján	3 368	675		5 408	553 916	136 500		70 000
Sopron	6 025				869 600			94 000
Szeged	4 671			20 005	2 618 267			
Székesfehérvár	8 758	9 074			2 201 215	16 000		
Szolnok	6 148	877			1 278 594	145 968		
Szombathely	3 849	8 348		Bus. 3 356	1 431 330	110 000		Bus. 25 500
Tatabánya	4 335	6 998			545 698	84 700		
Veszprém	1 887	7 882			1 009 990	295 140		
Zalaegerszeg	3 754				1 161 008			

Sources: Kaposvár (1998) and Garzon (1998).

Land parcel tax (plot tax)

This tax can be levied on the owner of undeveloped parcels of land situated in central areas within the area of jurisdiction of a local government. The tax is levied on the unimproved value of land plots larger in size than the average in a municipality, as set out in the master plan. The Act provides detailed specifications on exemptions. The local government may choose to use either the actual area of the parcel as calculated in square meters or the adjusted market value of the parcel as the tax base. The annual maximum rate of tax is HUF 200/m^2, or 3 percent of the adjusted 'corrected' market value. 'Corrected' or 'adjusted' market value is 50 percent of the market value as determined by the local government as set out in the Act on Local Taxes (1990). (Garzon, 1998, p. 5; Balas and Kovacs, 1999, p. 17). In 2001, this tax raised approximately 1.2 percent of local taxes levied.

Building tax

Tax can be levied on the owners of all types of buildings. The local government may choose to use either the useful surface area or the adjusted market value of the building as the tax base. The annual maximum rate of the tax is HUF 900/m^2 or 3 percent of the adjusted market value.[4] Virtually every municipality that uses this tax appears to employ the area basis.[5]

The Act sets out buildings which are exempt from this tax, including temporary residential dwellings, premises used for the purposes of social welfare, health care, child care and educational institutions, buildings owned by budgetary organizations, public service and religious organizations, and so on.

Tourism tax

The tourism tax may be levied on non-residential individuals who spend more than 48 hours in a municipality, or who own a holiday dwelling that does not qualify as a permanent home. The tax base is the number of guest-nights spent, or the lodging fee for a guest-night, or the net floor space of the building. The upper limit of the rate of tax is HUF 300 per person and per guest-night, or 4 percent of the lodging fee; or HUF 900/m^2 payable annually for the building.

Exemptions

Municipalities have unlimited rights to employ tax exemptions and tax allowances. However, the Act on Local Taxes terminated all previous tax exemptions except for the house-tax exemption, which shelters many houses from the building tax but not from the communal tax, which has a lower capacity to generate revenue. Before the termination of the house tax in 1991, local councils could give 30-year exemptions for new houses, a practice that will continue to reduce the tax base for years to come. Consequently, the communal tax on residential properties is more popular with municipalities.

Agricultural land
The tax treatment of agricultural land is optional at the local level. In Jaszberenyi, buildings up to 100 m² used for agricultural production were exempted from building taxes. The exemption was widened as the Act was modified. Farmers running small-scale businesses with net sales of up to HUF 250 000 are exempted from the communal tax on business (Hogye, 2000, p. 237).

Land transfer tax
Duties are payable on obtaining property by a gratis transfer (inheritance, donation) and when property is obtained for a consideration (OECD, 1999, p. 29). Generally the duty is based on the market value of the property. The County Duty Office (Illetek Hivatal) has the responsibility for determining the market value of the property being transferred. The Act on Local Taxes requires that the basis of assessment of an individual property in the case of *ad valorem* taxation should be calculated in the same manner. Further, municipalities also assess the value of some real property for certain legal purposes (and issue the so-called Tax Value Certification), but the Duty Office may revise this value specifically for the purpose of this tax.

With respect to property obtained for a consideration, the general tax rate is 10 percent. For residential property, it is 2 percent for the first four million forints (HUF) and 6 percent for the rest of its value.

The common feature of taxation on acquired property is that the tax is independent of the manner in which the property is obtained and is to be paid by the beneficiary in proportion to the actual ownership ratio. The tax law provides for tax allowances and even exemptions from the tax obligations. The method of base calculation is specified by statute and cannot be deviated from by the duty office. The revenues from this duty are shared with the central government.

Tax administration
In the context of imminent EU accession, concerns have been raised as to the capacity of local governments to administer new forms of taxation and to meet the eligibility criteria of possible new transfer payments. The development of administrative capacity has been hampered by the excessive decentralization of existing local governance arrangements. The possibility of establishing a regional level of governance throughout the country that would integrate existing counties has gained some support as well (OECD, 2000, p. 8). Szegvari (2002) explores the regional administrative imperatives

as these are related to eligibility for EU development subsidies and describe EU-motivated reforms to public administration. He also notes that a regional level of government would need access to its own sources of revenue. These themes have been taken up in more detail in Swaniewicz (2002) in an important cross-country study. The local capacity to administer a value-based property tax is also affected by existing national legislation concerning tax administration, the existing state of record-keeping with respect to properties and existing systems of tax appeals and collections.

The administration of all taxes is governed by a single law. Because an *ad valorem* property tax is not yet in place, this law has been designed to suit the administration of other forms of taxation, especially income and sales taxation. In considering a broader implementation of property taxation, the key impact of this statute is the legal requirement that each Hungarian tax process be based solely on the information collected from the taxpayer's tax returns. Although the municipality is entitled to some information on the ownership, physical parameters and the value of the property, the property may not be taxed and the tax base may not be determined unless the taxpayer files a tax return. A field investigation or 'valuation process' may be conducted only as part of the tax audit process if the taxpayer does not submit the return or the administration suspects that the return contains false information.

There is a general obligation applicable to the Hungarian taxation system that all data related to tax payment be confidential. Thus the value of real property in the case of a duty process is 'personal data', so the local tax administration is not allowed to use this specific information to assess the value of a specific property.

Local tax administration
Among the impediments to the implementation of a local property tax system in Hungary is the fact that the local tax administration generally does not have the capacity to administer such a tax. Some of the problems stem from gaps in the legislation and others from lack of experience in property taxation.

Identification of the tax base   The current local tax system in Hungary is based on the principle of self-identification. Taxpayers have the obligation to register and report their tax obligations to the local tax administration. In practice, the responsibility of self-registration is not fully effective as not all owners comply. Consequently, the number of potential local taxpayers or taxable assets is generally unknown (Kopanyi et al., 2000, p. 26).

The determination of tax liabilities also entails a verification of the self-assessment submitted by the taxpayer for the particular tax. For the current tax on buildings and on idle urban land (plots) the verification of the size of the properties rather than their market value is required. This verification has to be done at least once in the field. It appears that verification is required upon notification to the tax authority of a change to the property rather than on an annual basis.

In 1999, of 3200 local governments, only two municipalities used market valuation data in determining local taxes levied on business properties. There appear to be both legal and bureaucratic impediments to the use of market value information for land transfer tax purposes as the basis of the plot tax or the tax on buildings.

The assessment method   Municipalities do not have enough experts to appraise the value of all properties in their districts. While manpower issues can be resolved through training or contracts with outside assistance, the central government currently does not provide municipalities with enough information or legislative authority to make these assessments. In Hungarian legislation, the use of the term 'market value' is not a sufficient basis for the introduction of mass appraisal techniques for several reasons, including the fact that the legislation does not recognize that market value may in reality change from month to month and the law does not define the date of the base (Szalai and Tassonyi, 2000). The Law on Duty also requires that valuation be based on the sales comparison method, but in Hungary there is no tradition of property taxation so that an understanding of the technical issues involved in making comparisons is lacking (what does 'similarity' mean, how are different properties to be compared? and so on).[6]

Administration of information   The information to support a fiscal cadastre or mass appraisal on a consistent nationwide basis is fragmented between the two levels of government. The legal cadastre is managed by the Land Offices, which are deconcentrated agencies of the Ministry of Agriculture. They are organized by counties, with 109 local units under the county offices plus 22 district offices in the capital. The property information comprises the owner's identification, use of the property for both land and buildings, and legal information. The information is categorized by parcel numbers and maps. A digitalization program is under way. No information on value is retained by these offices (Davey and Peteri, 1998, p. 95). At the local level, the Duty Offices (Illetek Hivatal) keep records of transactions. The 19 county Duty Offices and the 22 offices in the capital operate within the local government administration, under the direction of the county notary. Information is gathered on the value of transactions (sales, inheritance or gifts) and work is done on valuations. However, the Duty Office may not provide the municipalities with precise information on the actual prices because of the legislative provisions for confidentiality. Tax departments and technical departments within local administrations also have access to property information. The tax departments collect information on residential units. Technical departments maintain registers of building permits, local master plans for land-use zoning and information on public utility infrastructure. Unfortunately, these databases are usually not integrated.

Given the lack of a governmental inventory process, citizens should probably be required to provide information about the physical parameters of the real property, but it is unlikely that each citizen would be able to correctly complete a very detailed tax return. Municipalities also lack the personnel to make field inspections (tax control process) of each property in the immediate future.

Municipalities have very little information that can serve as the basis for picking out 'false and suspicious' tax returns. Although local Building Offices have collected the main parameters of each building built or renovated since 1998 as part of the process of building permit documentation, these data are seldom stored in a computerized database, and the older information is incomplete and not readily available.

Collection issues

In the two Hungarian municipalities using a market-value-based tax system, tax returns are 'reconsidered' with the owners. Disputes are settled at this level as there is no tribunal mechanism to adjudicate further on the differences in the opinions of the two parties (Szalai, 2002, p. 10).

Tax arrears, according to a recent study (cited in Kopanyi et al., 2000), fluctuate broadly from one municipality to another, ranging from 11 percent of current local tax revenues to 2 percent. However, arrears in this context refers only to those taxpayers who have made partial payments of their tax obligations. They do not include the arrears of those who are registered but have made no payments at all, or those who have not even registered. Therefore, the potential magnitude of unpaid tax obligations is greater than the arrears reported by the cities.

Sanctions for non-payment are strict. The first step is to levy a penalty or fine related to the delay in payment. A failure to pay after a certain period may result in an immediate collection of the total tax due or the initiation of the process to withdraw a business license. For communal and building taxes, possible sanctions are to garnishee benefits, wages and pensions, or confiscate mobile assets. In cases involving large amounts of tax arrears, the taxpayer's property can be mortgaged or the local government can file a foreclosure request. In practice, these sanctions have rarely been used in any of the cities that have been the subject of comparative studies.

The problem of enforcement remains unsolved in the case of taxes on residents. At present, a large percentage of unpaid taxes relates to local businesses. This fact should make enforcement easier because the companies are required to inform the tax administration of their bank practices[7] and in many cases they have assets such as vehicles that can be seized. However, non-businesses do not have to register their bank accounts with the tax administration and do not always have high-value 'movable' properties to be seized. The seizure of the (movable and immovable) properties of non-payers (physically or by securing a lien) should serve as an adequate enforcement mechanism.[8] Garnishing from personal income should be made easier and the municipalities should get information about the employer of the taxpayers from the social contribution databases (from the Central Tax Office). Stopping PIT repayment could also be employed.[9]

Tasks for national legislation
Property tax policy has three main components: (i) the definition of tax liability (who pays taxes, on what basis and with which 'rates'), (ii) the assessment method and (iii) mitigation issues. This section summarizes the tasks of central legislation and municipalities in the policy-making and administrative process.

Tax liability
Current legislation defines the owners of each parcel of local real property as the taxpayer in the case of building, parcel and tourism tax. In the case of the communal tax the taxpayer is the private owner of the residential property and the tenant of a dwelling not owned by a private person (for example municipal flats).[10]

Rates
Some studies have suggested that there is capacity within the existing system to increase the tax yield from land and property-based taxation. Garzon (1998) summarizes the situation in six municipalities in which rates vary between 8 percent and 33 percent of the maximum rate set by the legislation. Other studies suggest similar patterns for different municipalities (Hogye, 2000, pp. 233–6). A significant feature of the Hungarian local tax system that will have to be confronted is the lack of a mandatory tax. The relative cost of maintaining an up-to-date assessment base is significant, and centralized assessment would be desirable, so a local property tax is only worth implementing when all municipalities have to implement it.

Market value (capital value)
Experience in Hungary emphasizes that a simple legal declaration of market value is not enough.

National versus local assessment

Current Hungarian law defines assessment as a local task. This seems to be one of the main impediments to the implementation of an *ad valorem* property taxation system. In the Hungarian case, it is rational to keep the assessment function under the control of the central government. This is also likely to be a more economical solution – there is evidence of economies of scale in property assessment.[11] This solution is also likely to be less vulnerable to local political pressure; in many cases local assessors may face political pressure to undervalue the property of politically important owners. The centralization of this function can also provide direct information for tax-base equalization.

A recent reform proposal

In 1996, the Ministry of Finance drafted an amendment to the Law on Local Taxes. The goal of this legislative proposal was to introduce an *ad valorem* local property tax. The draft bill defined a range of average unit values for 11 types of residential and commercial property in four types of local governments (large city, village, and so on) by counties. Within this range a local government decree would specify the unit value for the urban zones within the area of a municipality. There were 17 predetermined factors with a given multiplier, which could be used for modifying the sub-averages (age, utilities, building materials and so on). The minimum and maximum rates are also defined by the draft law (0.5–1.5 percent). Two options were designed for deducting local property taxes (partially or totally) from the personal income tax or from the PIT base (Davey and Peteri, 1998, pp. 90–91). While the proposal was not presented to Parliament, it was tested on a sample of municipalities.

This legislative proposal tries to combine both a central and a local role in assessment: the central government would define the calculation method through the relative values of different types of property (within a class), while the local government would define the base or starting-point value based on current real property prices.[12] However, this method has several disadvantages as well.

For example, this structure may induce municipal decisions to be politically biased, providing representatives with a strong incentive to undervalue the properties in their electoral districts and those of their party members.

According to the proposal, the value of a basic property should be based on the actual market price. This would require frequent reassessment, a feature of the system that incurs higher administrative costs as a result. With every reassessment local governments will have no choice but to replay the political debates around the existing local taxes and the level of the local rates (Garzon, 1998, p. 14).

According to the proposal, each property should have a unique calculated value, a system far more complicated and expensive (in terms of appeals and so on) than the existing lump-sum tax. Many municipalities have already expressed their preference for the communal tax rather than the building tax because of its simplicity. The Bill, similar to the current legislation in the Law on Duty, does not distinguish between the assessment of residential and non-residential properties. This is unrealistic. The assessment methodology for residential and non-residential property varies considerably as there is usually a very limited market in industrial properties and thus various methods are used to obtain an estimate of value. Consequently, any assessment method which works using fixed price ratios as a method of comparison would lead to serious inequities in the assessment roll.

Tax abatements are a special form of tax exemption when the municipality does not levy and collect tax on the higher value of property after the completion of an improvement. In Hungary there was a similar abatement program – the house-tax exemption for a 30-year period. Although such an exemption constrains the (disincentive) effect on investment, it arguably makes the system unfair. Abatements also have the effect of exempting the part of hidden income invested in real property from the property tax, and the owner does not contribute to the financing of the new infrastructure required by his/her new investment. The problem of investment incentives can be solved through a higher tax on vacant lands and increasing the period between reassessments. Another solution is to use supplementary assessments to update the assessment roll on a timely basis.

If the central government declares the *ad valorem* property tax to be mandatory, and other taxes are reduced to create tax room or an ability to pay for this tax, it is essential that some national tax relief policy be enacted as well. Such a central policy would be essential in order that Parliament accept the new tax structure. (A weakness of the current proposal is that it considers neither the issue of a national mitigation system nor the issue of reducing other taxes.)

Property taxation is also recommended as a means of exerting influence on the real estate market to encourage efficient land use. However, this may be hampered due to several weaknesses in the current functioning of Hungarian land markets: (i) the cost of real property transactions is relatively expensive, and (ii) the Hungarian financial market is not prepared to be involved in this market without a well-functioning mortgage system (or governmental guarantees of security of tenure and value). The real estate market may be too rigid to adjust to tax incentives. Nonetheless, Garzon (1998) suggests that more than 50 percent of housing units are privately owned and market transactions occur with frequency. A recent study of the relationship between land-use planning and infrastructure finance in the Hungarian context advocates more reliance on value-based property taxation as the real estate market matures (Locsmandi et al., 2000).

Conclusion

The Hungarian local tax system needs reform. Municipalities are not required to impose any local tax and the system in effect is largely a residue of the tax options in place during the pre-transition period. The hodge-podge of available local tax options is perceived as being too weak to raise the revenues that will be required by local governments to manage EU accession. The implementation of a value-based property tax at the subnational level could usefully augment local tax capacity and local accountability.

Notes

1. This chapter is partly based on earlier work done with Akos Szalai for the Canadian Urban Institute with the assistance of the Canadian International Development Agency. It does not reflect the official position of the Ontario Ministry of Finance.
2. See Hogye (2000), p. 215. A two-tier municipal system consisting of local and county municipalities exists. The exceptions are cities with county rights and Budapest, the capital. Most of these cities are the capital of the county. They have special functions that have to be fulfilled at the county level as well as within their boundaries.
3. If the entrepreneur has permanent commercial activities in the areas of more than one jurisdiction, the tax base is divided.
4. According to Peteri and Lados (1999, p. 430), if value assessment is used, the 'assessed value' is mandatorily set at 50 percent of the market value, reportedly because 'it is reasoned by the legislators that to levy a tax based on full market price would be unfair, given that there have been relatively few market related transactions.'
5. Peteri and Lados (1999, p. 431), state that 'the only exception is the municipality of Nyiregyhaza, which introduced a value based property tax for non-residential buildings. Here, the tax administration has a unique administrative arrangement where the tax department and the Fee Department [Duty Office] are part of the same organization sharing a common database system. This enables the municipality to be able to administer the ad valorem property tax because of the provision of adequate technical expertise.'
6. Administrative considerations seem to have been important in governing the preference of municipalities for simpler tax systems. Peteri and Lados (1999, p. 434) report that the buildings tax was the most costly local tax to administer and that costs were highest in smaller municipalities. The average reported administrative costs of all local taxes in 1991 was an astounding 12.0 percent of tax revenue, with the tax on buildings being the highest (13.1 percent) and that on business the lowest (11.0 percent).
7. The administration has the right to stop payment from the bank account until the tax is paid.
8. The seizure of movable properties appears to function well, especially in the case of vehicles.
9. Stopping company tax repayment is often used to collect unpaid business receipts tax.
10. The other option would be that the first liability is on the occupier (tenant) in the absence of owner-occupancy. Such a change could have a positive effect in Hungary, as owners would have an incentive to inform the tax authority about their rental contracts (currently, most rental income is in the grey economy as owners try to evade income taxation), but as there are more tenants than owners, administrative costs would likely increase.
11. Sjoquist and Walker (1999) found that a 10 percent increase in the volume of assessments reduces the average cost of assessment by approximately 6 percent in Georgia, where assessment is conducted at the county level.

12. To list some examples: standard property: 10–30 years old, brick, stone or concrete block construction, habitable, two rooms, one level or having an elevator if more than three stories. Rooming house: same characteristics but must have private bathrooms in one-quarter to two-thirds of the rooms, central heating. Offices are required to be centrally heated. Stores do not always have underground central heating, street access and the entrance and store space ratio: 0.85–1.25. Manufacturing plant must have water and electricity but not gas. Lot values must reflect road access and access to water and electricity.

References

Balas, G. and R. Kovacs (1999), 'Prospects for the Introduction of Value-Based Property Tax in Hungary,' The Urban Institute/USAID, Washington.

Bird, R.M. and C.I. Wallich (1992), 'Financing Local Government in Hungary,' WPS 869, World Bank, Washington.

Bird, R.M., C. Wallich and G. Peteri (1995), 'Financing Local Government in Hungary,' in R.M. Bird, R.D. Ebel and C.I. Wallich (eds), *Decentralization of the Socialist State*, Washington: World Bank, pp. 69–112.

Davey, K. and G. Peteri (1998), *Local Government Finances: Options for Reform*, Nagykovacsi: Local Government Know-How Programme.

Ebel, R., I. Varfalvi and S. Varga (1998), 'Sorting Out Intergovernmental Roles and Responsibilities in the Hungarian Transition,' in L. Bokros and J.-J. Dethier (eds), *Public Finance Reform during the Transition*, Washington, DC: World Bank, pp. 424–46.

Fekete, E., M. Lados, E. Pfeil and Z. Szoboszlai (2002), 'Size of Local Government, Local Democracy and Local Service Delivery in Hungary,' in P. Swianiewicz (ed.), *Consolidation or Fragmentation? The Size of Local Governments in Central and Eastern Europe*, Budapest: Local Government and Public Service Reform Initiative, pp. 31–100.

Garzon, H. (1998), 'Local Revenues and Policy Implications,' USAID, The Urban Institute, paper presented at the the Six-City Seminar, Budapest, Hungary, March.

Hogye, M. (ed.) (2000), *Local and Regional Tax Administration in Transition Countries*, Budapest: Open Society Institute.

Kaposvár, (1998), 'Kaposvár Megyei Jogu Város Jegyzöjének Tájékoztatoja a helyi adoztatás tapasztalatairol' (Information on the Experience of Local Taxation from the Notary of Kaposvar to the Local Government).

Kopanyi, M., S. El Daher, D. Wetzel, M. Noel and A. Papp (2000), 'Hungary: Modernizing the Subnational Government System,'World Bank Discussion Paper No. 417.

Locsmandi, G., G. Peteri and B. Varga-Otvos (2000), *Urban Planning and Capital Investment Financing in Hungary*, Budapest: Open Society Institute. Local Government and Public Service Reform Initiative.

OECD (1999), 'Fiscal Design Across Levels of Government Country Report: Hungary,' Paris: OECD.

OECD (2000), *Economic Surveys: Hungary*, Paris: OECD.

Peteri, Gabor and Mihaly Lados (1999), 'Local Property Taxation in Hungary,' in W. McCluskey (ed.), *Property Tax: An International Comparative Review*, Aldershot, UK: Ashgate.

Sjoquist, D.L. and M.B. Walker (1999), 'Economies of Scale in Property Tax Assessment,' *National Tax Journal*, **52**, 207–20.

Swianiewicz, P. (ed.) (2002), *Consolidation or Fragmentation? The Size of Local Governments in Central and Eastern Europe*, Budapest: Local Government and Public Service Reform Initiative.

Szalai, A. (1999), 'Az értékalapu ingatlanado Magyarországon Kézikonyv a magyar önkormányzatok számára' (Value-Based Property Taxation for Hungary: A Handbook for Hungarian Municipalities) Toronto: Canadian Urban Institute, CIDA.

Szalai, A. (2002), 'Intergovernmental Finance System in Hungary,' Policy Paper for Serbia Local Government Reform Program (SLGRP), mimeo.

Szalai, A. and A. Tassonyi (2000), 'Value Based Property Taxation: Options for Hungary,' Toronto: Canadian Urban Institute.

Szegvari, P. (2002), 'Methods and Techniques of Managing Decentralization Reforms in Hungary,' in G. Peteri (ed.) (2002), *Mastering Decentralization and Public Administration Reforms in Central and Eastern Europe*, Budapest: Open Society Institute. Local Government and Public Service Reform Initiative, pp. 137–62.

Temesi, Istvan (2000), 'Local Government in Hungary,' in Tamas M. Horvath (ed.), *Decentralization: Experiments and Reforms*, OSI, LGI Studies, Budapest, pp. 343–84.

Youngman, Joan M. (1999), 'Property Taxes in an Age of Globalization,' *State Tax Notes*, pp. 1897–900.

Youngman, Joan M. and Jane H. Malme (1994), *An International Survey of Taxes on Land and Buildings*, Boston: Kluwer Law and Taxation Publishers.

20 Land and property taxes in Russia[1]

Andrey Timofeev

The Russian Federation has a population of 144 million, of which 73 percent reside in urban areas. The Federation comprises 89 'subjects of the federation': ethnic republics, *krais*, *okrugs*, *oblasts*, and autonomous areas – all of which are hereafter referred to as 'regions.' Below the regional level, there are one or two levels of local government, depending on the region. The prevailing one-tier system has local government established at the level of cities and 'rayons' (an equivalent of the US county) with an average size of 579 000. However, in about fifteen regions local government is established at the level of sub-rayon townships and rural districts, with an average size of 5400. In this case, at the rayon level there is either an overlapping local government or a deconcentrated arm of the regional government. All formally established governments have their political autonomy secured in the constitution. However, as shown below, this autonomy is constrained by the *de facto* monopolization of tax policy by the federal government.

Federal legislation[2] prescribes a closed list of taxes that can be levied in the Russian Federation. This list comprises three groups: federal taxes, regional taxes and local taxes. The criteria to classify a tax as belonging to a particular level of government are (a) the territory covered by the tax and (b) the level of the government that introduces the tax. The criteria do not include the level that ultimately receives the revenue or the level defining a tax base or rate. In some instances, neither localities nor regions have any control over whether to adopt a tax or what its rate or base will be. This is the case with the land tax. Classified as a local tax, this tax is split between the three levels of budgets (federal, regional, local) in proportions set by the federal government. The tax rate is set by local governments within a narrow range established by the federal and regional governments.

Regional and local governments must fit tax bases to the federal law, and may levy rates only within federal limits. Certain taxes introduced by one level of government are shared on a derivation basis with another level of government. Revenue from some taxes is split between levels of government in proportions fixed in the federal legislation, while for other taxes the sharing rate is adjusted annually (such tax revenue is called 'regulated').

Besides the land tax, the list of authorized taxes contains three other items related to property: individual property tax, enterprise assets tax, and succession and gift tax. The individual property tax is classified as local, the enterprise assets tax is classified as regional, and the succession and gift tax is classified as a federal tax. However, 50 percent of revenue from the enterprise assets tax is to be allocated to the local government at the point of collection. All revenue from the succession and gift tax is allocated to the local budget at the point of collection.[3] In all localities, tax payments to all levels of government are collected by a local branch of the federal tax service (tax inspectorate). Proceeds from taxes assigned exclusively to localities and regions are then transferred to an appropriate budget, while exclusive federal and shared tax revenue is transferred to a local branch of the federal treasury. It is the local treasury office that splits the shared tax revenue between the budgets of the different levels of government according to legislated sharing rates.

Since January 1999, the federal parliament has been enacting separate parts of the draft Tax Code. As of January 2003, besides the general part of the Code dealing with tax administration issues and taxpayer rights and obligations, only those parts that develop federal taxes and the regional sales and transport taxes are in force. The parts of the Code that develop the structure of other regional and local taxes have yet to be discussed and approved by the federal parliament. In the original draft of the Tax Code, Chapter 40 provided for the introduction of a western-style real estate property tax at the regional level, which was to be shared with local governments. According to the draft Code, as soon as representative branches of regional governments put into effect the real estate tax, the three existing property taxes (land tax, individual property tax and enterprise assets tax) will cease to be levied in their jurisdictions.

Two pilot cities (Novgorod and Tver) have been working on the introduction of the real estate tax since 1997.[4] The city of Novgorod created a municipal register of property specifically for taxation purposes. For every property object the register contains data on its technical characteristics, legal status and holders of property rights. These data are used for mass appraisal of the registered property objects. In Novgorod, the introduction of the real estate tax is to be made stage by stage. At the first stage the existing property taxes are replaced by the real estate tax only for those legal entities that own land plots and improvements. At present, for about ten large enterprises, which own the land under their facilities, the two property taxes are replaced by the real estate tax. Although the property register covers all property objects, the present system of revenue-sharing reportedly discourages city officials from tapping this tax base. The idea is that at later stages the experiment will also cover legal entities that lease land plots. The experiment in the city of Tver lags behind the one in Novgorod.

Both experiments are to be completed by 2003 and the results are to be reported by the two city governments to the federal parliament as inputs for developing the federal legislation on this tax. However, in the summer of

2003, the federal government submitted to the parliament a new draft of Tax Code Chapter 30, which essentially reanimates the existing enterprise assets tax. At the same time the federal government is finalizing bills that would modernize the existing land tax and individual property tax. While this is likely to boost revenue from the existing property taxes, it may indicate a delay in the introduction of the real estate tax.[5]

Payment for the use of land

In Russia, land use requires payment to the government. There are two forms of payment: the land tax and the land lease fee. The land lease fee is paid by lessees of the state (federal and regional) and municipal land. The amount and terms of payment are set separately in every lease. For state and municipal lands, the respective legislatures set basic rates by type of use and category of lessee. Land plots and shares of land plots in ownership, possession, or use of legal entities and physical persons are subject to the land tax. Separate rates for agricultural and non-agricultural land are applied to the area of land plots. Tax rates are doubled for land plots not in use or used for purposes different from intended.

Tax rates on agricultural land

These rates vary by composition, quality and location. Moreover, differentiation with respect to different factors is carried out by different levels of government. The average tax rate (in rubles per hectare of plowed field) is set for each region in the Federal Law On Payment for Land (N 1738-1, 11 October 1991). These rates are indexed annually in the federal budget law. Based on the average rate, regional legislatures differentiate rates on plowed fields by type of soil, and set rates for plantations, hayfields and pastures. Regional legislatures also set the minimal rate for agricultural land. Plots of land in the territory of rural settlements provided to physical persons for uses different from farming are taxed at a rate (per m^2) fixed in the Law On Payment for Land. For advantageously located plots in the territory of a rural settlement, the respective local government can increase the rates set by the higher-level governments but no more than by a factor of 2.[6] Payment for land used for forest utilization is charged as part of the forestry fee and equals 5 percent of the total fee.

Tax rates on non-agricultural land

The Federal Law On Payment for Land sets the average rate for each of the 11 economic zones of Russia and ten categories of sizes of urban settlements. The law also prescribes adjustment coefficients for resort and recreational areas, and advanced cities (for example, regional capitals). Based on the average rate resulting for a given urban settlement, local governments set differentiated rates for particular urban zones depending on their location, distance from the downtown area, level of development, environment and geological characteristics. According to the law, local governments can set these rates as they wish. However, an order from the federal Ministry of Taxation requires that the differentiated rates generate the same revenue as if the average rate (set in federal law) were applied to the total area.[7] The portion of land plots in excess of the 'standard lot size' is taxed at a double rate.[8]

Plots under residential structures and personal subsidiary plots are taxed at a rate equal to 3 percent of the rate set for a given urban zone. However, the Federal Law On Payment for Land sets a minimal rate on plots under residential structures, and this minimal rate is indexed annually in the federal budget law. In year 2003, the minimal rate was equal to RUR 0.52 (US$0.017) per m². Personal gardening plots located within urban settlements are taxed at a rate set in the Federal Law On Payment for Land and indexed annually in the federal budget law. Agricultural land located within urban settlements is taxed at double the rate set on agricultural land in rural areas of the same region.

Billing and collection
For physical persons, the tax inspectorate at the location of the plot sends tax advice to the owner by 1 August. Information on the area of plots comes from the State Register of Land and information on their ownership from the State Register of Property Rights.[9] Legal entities make tax computations themselves and file tax returns by 1 July. Both legal entities and physical persons pay the tax in two equal installments by 15 September and 15 November. The payments are made to the local branch of the federal treasury, where it is then allocated to the three budgets. Late payment is penalized by charging interest on the overdue amount equal to 1/300 of the refinancing rate of the Central Bank for each day of delay.

Revenue allocation
Payments for land located within rural settlements are allocated to the budget of the local government. Payments for land located within urban settlements are split between the federal, regional and local budgets in proportions set in the federal legislation. In 2003, the law on the federal budget decreed payments for urban lands to be shared in proportions 0:50:50 between the federal, regional and local budgets. The regional government's share of payments for agricultural land is set by the regional legislature but cannot exceed 10 percent. The remaining share is allocated to the local budget. Since 2003, the federal legislation earmarks the regional share of the land tax revenue to the regional road programs. Regional governments can provide tax preferences to different categories of taxpayers and single taxpayers on the portion of the

tax liability due to the regional budget. At the same time, local governments are allowed to provide tax preferences on the portion of the tax liability due to their budgets but only with respect to single taxpayers.

Proposed modernization

The new Land Code of 2001 establishes that taxation of land should be based on the cadastral value. The estimation of the cadastral value is commissioned by Russia's Federal Service of Land Cadastre (*Roszemkadastr*) and based on the mass appraisal methodology developed by this federal agency. The federal government developed a new chapter of the Tax Code aiming at changing the taxable base from the acreage to cadastre value in January 2005. However, as of 2003, six out of 89 regions do not have a developed land cadastre.

The individual property tax

This tax, assigned to local governments, applies to structures (houses, apartments, cottages, garages and so on) owned by physical persons. For structures, the tax rate applies to the sum of inventory values of all structures located in the jurisdiction and owned by one individual. If tax rates vary by type of structure, the tax rate is applied to the total value of all structures of one type and then liabilities are summed over all types. The rates are set by the local government but with low federal maxima, which vary by the total value of structures (see Table 20.1). Regional governments can provide tax preferences to different categories of taxpayers as well as single taxpayers, while local governments are allowed to provide tax preferences only to particular taxpayers.

Table 20.1   Russia: federal limits for individual property tax rates

Total value of property	Tax rates (%)
Below RUR 300 000 (US$10 000)	up to 0.1
RUR 300 000–500 000	0.1–0.3
Over RUR 500 000 (US$17 000)	0.3–2.0

Source: Federal Law On Individual Property Tax (No. 2003-1; 9 December 1991) amended by Federal Law No. 178-FZ of 17 July 1999 and No. 100-FZ of 24 July 2002.

The inventory value of structures is determined by a local Bureau of Technical Inventory (*Gosstoi*)[10] as the cost of reconstruction depreciated for the deterioration of the structure. These bureaux are obliged to send information on the value and ownership of all registered structures to a local tax inspectorate by 1 March. By 1 August, tax inspectorates send tax advices to the owners.

Payment should be made in two equal installments by 15 September and 15 November. Late payment penalty is overdue amount times 1/300 of the refinancing rate of the Central Bank for each day of delay.

The proposed Tax Code chapter on the individual property tax reduces the tax rate ceiling to 0.1 percent of the inventory value. At the same time, *Gosstoi* is to update its ten-year-old methodology for assessing the inventory value of structures owned by individuals. The proposed bill significantly shortens the federal list of individuals exempted from this tax. At the same time, the federal government mandates abatements for the same category of individuals on structures valued under RUR 100 000 (US$3334) and land plots valued under RUR 10 000 (US$334).

The enterprise assets tax

This tax applies to the annual average balance sheet value of assets (fixed, intangible and inventories) of legal entities. Assets used for agricultural production are exempted from taxation. Rates are set by regional legislatures and can vary by type of production that the assets are used for. However, it is prohibited to set individual rates for single enterprises. The maximum rate is set at 2 percent.[11] The tax is essentially self-assessed: each quarter, legal entities make tax computations and file tax returns along with accounting reports to the tax inspectorate at the location of the legal entity itself and each of its detached subdivisions. Tax advances are paid quarterly within five days of filing tax returns. The final payment is made within ten days of filing the annual accounting report. Tax revenue is split equally between regional and local governments. Since 1998, enterprises have been required to pay taxes on the assets of their detached subdivisions (not registered as separate enterprises and not maintaining separate accounts) to the jurisdictions in which those subdivisions are located. It may, however, be difficult to enforce this provision since neither the federal administration nor the enterprises have any incentives to split tax payments in this way.

In June 2003, the Tax Code chapter dealing with this tax passed the second (essential) reading in the Lower House of Parliament. It is proposed to increase the ceiling on the property tax rate to 2.2 percent. At the same time inventories, intangibles and capital outlays are taken out of the tax base. In addition, the federally imposed list of tax exemptions is to be significantly shortened.

The succession and gift tax

This tax is paid by physical persons who receive property as a gift or by right of succession. Taxed objects include houses, apartments, cottages, garages, land plots, land shares, automobiles, motorcycles, motorboats, aircraft and other vehicles, as well as bank deposits and securities. Structures are taxed according to the technical inventory value or insurance value. Vehicles are taxed according to the insurance value. Other property is appraised by special experts. The tax rate is set in the federal law, as this tax is classified as federal. The rate varies by the degree of relationship and by the value of the gift or bequest. Bequests valued over RUR 85 000 (US$2900) are taxed from 5 to 15 percent for the first devisees, 10 to 30 percent for the second devisees, and 20 to 40 percent for other devisees. Gifts valued over RUR 8000 (US$270) are taxed from 3 to 15 percent for gifts between parents and children, and from 10 to 40 percent in other cases. Tax computations and billings are made by the tax inspectorate at the location of the property. Russian residents are to pay the tax within three months of receiving the bill. Late payment is penalized at the rate of 0.7 percent of the overdue amount for each day of delay. All revenue is allocated to the local government.

In June 2003, the Tax Code chapter dealing with this tax passed the second (essential) reading in the Lower House of Parliament. The resulting draft narrows the list of tax objects to real estate and vehicles. The proposed tax rate is to range from 5 to 13 percent. The value of exempted objects is to be raised to RUR 200 000 (US$6667) for succession and RUR 2000 (US$667) for gifts.

Revenue and arrears
The data in Table 20.2 show that, over the 1997–2000 period, revenue from the property-related taxes ranged from 8.7 to 18.4 percent of total local revenue including intergovernmental transfers. Until 1998 this share was growing steadily. However, from 1998 to 2001 it declined by more than 50 percent. There are two reasons for this. First, because property taxes are an inelastic source of revenue, their share in total revenue grew during the years of economic decline until 1997 and then decreased when economic growth started in 1999. Second, the yield of the property-related taxes depends on how the land tax rates and the balance value of assets are indexed relative to the level of inflation. Table 20.3 reveals that land tax rates were indexed below the inflation level in 1995, 1998, 2000 and 2001. Therefore, the yield of the land tax and land lease dropped during those years.

Structures owned by legal entities are taxed according to the balance sheet value. This value can be reappraised either through direct calculation of the cost of reconstruction or by indexing the previous year's value by the indexes reported in Table 20.3. In 1992–97, when inflation was high, annual reappraisal was mandatory, using one of these procedures. Since 1998, while enterprises have the right to reappraise property once a year, it is not mandatory. The index of asset appraisal was above the inflation level in 1995, 1996 and 1998. Hence the yield of the enterprise assets tax was increasing during these years. However, in 1997 and 1999–2001 the appraisal index fell signifi-

Table 20.2   Russia: share of local revenue accounted for by taxes on land and property, 1995–2002 (%)

Revenue source	1995	1996	1997	1998	1999	2000	2001	2002
Property taxes	9.04	n.a.	13.90	14.59	10.52	8.09	6.80	7.05
Individual property tax	n.a.	0.20	0.25	0.31	0.28	0.26	0.23	0.26
Enterprise assets tax	n.a.	14.49	13.62	14.24	10.19	7.79	6.53	6.75
Succession and gift tax	n.a.	n.a.	0.03	0.04	0.04	0.04	0.03	0.03
Land tax and land lease fee	n.a.	n.a.	3.20	3.78	3.88	3.24	2.44	3.37
Agricultural land tax	n.a.	n.a.	0.44	0.43	0.32	0.19	0.12	0.12
Non-agricultural land tax	n.a.	n.a.	2.01	2.24	2.40	2.03	1.44	1.85
Agricultural land lease fee	n.a.	n.a.	0.05	0.05	0.05	0.04	0.03	0.04
Non-agricultural land lease fee	n.a.	n.a.	0.48	1.06	1.11	0.99	0.85	1.36

Source: Calculated from Russian Ministry of Finance data.

Table 20.3   Russia: annual indexes

Index	1995	1996	1997	1998	1999	2000	2001	2002
GDP growth	0.96	0.97	1.01	0.95	1.05	1.09	1.05	1.04
GDP deflator	2.8	1.4	1.1	1.2	1.6	1.4	1.2	1.15
Land tax rate index	1.5–2.0	1.5	2.0	1.0	2.0	1.2	1.0	2.00
Balance sheet value of assets index	2.8–3.9	1.67–1.80	1.03–1.08	0.96–1.23	1.3	1.2	1.14	–

cantly below the inflation level and the share of revenue from the enterprise assets tax almost halved. The inventory value of structures owned by physical persons is indexed by local Bureaux of Technical Inventory according to indexes set by regional governments.

The major property tax – enterprise assets tax – generated about 7 percent of the total revenue of local government in 2002. This accounted for 65 percent of all revenue from the property-related taxes. The second largest source of property-related revenue was the tax on non-agricultural land. In 2002 this tax generated about 2 percent of the total revenue of local government or 18 percent of revenue from the property-related taxes. Non-agricultural land lease fees accounted for additional 1 percent of the total revenue of local government and the yield from each of the remaining four sources did not exceed 0.5 percent of the total revenue of local governments.

There is only limited information on the extent of arrears for these taxes. At the beginning of 2000 the stock of overdue payables on the land tax was equal to 69 percent of the estimated annual flow of land tax payables (tax collections plus the flow of tax arrears). The stock of rescheduled payables accounted for an additional 6 percent of the annual flow of payables. During the year 2000 the stock of overdue payables increased by 20 percent of the annual flow of payables. Data on other property taxes in arrears are not available after 1998, when the federal Ministry of Taxation stopped reporting these figures. By the end of 1997 the stock of overdue payables on the property taxes (individual property tax, enterprise assets tax and succession and gift tax) reached the level of 30 percent of the estimated annual flow of the property tax payables. Tax compliance on these taxes was 93 percent in 1997 and 85 percent in 1996.[12]

The value of structures owned by individuals, as set by the Bureaux of Technical Inventory, cannot be appealed. Some enterprise taxpayers tried to appeal the reappraisal indexes (Table 20.3) issued by the State Committee of Statistics, but the courts ruled that taxpayers could do their own object-by-object reappraisal based on the cost of reconstruction if they are not happy with the average indexes. The mass appraisal procedure used in Novgorod allows for appeal but so far none have been made. On the other hand, as noted above, at present these values are only used for about ten (enterprise) taxpayers.

Notes

1. For some general background, particularly with respect to difficulties in establishing clear property rights in land in Russia, notably in rural areas, see Malme and Kalinina (2001).
2. Articles 18–21 of the Federal Law On the Basic Principles of Taxation (No. 2118-1; 27 December 1991).
3. The City of Moscow and, until 1999, the City of St Petersburg had no local governments and thus all revenue from the succession and gift tax was allocated to the city budget. In

addition, the Republic of Sakha's budget in 1997 and the Orenburg and Penza Regions' budgets in 1999 received minor portions of revenue from the succession and gift tax collected in their constituent localities.

4. Federal Law On Real Estate Tax Experiment in the Cities of Novgorod and Tver (110-FZ; 20 July 1997). For a more detailed account of this experiment, see Malme and Kalinina (2001, pp. 76–80).

5. Inclusion in the new Tax Code does necessarily guarantee a long life for a tax. Thus, in November 2001, the Parliament enacted the Tax Code chapter on the regional sales tax. However, at the same time this tax was scheduled for abolition on 1 January 2004.

6. 'Advantageously located plots' are as defined by the local government. This provision applies only to plots in rural settlements. It seems unlikely that any such differentiated rates have actually been applied.

7. Federal Ministry of Taxation Instruction No. 56 On Application of the Federal Law 'On Payment for Land' (21 February 2000).

8. The 'standard lot size' is the norm set out in the city development plan to guide the issuance of building permits and the leasing of public land.

9. All property rights acquired after the enactment of the federal law On the State Registration of Property Rights and Transactions (No. 122-FZ; 21 July 1997) are subject to state registration. State registration of property rights is carried out by justice offices established by regional governments in accordance with the federal legislation and under the supervision of the federal government. According to Malme and Kalinina (2001, p. 68), this registration process has been 'burdensome for new owners and costly for governments. ... As a result, much property remains unregistered, including valuable new construction.'

10. An authorized agent of the State Committee of the Russian Federation on Construction and Housing and Utilities.

11. A review of 1998 budgets for 77 regions found that 55 levied the maximum 2 percent rate. Other rates levied included: 1 percent (three regions), 1.2 percent (one region), 1.5 percent (two regions), and 1.8 percent (one region). Fourteen other regions levied rates that were differentiated by type of enterprise, with rates ranging from 0.05 to 2 percent.

12. Malme and Kalinina (2001, p. 68) report a 'collection ratio' of 60 percent for 1998, but this appears to be the ratio of collections to budget estimates.

References

Malme, J.H. and N. Kalinina (2001), 'Property Tax Developments in the Russian Federation,' in J.H. Malme and J.M. Youngman (eds), *The Development of Property Taxation in Economies in Transition*, Washington, DC: World Bank.

21 Property tax in Ukraine[1]

Richard M. Bird

Like most countries that emerged from the former Soviet Union, Ukraine has faced very substantial difficulties in maintaining economic growth while at the same time organizing an effective national government and national fiscal structure and administration. An important aspect of this task has been to establish clearly defined property rights, including those in land, in order to facilitate market activities while also providing an appropriate fiscal base for government. Simultaneously, Ukraine has had to deal with establishing viable local and regional governments and coping with their demands and needs.

Although Ukraine has a unitary system of government, it has 27 regional or *oblast*-level governments (including the Crimean Republic and the Cities of Kiev (Kyiv) and Sevastapol, which have *oblast* status), as well as close to 500 *rayon* (district) governments, almost as many municipalities, and many settlements and villages. Rayons and cities are subordinated to oblasts, which are in turn subordinated to the central government. Under the current Budget Code, however, rayons and larger cities are no longer subordinated in fiscal terms to the oblasts since they receive transfers directly from the central budget. The lower levels of local government are controlled by locally elected councils (radas). In principle, the development of a feasible and appropriate local tax base is an important component of any sustainable long-term solution to the complex problem of establishing a viable intergovernmental fiscal system. This need has clearly been recognized in Ukraine, but as yet little progress has been made in this respect.

At present, there is essentially no significant local tax autonomy in Ukraine and almost all local revenue comes from shares of national taxes on a derivation basis. Since the Budget Code adopted in 2001, these shares are fixed rather than discretionary as in earlier years. Although a 1993 Decree On Local Taxes and Duties established a number of 'local taxes', none of these levies produces much revenue. Moreover, although these local taxes are administered by local tax offices, these offices are under the national State Tax Administration (STA).

Many changes in intergovernmental fiscal relations have been discussed in Ukraine over the last few years, including possible changes in property taxation, but the situation in Ukraine remains highly centralized, with all significant taxes on land and property being entirely under central government control, even though in most cases the proceeds are channeled to local budgets on a derivation basis.

Current taxes and charges on land and property

The only 'local taxes and duties' affecting land and property are the following minor levies:

1. Fee charged for authorization for the extension of private apartments.
2. Resort fees charged to persons who visit holiday resort areas.
3. Fees charged to legal entities for permission to establish facilities in densely populated areas and to individuals who receive permission to build residential constructions in such areas. These fees are based on the size of the area used for construction purposes.
4. There is a similar fee charged to legal entities that operate in the central parts of densely populated areas and in buildings of historical or architectural value.

These minor fees are of little revenue importance. In 2002, for example, only a bit more than UAH 0.5 billion was collected from all local taxes and charges.

The land tax

Much more important are land payments and taxes imposed by the central government.[2] Although both a land tax and a real estate tax are specifically enumerated as state taxes, in fact the main tax on land is that imposed by the 1992 Law On Payment for Land in the form of a charge on legal entities and physical persons who own or use land.[3] Unlike Russia, there is no tax on buildings as such (other than the small local fees noted above). Land tax rates vary depending upon whether the land is intended to be used for agriculture or not. Agricultural land is taxed at rates depending upon what it is used for – arable land and plantations or hayfields and pastures – and upon its fertility according to the land cadastre.[4] Non-agricultural land is taxed at rates depending upon the category of the settlement – number of inhabitants – and its location within the settlement. Rates varied in 1999 from UAH 0.015 (in localities with populations less than 200) to 0.21 per m^2 (in cities over one million), or 1 percent of land valuation.

As the State Committee on Land Resources has progressed with its task of valuing land, the fixed levies have become less important and the tax on land values more important. In rural areas, the tax rates are lower – 0.1 percent on annual cropland and only 0.03 percent on land used for perennial crops. Although little is known about the techniques used to appraise land, in Kyiv the city was divided into 1483 zones and a value was ascribed to each.

Applying the standard rate of 1 percent resulted in tax rates in the city varying from about UAH 4 to 4000 per m^2 of land (Thirsk, 2003).

Land tax is self-assessed by legal entities and due on 15 July each year. With respect to agricultural enterprises, the tax is payable on 15 August and 15 November, and all others pay it quarterly. The tax is imposed on physical persons by the tax office.[5] In 2003, the Budget Code assigns 60 percent of land tax revenues to towns and settlements, 15 percent to rayons, and 25 percent to oblasts, or alternatively 75 percent to cities of 'oblast significance' and 25 percent to oblasts. Legally, the proceeds of the land tax are earmarked for 'land improvement purposes.'

Exemptions include enterprises in the state sector as well as cultural, scientific, education and health care organizations, charitable foundations and military units. Those subject to the fixed agricultural tax are not subject to the land tax. In addition, land tax exemptions are often granted as part of the package of tax incentives (for example in 'free zones'). The estimated revenue cost of land tax exemptions in 2002 was UAH 1.3 billion, or about 72 percent of land taxes collected. Local governments may exempt taxpayers from paying the share of taxes due to local governments, but such 'local exemptions' appear to account for no more than 2–3 percent of total land taxes forgone.

In 2000, 168 411 land tax payees were registered with the State Tax Administration, of whom 149 537 (88.8 percent) actually filed tax declarations. The total land tax assessed in that year was UAH 1.6 billion, compared to arrears of UAH 0.5 billion. In 2002, the total stock of arrears amounted to 29 percent of actual collections.

The law simply says that disputes are to be settled in the courts. Reportedly, appeals of land tax assessments are very rare.

Simplified taxes
Small businesses that choose to be taxed under a 'simplified' tax system introduced in 1998 (On Simplified System of Taxation, Registration and Reporting of Small Business Entities) are not subject to the land tax (or to duties for special utilization of natural resources). Physical persons who employ fewer than ten people and have sales less than UAH 500 000 (less than US$100 000) and legal entities with fewer than 50 employees and sales less than UAH 1 million may opt for this system. Legal entities under the simplified system pay a single tax of 6 percent on sales (plus VAT) or 10 percent (and no VAT). Physical persons are taxed at fixed rates set for different activities by local councils, within the range of UAH 20–200 per month (less than US$50–500 per year). Twenty-three percent of proceeds from this 'single tax' goes to local budgets. Reportedly, depending upon the sector, from 45 to 65 percent of businesses can choose to adopt this system, and

Table 21.1   Ukraine land tax data from the State Tax Administration

	1995	1996	1997	1998	1999	2000
Registered taxpayers	190 426	214 766	190 067	196 846	178 158	168 411
Reporting taxpayers (as %)	73.7	75.2	91.0	90.1	87.3	88.8
Collections (UAH '000)	649	815	1005	1105	1104	1375
Arrears (UAH '000)	81	166	220	419	332	494
Exempt enterprises				31 141	23 889	
Revenue loss (UAH '000)				1642	1004	871

Note: All land tax revenue went to local governments in 1997 and later years, but that in 1995 only 84.2% and in 1996 73.4% went to local budgets.

Source: State Tax Administration.

about half of those eligible have done so. Total collections (net of payments to the Pension Fund) from this tax in 2002, however, were only UAH 0.6 billion. As can be seen in Table 21.1, it seems likely that both the fall in the number of land taxpayers and the stagnation in collections from this source in 1999 may be attributed at least in part to the introduction of the simplified tax.

Along similar lines, a 1998 law On Fixed Agricultural Tax replaced land tax, payment for use of natural resources, and many other taxes. This tax applies to agricultural enterprises including food processors so long as such sales do not exceed 50 percent of gross revenues. The rates are based on estimated land values per hectare as established in the land cadastre and vary by the type of land between 0.1 percent and 0.5 percent. The tax is paid quarterly, and 30 percent of its proceeds go to local budgets. In principle, since this tax was imposed for a five-year period, it is scheduled to lapse in January 2004.

Revenue importance
Tables 21.1–21.3 depict the importance of these various levies from different perspectives.[6] Table 21.1 shows, for 1995–2000, the land tax collections and other information reported by the State Tax Administration (STA), which collects all local taxes. The STA does not, however, collect all revenues in Ukraine, so Table 21.2 places the land tax (still based of course on the STA data) in the context of all government revenues (net of Pension Fund) and GDP for 1998–2000. Finally, Table 21.3 shows the importance of all the taxes mentioned above in local budgets in 2000 and 2001. While not all these figures are easily comparable, they show clearly that taxes on land and property are not very important in Ukraine. An additional important piece of

Table 21.2   Ukraine: revenue importance of land taxes

	1998	1999	2000	2001	2002
Land tax (UAH million)	1115	1094	1377	1619	1806
Local taxes and charges (UAH million)	392	440	485	514	542
Land tax as % total revenues	3.9	3.3	2.8	3.0	2.9
Land tax as % GDP	1.1	0.8	0.8	0.8	0.8

Source: Ministry of Finance.

Table 21.3   Ukraine: local revenues, 2002

Total revenues (general fund): UAH 19.4 billion
Of which: Personal income tax   56.0%
             Land payments (tax)   9.3%
             User charges   8.2%
             Local taxes and fees   2.0%
             Simplified tax   3.3%
             Fixed agricultural tax   0.6%
             Other   19.9%

Source: 2002 Treasury Report.

information is that local revenues accounted (in 1998) for 14.4 percent of GDP and 40.1 percent of consolidated government expenditures (World Bank, 1999). As in other former Soviet countries, the size of the government sector has shrunk over the last decade, but the share of the local sector has remained relatively constant, at around 40 percent of the total. Interestingly, the share of land taxes rose from less than 5 percent of total local revenues in 1993 and 1994 to 8 percent by 1998. Table 21.3 suggests that this trend has been sustained. 'Local' taxes and fees, on the other hand, have never yielded more than 3 percent of local revenues.

Proposed reforms in land taxation
An earlier examination of property tax reform in Ukraine reviewed several unsuccessful attempts in 1995, 1996 and 1998 to introduce a real estate tax (Slack et al., 1998). The version contained in the proposed Tax Code in 2001 included a tax on all forms of immovable property, including agricultural land, land plots, buildings and constructions, assuming that valuation data are available for all. Taxpayers were identified as owners and land users. The tax base for land was to be value or area, where value has not been established.

For buildings, the base was to be capital value, with values to be revised every five years (and perhaps indexed if inflation exceeded 10 percent in any tax year). The rate on land in populated areas was set at 1 percent or different fixed rates per m² if no values, with surcharges applied in cities. Buildings were to be taxed from 1 percent to 2 percent. Local radas would be allowed to impose surcharges up to twice the established rate. Agricultural land was to be taxed differently, with the rates set as a percentage of value adjusted by a coefficient varied by the usage of the land and farmers allowed to credit property tax against enterprise profits tax. There were many other special rates (for railways, recreational land, water reserves and so on). Many exemptions were provided in the draft legislation: one estimate, for example, is that 80 percent of all residential property would be exempted (Downey, 2000).

Reviewing an earlier version of this scheme, Slack et al. (1998) suggested that, since it would be neither easy nor quick to set up a market-value-based tax, the best approach might be to begin with a unit value assessment system. As Thirsk (2003) notes, despite some advances in land valuation in recent years (and the potential of using building information from the Bureaux of Technical Inventory), this advice still seems sound. Although proposals for property taxes still surface from time to time, however – in 2002, for example, the Ministry of Finance proposed a levy of 1 percent on property sales – the introduction of an effective local property tax does not, at the moment, appear to be a priority item on Ukraine's tax reform agenda.

Notes

1. We are grateful to Svetlana Budagovskaya, Wayne Thirsk and Ihor Shpak for information and helpful comments.
2. Parenthetically, it should perhaps be noted that Ukrainian statistics sometimes show 'property taxes' as a revenue source. As a rule, this item refers solely to taxes on vehicles. Land tax revenue is sometimes labeled 'royalties for use of natural resources.' The 'fixed' taxes noted below are usually classified as 'other tax revenues.' Rental revenues received by local radas from land retained by them when collective farms were dissolved are often reported as 'land tax' in revenue accounts.
3. Since 1996, there have been 30 amendments to this law. An interesting recent provision is Art. 7.1.2 of a 2002 Law On Procedure for Satisfying Taxpayer Liabilities to the Budgets and Government Target Funds (the 'Payments Law') which specifies that if no person responsible for paying taxes and charges on immovable property can be located, the taxes and charges may be 'applied directly to objects of such property.'
4. The State Committee on Land Resources is responsible for land assessment.
5. Under other laws, special charges are imposed on the use of forestry resources (essentially based on wood cut), on freshwater resources (essentially on water used), and on mineral resources (essentially on extraction).
6. In addition to the taxes discussed in the text, there is a 5 percent stamp tax imposed on the registered value of land sales.

References

Downey, Maurice (2000), *Property Tax in the Government Draft Tax Code*, European Union Tacis Programme, Kyiv, November.
Slack, Enid, John La Faver and Ihor Shpak (1998), 'Property Tax Reform in Ukraine: Third Attempt,' *Budget and Fiscal Review* (kgiv), second quarter, August.
Thirsk, Wayne (2003), 'Prospects for the Property Tax in Ukraine,' Kyiv.
World Bank (1999), *Intergovernmental Finance in Ukraine: An Agenda for Reform*, Washington, DC: World Bank, April.

22 Land and property taxes in Poland[1]

Richard M. Bird

In 1999, subnational taxes accounted for 24.5 percent of subnational revenues in Poland, and subnational revenues accounted for 28.8 percent of total government revenue and 12.0 percent of GDP. In other words, subnational taxes were 2.9 percent of GDP. Since taxes on property accounted for 39.7 percent of subnational taxes, property taxes in 1999 thus came to 1.2 percent of GDP. Property taxes accounted for 13.9 percent of local revenues and 31.8 percent of local 'own' revenues.[2]

Poland has several levels of subnational government, with different degrees of autonomy and different fiscal bases. The municipal (*gmina*) level has had considerable autonomy since the dawning of the post-communist era in 1990 saw the creation of almost 2500 municipalities. A major reform in 1999 created a new regional (*powiat*) level with some degree of autonomy but did not in any way reduce municipal autonomy. This reform created 308 *powiats*, with an average of about eight *gminas* per *powiat*, along with 65 cities with *powiat* status (Wojcik, 2000). These new entities, however, have little revenue autonomy and are largely financed by transfers.[3] Finally, there are 16 vovoidships, which are essentially regional administrations of the national government.

Since the Law on Local Taxes and Duties of 1991, there have been essentially three taxes on property in Poland: the urban property or real estate tax, the agricultural tax and the forest tax. By far the most important of these taxes is the real estate tax, which accounts for 85 percent of total property taxes, compared to 13 percent for the agricultural tax, and only 2 percent for the forest tax. There are also significant charges imposed by the central government on the transfer and registration of property, estimated to amount to 10 percent of transaction prices (Malme and Brzeski, 2001). Local (*gmina*) governments can set the rates of the real estate and agricultural tax, subject to a maximum limit set by the central government.

The real estate tax
The real estate tax, originally imposed in 1986, was assigned to municipalities in 1991. This tax is levied on all property other than that subject to the agricultural or forest taxes. Although, unlike many other former communist countries, Poland never abolished private property rights, many aspects of property rights are nonetheless still unclear, thus making it rather difficult to

establish a market-value-based property tax. The real estate tax is based not on value but on the area of the land and the area of the building (measured on a net internal basis, that is, deducting staircases, corridors, and so on). Plant and machinery (improvements, not buildings, claimed by businesses for income tax depreciation purposes) are taxed at cost. The tax base is reviewed annually. In effect, the real estate tax thus has three components: the land tax, the building tax, and the 'structures' tax.

The tax is administered by local governments although the basic information used to determine the tax base is found in two central registries. One registry is on Land and Building Evidence for technical cadastral information (land maps, land area, parcel identification, building descriptions) and one, the Land Title Registry (Perpetual Books), is on title registry (owner/taxpayer identification). Local governments collect and administer property taxes by connecting their tax rolls to these two registers and by gathering information on building construction from municipal planning and architecture departments. They have legal access to this information, but it does not come to them automatically: they have to collect it. Legal entities are responsible for self-assessing their real estate tax.

Tax rates are set annually by the local government, subject to prescribed minimum and maximum rates linked to the rate of inflation. In 2002, the rates varied from US$0.02 per m^2 for residential and other land, to US$0.74 per m^2 for land 'under lakes, reservoirs, and power stations.' The rates per m^2 for buildings ranged from US$0.11 for residential buildings to US$3.69 for commercial and industrial buildings.[4] The rate was 2 percent of the depreciated book values for income tax purposes for fixed installations (plant and machinery).

Given the rate structure, it is not surprising that business buildings reportedly produce over half of the property tax revenue, although they constitute less than 5 percent of the total capital value of real estate, while residential property, which accounts for over 70 percent of value, accounts for less than 10 percent of property tax revenues.[5] A study made in 2000 estimated that, for smaller cities in Poland, business buildings provided 36 percent of taxes (and were taxed at a rather startling 7.8 percent of capital value), while business land provided another 23 percent (but was taxed at only 1.4 percent of its value). In contrast, residential land (7.8 percent of collections) was taxed at less than 0.05 percent of market value and residential buildings (3.4 percent of collections) at little more (about 0.06 percent). The main difference in larger cities was that much more of the real estate tax (64 percent) came from business buildings and less (11 percent) from business land: residential buildings accounted for only 3.7 percent and residential land for only 2.1 percent. Moreover, within the business sector, it appears that industrial companies with large areas of land are taxed relatively more heavily than commercial enterprises (which have generally done much better in the transition economy).

Although 5.5 million taxpayers are subject to real estate tax, there are many exemptions. Exemptions include property used for public purposes (local governments, schools, hospitals, charitable institutions and so on) and that used by religious groups, railway and other transportation installations (including pipelines), and 'historic monuments.' In 1997, generating facilities of electric, gas and water utilities that were experiencing financial difficulties were exempted. This exemption was ended in 2001, but to mitigate the rise the tax rate on these facilities (which would normally be the 'structure tax' of 2 percent) was temporarily set at 1 percent. In addition to the exemptions set out in the law for the elderly, veterans and others, local governments can grant reliefs, and they appear to do so to a considerable extent. In 1999, 78 percent of local tax relief took the form of reductions in real estate tax, and the revenue of that tax was reduced by 18.1 percent for this reason (OECD, 2001, p. 35). In addition, there are numerous 'special economic zones' intended to encourage investment that provide, among other benefits, exemption from property tax. One estimate is that the 'national' exemptions alone reduced property tax revenues by 14.6 percent in the city of Krakow (Brzeski, 2003).

On the other hand, national government property is not exempted unless done by the municipality itself. The state treasury is supposed to make payments on such property like any other taxpayer. Even municipally owned property such as utilities is supposed to be taxed, unless specifically exempted.

The real estate tax is payable by owners, whether in occupation or not. The tax is payable quarterly by individuals and monthly by corporations. The latter are required to self-assess the tax. Most large municipalities are responsible for tax collection although for smaller ones, the national tax office may collect the tax. Unpaid taxes (arrears), except in the largest cities, are, interestingly, turned over to the national tax office for collection. Unsurprisingly, this office seldom seems to pursue the collections of 'other people's revenue' with enthusiasm. In the city of Krakow, 8.0 percent of taxes billed to legal entities (86 percent of total property taxes) were in arrears in 2000, compared to 9.5 percent of taxes billed to natural persons (Brzeski, 2003).

Appeals may be lodged first with local governments, then with a regional appeal board, and then, finally, with the Administrative Appeals Court.

Agricultural tax

The agricultural tax dates from 1985. This tax applies to land used for crop growing on farms exceeding one hectare. It is imposed on individual farmers, cooperatives and state farms and is in fact the only tax imposed on the latter two. There are 2 million taxpayers. The tax is based on a 'conventional hectare' (or 'conversion hectare'), defined as the actual number of hectares multiplied by a coefficient related to the fertility of the land, the location of the farm and the type of agriculture. The fertility factor is based on the information in the technical cadastre and the zone allocation is determined by the Ministry of Finance. Four zones depending on economic and production (climatic) conditions have been established, and there are two types of land (arable land and meadows and pastures), and ten usage classes as well as 14 classes of soils. The tax rate is set as the value of 2.5 quintals (a measure of quantity) of rye per conventional hectare (that is, indexed to the average market price per quintal of rye paid on wholesale markets for the first three quarters of the preceding year), but there are various reliefs (for example, for farm improvements and military service) that lower this rate by up to 75 percent. The agricultural tax is payable quarterly.

Forest tax
The forest tax is paid by owners of forests and occupiers of state or communal forests on land of at least 0.1 hectare used for the production of forest vegetation. There are 1.2 million forest taxpayers. Like the agricultural tax, this tax is based on a 'conventional hectare' defined in much the same way to reflect fertility and the main tree species as set out in the forest management plan. The coefficient ranges from 2.3 for firs to 0.2 for aspen, and the tax rate is the average sawmill price of 0.2 m^3 of the timber in question per conventional hectare except for lands without a management plan and land in national parks, natural reservations and protected forests, where the rate is set at the price of 300 kg (0.3 quintals) of rye per hectare per half year. Some reliefs are granted for forests that are at least 40 years old and for those that are 'historical monuments.'

Other taxes on property
There are three transfer taxes: (1) a 5 percent stamp duty (2 percent on interests in cooperatives) collected by notary offices on executed deeds; (2) a 3 percent average notarial fee on the same base; and (3) a 1.6 percent fee (on reported price) by the Land Title Registry for recording new ownership titles.

Local governments may impose an 'adjacency fee,' which is essentially a betterment tax for partial cost recovery of infrastructure investments. The cost imposed on an individual property may not exceed 50 percent of the increase in value attributable to the improvements. The fee is payable (with interest) over a period of not more than ten years.

A tax of up to 30 percent of the value increase attributable to a land use change may be imposed on the sale of affected property within five years of the change. On the other hand, owners whose property values decrease as a result of land use plan changes have a right to compensation.

Real property is subject to inheritance and gift taxes at rates between 3 and 12 percent, depending on the relationship of the parties and the value of the property. Small residences occupied by those who receive them are exempted.

Reform proposals

As in most post-communist countries, there has been no shortage of proposed reforms of the property tax system described above. Although, as shown above, property taxes are important sources of local revenue in Poland, they have been decreasing in importance in recent years. This decrease has been attributed largely to the lack of elasticity of the area-based assessment system.[6] Unsurprisingly, a move to a more conventional *ad valorem* property tax has thus been at the top of the reform list. In 1994, the national government ordered the Ministry of Finance to create a national fiscal cadastre, to serve as the basis for mass appraisal of property for an *ad valorem* tax by 1999. The original idea was to have a national cadastral office. By 1996, when a detailed proposal was prepared, it provided for local management of the cadastre by the larger cities and by municipal unions designed to achieve sufficient scale, with an implementation date of 2001. In 1998, a Department of Local Government Taxes and Cadastre was established in the Ministry of Finance to move matters along, and in 1999 a new proposal to replace the three existing taxes by a new tax based on a unit value system was presented.

Subsequent discussions, and explorations of how the proposed system would work in several selected cities, have continued. The most recent strategy under consideration appears to be to use an area-based formula for land, modified by location coefficients reflecting market factors. Buildings would at first be taxed as now, but would subsequently be taxed on a depreciated replacement cost basis for non-residential structures. As elsewhere in Central and Eastern Europe, it thus appears that Poland still seems to have some distance to go before it achieves anything close to a market-value-based property tax system.

Notes

1. We are grateful to Jan Brzeski for supplying many useful materials.
2. OECD (2001, 2003). For the 1996–97 period, property taxes were a bit less than 1 percent of GDP (Maurer and Paugnam, 2000, p. 2).
3. As Kulesza (2003, p. 202) says, 'a real decentralization of public finance in Poland has not been made yet.'
4. The much higher rates on business 'can be explained by the political reality of business taxpayers being seen by politicians as a non-voting public, as well as by the widely held popular view that businesses have money while individuals (voting taxpayers) do not' (Brzeski, 2001a, p. 7).
5. This estimate (by Brzeski, 2001a) is based on the depreciated book value of business capital, but he notes (1) that most of business capital stock is obsolescent so this figure is probably not too far off, while (2) since owner-occupied residential property is not subject to depreciation, its reported value is probably closer to market values.

6. Malme and Brzeski (2001, p. 13). For more on the problems of the area-based property tax, see, for example Brzeski (2001a, p. 8), who refers to the residential portion of the tax as 'resembling a low rate poll tax' (p. 8).

References

Brzeski, Jan (1999), 'Real Property Taxation in Poland,' in W. McCluskey (ed.), *Property Tax: An International Comparative Review*, Aldershot, UK: Ashgate.

Brzeski, W. Jan (2001a), 'Reforming Residential Property Taxation in Poland,' paper presented at 8th European Real Estate Society Conference, Alicante, Spain, June.

Brzeski, W. Jan (2001b), 'Property Taxes in Poland and the Recent Reform Efforts,' paper prepared for OECD Seminar on Property Tax Reforms and Valuation, Vilnius, October.

Brzeski, W. Jan (2003), 'Property Tax Administration in the City of Cracow, Poland,' presentation to World Bank Workshop on Innovations in Local Revenue Mobilization, 23–24 June.

Brown, P.K. and M.A. Hepworth (2000), 'A Survey of European Land Tax Systems,' Cambridge, MA: Lincoln Institute of Land Policy Working Paper.

Kulesza, Michal (2003), 'Methods and Techniques of Managing Decentralization Reforms in the CEE Countries: The Polish Experience,' in *Mastering Decentralization and Public Administration Reforms in Central and Eastern Europe*, Budapest: Local Government and Public Service Reform Initiative.

Malme, J.H. and W.J. Brzeski (2001), 'Property Tax Developments in Poland,' in J.H. Malme and J.M. Youngman (eds), *The Development of Property Taxation in Economies in Transition*, Washington: World Bank.

Maurer, Robert and Anne Paugam (2000), 'Reform toward Ad Valorem Property Tax in Transition Economies: Fiscal and Land Use Benefits,' Background Series 13, Land and Real Estate Initiative, World Bank, June.

OECD (2001), *Fiscal Design Across Levels of Government, Year 2000 Surveys*, Paris: OECD.

OECD (2003), 'Fiscal Decentralisation in Europe: Overall Status in Selected Countries,' Informal Meeting on Fiscal Relations Across Levels of Government, Paris, March.

Wojcik, Marek (2000), *The Powiat (County) Local Government Public Administration Reform Implementation Experience in Poland in 1999*, Szczecin, Poland.

23 Real estate tax in Latvia[1]

Richard M. Bird

Latvia has a population of 2.4 million, of whom 69 percent live in urban areas. Unlike the other Baltic States, Latvia has several layers of subnational government – rural municipalities and towns, local urban governments (called Republican or big cities), and regional governments. In 2000, there were 486 rural municipalities, 70 town municipalities and 7 city municipalities. In addition, there are 26 rajon or district-level governments as well as, again, the seven cities, which perform both regional and municipal functions. Regions have their own budgets, and indirectly elected councils, but financially they are almost entirely dependent upon transfers. Rural municipalities govern less developed areas and have fewer functions than their urban counterparts.

As in a number of other countries in Eastern Europe, among the earliest laws introduced in Latvia after achieving independence were several on local governments introduced in 1990 and intended to replace the old Soviet-type municipalities, which were essentially parts of the central government, with local elected self-governments. The many small municipalities created – the average size of a rural municipality was less than 2000 people – could not really organize and provide many public services, however, so a further reform in 1998 (Law on Administrative Territorial Reform) provided for amalgamations of small municipalities into more sustainable units, on a voluntary basis through 2003, after which the central government will take over the process. The intention is apparently to end up with about 100 municipalities, but little has yet been accomplished in this direction in part because of significant local resistance.

Interestingly, despite the emphasis on increasing the effectiveness of local government, Latvian municipalities have no revenue autonomy since all local taxes are entirely determined by the central government, which sets both the tax base and the tax rate. The municipalities do, however, have significant 'own' tax revenue, and all revenue from land and property taxes accrues to those governments. This source of funds is not trivial since Latvia probably has the highest taxes on land and property of any transitional country in Europe.[2] In 1999, when subnational revenues accounted for 7.3 percent of GDP, 6.6 percent (91 percent of subnational revenues) came from taxes and 21 percent of those taxes were property taxes, which were therefore 1.4 percent of GDP.[3] Table 23.1 presents information on the importance of these taxes over the last few years.

Table 23.1   Revenue from property taxes (millions of LVL)

	1994	1995	1996	1997	1998	1999	2000
Land tax	9.5	10.8	12.9	16.9	–	–	–
Property tax	12.2	15.1	18.2	20.3	27.4	24.5	–
Real estate tax	–	–	–	–	20.9	22.1	42.8
Total property tax revenue	21.7	25.8	31.1	37.2	48.3	46.6	42.8
Total local taxes	115.0	162.8	188.2	175.3	203.2	221.5	234.6
Property taxes as % local taxes	18.9	15.8	16.5	21.2	23.8	21.0	18.2
Property taxes as % all taxes	3.6	3.5	3.5	3.3	3.8	3.6	3.1

Source: Ministry of Finance.

The current property tax in Latvia came into force only in 1998 and more fully in 2000. Before then (see Table 23.1), separate taxes were imposed on land and property (mainly buildings) under two 1991 acts on land tax and property tax respectively. The real estate tax imposed by the 1998 law is imposed on both land and buildings at a rate of 1.5 percent of cadastral value for land and inventory value for constructions until 2007. Thereafter, the tax is to be applied only on the cadastral value for land. The rate is set by the national government, and local governments cannot alter it. However, local governments are empowered to grant reliefs up to 90 percent for some classes of taxpayers. Reportedly, the possibility of giving municipalities the right to set the real property tax, within limits, is being considered (OECD, 2001).

The cadastral value is supposed to be 'market-based' capital value, calculated in accordance with mass valuation principles taking into account price levels realized in the real estate market as determined from analysis over at least a two-year period. Revaluation is required at least every five years. Land and buildings are to be valued separately. As mentioned, buildings ('constructions') are taxed on book or inventory value, but are to be exempt after 2007.

As of 2000, approximately 50 percent of all real estate was reported to be registered in the Title Book (Land Register) for the Baltic States as a whole. In Latvia, the State Land Service is responsible for both the land cadastre and the building register, while the real property rights record (register) is maintained by the Title Book Office. Registration of land and property began in 1993 and was completed in 1999. While registration of legal ownership is not complete, rights on some 610 000 properties were registered in the Title Book at the end of 2001. Reportedly, in rural areas the value of land is proportional to the average cadastral values (with values ranging from €400–440 per hectare in the south to €150–380 per hectare elsewhere). Forest land, which accounts for 30 percent of the total (compared to 63 percent in agricultural land), is valued generally from €517 to €862 per hectare, with values linked to timber value and accessibility, but some land is valued as high as €1034 per hectare. Standard urban residential plots (500–1400 m^2 in Riga and 700–2000 elsewhere) are valued at €7–40 per m^2.[4]

Although the real estate tax is a national tax, both local and national governments are responsible for its administration. The State Revenue Service is responsible for collecting data on taxable properties and for assessment. Local governments are responsible for calculating the tax, billing it, and collecting it. Tax payments are due quarterly.

Exemptions include the property of state and local governments, religious organizations (used for religious activity), cultural monuments, recreational and sports facilities (as regulated by the cabinet). Individual residences (including private apartments) are exempted. The value of forests is excluded from cadastral value. A special relief – 50 percent reduction – is provided in the law for residences of 'politically repressed persons' in their possession for at least five years. Buildings and constructions used for agricultural activity, communications lines, local pipelines and cables, and a variety of other activities are exempted until 2007. After that, no constructions are apparently to be taxed.

Taxpayers may appeal to the head of the relevant local government council if they do not agree with the tax assessed.

Notes

1. We are grateful to Andrey Timofeev, and especially to Mudite Priede of the Union of Local and Regional Governments of Latvia, for supplying some of the information.
2. See, for example, the comparisons in Maurer and Paugam (2000). Latvia is the highest country reported in this study, with property taxes in excess of 1 percent of GDP. Next highest, a bit below 1 percent, is Poland. The CEE (Central and East European) average is 0.55 percent, and some countries, notably Hungary (0.15 percent), are much lower.
3. Calculated from data in OECD (2000).
4. Value information from *Review of Baltic States Real Estate Market*, Spring 2000.

References

Maurer, Robert and Anne Paugam (2000), 'Reform Toward Ad Valorem Property Tax in Transition Economies,' Background Series 13, Land and Real Estate Initiative, World Bank, June.

OECD (2000), *Fiscal Design Across Levels of Government Year 2000 Surveys*, Paris: OECD.

OECD (2001), 'Fiscal Design Across Levels of Government Year 2000 Surveys, Country Report: Latvia,' May.

Proskurovska, Svetalana (2002), 'Structural and Organizational Reform: The Experience of Latvia,' in *Mastering Decentralization and Public Administration Reforms in Central and Eastern Europe*, Budapest: Local Government and Public Service Reform Initiative.

Vanags, Edvins and Inga Vilka (2000), 'Local Government in Latvia,' in T. Horvath (ed.), *Decentralization: Experiments and Reforms*, Budapest: Local Government and Public Service Reform Intitiative.

PART V

LATIN AMERICA

24 Land taxes in Colombia[1]

Richard M. Bird

In 2000, Colombia had 1098 municipalities. All these municipalities, from the largest (Bogotá, the capital) to the smallest, are in principle fully entitled to administer their own resources and to collect the taxes necessary to the performance of their functions 'within the limits imposed by the Constitution and the law' (Constitution, Art. 287). Moreover, Article 317 of the Constitution provides that only municipalities can levy taxes on property. This provision has, however, been interpreted to apply only to taxes based solely on the existence of land and does not apply to other taxes related to land, such as gains derived from the sale of real estate.

In practice, the taxing powers of local governments depend upon the terms of the laws authorizing each specific tax. As a general rule, the national Congress defines the basic elements of a local tax such as its base and rate. Often, a range of rates is established within which municipalities are free to choose. With respect to fees and special levies (*contribuciones*), however, the rate can be determined directly by a municipality as long as it follows the procedures established by Congress. Bogotá, Colombia's largest city, is in a special position: in effect, it is both a municipality and a department (region) at the same time and hence has a unique tax regime.

Revenues

A recent World Bank report notes that property taxes accounted for 35 percent of Colombian local taxes (Giugale et al., 2003). An earlier report (World Bank, 1996) noted that property taxes accounted in 1994 for 23.5 percent of own-source local revenues in Colombia. The comparable figure for Bogotá, Medellín and Cali, the three largest cities, was 21.9 percent. In smaller municipalities – those with less than 20 000 inhabitants – the property tax was relatively more important (over 30 percent), essentially because local business taxes were less important in less populous areas.[2] The amount collected in valorization levies (see below) in the same year amounted to 11.0 percent of property taxes, with most collections being in the larger cities. Departmental (regional) governments collected about 40 percent as much in valorization as municipal governments. The average effective property tax rate (taxes as a ratio of assessed values) was estimated in this report to be 0.41 percent. A more recent estimate for a sample of municipalities is that the effective rate for 1999 was 0.53

percent (Leibovich and Nuñez, 2002), with the effective rate being highest in the smallest municipalities.

Leibovich and Nuñez (2002) also estimate that property tax collections for Colombia as a whole rose from a level of 0.24 percent of GDP in 1985 to 0.65 percent of GDP in 2000. This astounding performance was clearly attributable in significant part to the performance of Bogotá during the 1990s, as discussed further below, although property tax revenues in real per capita terms rose substantially in municipalities of all sizes during this period, largely because of a relatively good effort at expanding the tax base, despite some difficulties discussed further below.[3] Table 24.1 presents some recent data for Bogotá, showing the prominence of the most important local taxes on land and property. Although Bogotá is unique in receiving revenue from the 'registry tax' (because of its 'dual' status as, in effect, both a department and a municipality), all municipalities can levy the other three taxes shown in this table, each of which is outlined below.

Table 24.1   Revenues from taxes on land and property in Bogotá, 1997–99 (billions of Colombian pesos and as a percentage of local revenue)[4]

	1997	1998	1999
Unified property tax	233.9 (26.1)	277.7 (25.2)	305.8 (25.9)
Urban outlining tax	9.2 (1.0)	9.6 (0.9)	4.7 (0.4)
Registry tax	22.6	21.7	19.5
Contribution for valorization	51.6	33.4	97.8
Total	317.2	342.4	427.8

Sources: Departments of Cadastre and Treasury of Bogotá, Government of Cundinamarca, and DIAN (National Tax Administration).

Urban outlining tax

Decree 1333 of 1986 authorized all local governments to levy an 'urban outlining tax' on the construction of new buildings or the repair of existing buildings. In Bogotá, the urban outlining tax actually combines this tax and a charge for the occupation of public streets and roads. This tax applies to owners who seek licenses for the construction, extension, modification, adaptation or repair of any kind of building, or for the urbanization of land. The tax is calculated at a rate of 2.6 percent on the budgeted costs of the construction or urbanization, as established in accordance with the instructions provided by the planning agency. Although the Bogotá urban outlining tax is self-assessed by the taxpayers, the planning agency can fix the minimum costs per m².

In other municipalities this tax operates differently. Medellín, for instance, imposes a tax on the construction or repair of buildings located in its territory (construction tax, or *impuesto de construcción*), which differs in several ways. The construction tax is based on an official valuation that takes into account the zone in which the property is located as well as its area. There are four zones, with values per m² ranging from 18 000 pesos to 321 000 pesos. The tax rate is 20 percent of the value established. In addition, Medellín imposes a separate charge for the occupation of public streets and roads (in the course of construction) at a fixed amount – a recent example is 13 000 pesos per large vehicle – indexed annually by the CPI.

Since Law 388 of 1997, those seeking a license for the construction or urbanization of a property must pay an additional levy to the *Curadores Urbano*. These are persons designated by the local urban planning entity to monitor compliance with urban planning rules and to issue such licenses. This charge is calculated according to a formula established in the law and is based on the area and location of the property.

Registry tax
To be legal, all land transfers must be registered by the Public Registry Office.[5] A registry tax is calculated on the amount of the transaction[6] at a rate ranging from 0.5 percent to 1 percent, as set by the Departmental Assembly. In Cundinamarca, the rate is 1 percent. The registry tax is assigned to the departments. However, since Bogotá is both the capital district and capital of the Department of Cundinamarca, it is entitled to 30 percent of the revenue collected from the registry tax within its territory.

In addition to the registry tax, taxpayers must pay fees (*derechos notariales*) for registry services, which are considered as public services. The rate of this fee is set annually by the *Superintendencia de Notariado y Registro*. The fee is collected at the same time as the registry tax, but goes to the Superintendencia.

Valorization contribution
Since 1921, Colombian municipalities have been authorized to impose special charges to pay for certain public works. The present 'valorization' system (*Contribución por Valorización por Beneficio Local y General*) was set out in Decree 1604 of 1966 and in the Municipal Code (Decree 1333) of 1986. The central government, the departments (states), and the municipalities can all levy contributions on any benefit or appreciation of property (urban or rural) arising from public works, such as roads.[7] The objective is that those whose properties benefit from such works should help finance the works from which

they benefit. Such contributions may be imposed before, during, or after the construction of public works. The amount to be charged is equal to the cost of the works plus 30 percent, divided among affected properties in proportion to benefit. The law provides for participation of the representatives of the owners of the properties subject to the tax both in establishing the budget and in assessing the contributions.

For example, some of the parameters (*factores de beneficio*) taken into account in Bogotá are the economic use of the property, the social and economic conditions of the owners of the property, the distance of the public work from the place where the property is located, and the area of the property. The law in the case of Bogotá (Decree-Law 868 of 1956) provides that in the case of rural land the factors that must be taken into account for the establishment of the benefit include, among others: (i) the potential agricultural productivity of the property; (ii) its proximity to the places where retail sales take place; and (iii) the distance to communication facilities.

In principle, valorization contributions are imposed only on the owners of those properties that directly benefited from public works (for example, those that are close to them). In 1956, however, the larger municipalities such as Bogotá were authorized to levy a so-called 'Contribution for Appreciation for General Benefit'. This contribution is based on the idea that any public good constructed within the jurisdiction of a municipality benefits all its inhabitants. Thus, such a contribution may be imposed throughout the area in proportion to the estimated benefit to property.

Unified property tax

Law 44 of 1990 created the unified property tax, replacing four previous taxes on land and property: the property tax, the parks and forest tax, the tax on the socioeconomic strata, and the surcharge for the formation of the cadastre. Only major municipalities could levy the parks and forest tax, which in most cases was in effect an additional tax based on the value of the property. Rates could be set freely, but revenues from this tax had to be directed to the construction of new parks, the improvement of existing parks, and housing development for the working class. Municipalities with more than 100 000 inhabitants could levy the tax on socioeconomic strata on owners or tenants of houses classified in the 'medium' or 'high' strata. Rates could be set between 0.15 percent and 0.50 percent of the value of the property. Revenues were again earmarked, in this case to finance works on houses of low socioeconomic strata lacking sewerage services and the acquisition of land for the development of social interest housing. Finally, a surcharge of 10 percent on the amount of property (and registry) taxes was imposed to finance the expenses incurred for the formation of the land registry and the maintenance of cadastral offices.[8]

The tax base
The base of the unified property tax can be either the *avalúo catastral* or the *autoavaluo*, if a municipality has implemented the system of self-assessment.

Cadastral value   The *avalúo catastral* (cadastral value) is an official valuation of the property made by the Cadastral Office. In determining this value, the Cadastral Office must take into consideration the value of the land, the buildings on it, the appreciation of the property because of nearby public improvements, the appreciation of the property because of any nearby spring of water, and any material from a building located in the property that has been demolished or whose demolition is expected. On the other hand, cadastral value explicitly excludes the following: agricultural or industrial machinery located on the property; plantations or the crops grown on the property; use rights over the property, and, importantly, the expected appreciation of the property due to its future use.

The process of incorporating a property into the cadastral register is called *formación catastral*, whereas the process of updating information regarding a property is called *actualización catastral*. Cadastres are supposed to be updated every five years. Between updates, the cadastral value is indexed annually, in accordance with an index established by the national government.[9] This index cannot be higher than that established by the Central Bank as the inflation target for the taxable year. When real asset values fell sharply in Bogotá at the end of the 1990s owing to the general financial and economic crisis, however, there was no provision for downward adjustment, so that taxable values, it has been argued, ended up sharply different from real values (Leibovich and Nuñez, 2002). As mentioned later, Bogotá made an adjustment in 2000 in an attempt to deal with this problem.

The cadastral value can be modified upon request of the owner of the property, at the discretion of the Cadastral Office.

Among the larger municipalities that have adopted a system of officially assessed unified property tax based on cadastral valuations are Medellín, Barranquilla and Cali.[10] The three largest cities in Colombia – Bogotá, Medellín and Cali – have their own Cadastral Departments, as does the Department of Antioquia (in which Medellín is located). Whenever there is no local Cadastral Office, the cadastral register is that maintained by the Agustin Codazzi Geographic Institute (Instituto Geográfico Agustin Codazzi or IGAC), a national agency which is responsible for geographical information on all Colombian territory. In part because of severe budgetary problems, IGAC has fallen well behind in updating cadastral values in much of the country. Although the technical quality of assessments is reportedly good, there appears to be no systematic attempt to revalue. Instead, the IGAC appears to respond largely to financial incentives and to revalue where it is paid to do so, by the municipality, by foreign aid agencies, or whoever. In 2002, for example, only 70 of Colombia's more than 1000 municipalities were revalued. In some 140 municipalities that are not controlled by the government at all (owing to guerrilla activity), there is, unsurprisingly, no effective land survey.

Self-assessment   An interesting feature of the Colombian property tax system is the importance of self-assessment. A self-assessment is a valuation made directly by the owner. In those municipalities that have adopted this system, taxpayers submit a unified property tax return in which they declare the value of property, as well as calculate the amount of the tax due. To support the self-assessment system, Law 44 of 1990 authorized those municipalities that adopted it to establish a minimum presumptive base. This minimum presumptive base is to be determined taking into account the location of the property and some technical parameters that serve to settle the price per m^2 of construction. When a minimum presumptive base is established, the self-assessed value cannot be less than the price determined as the minimum presumptive base times the area of the property. In the case of Bogotá, however, although the city's Tax Code provides for the establishment of such a minimum presumptive base, none has so far been established.

Self-assessed values can be used not only as the tax base of the unified property tax, but also as the basis for the determination of the taxable income or capital gain derived from the disposition of the property (including property acquired by inheritance).[11] This is probably why the self-assessment system was relatively successful initially in the early 1990s and was adopted by a number of larger municipalities, including, notably, Bogotá. More recently, however, some cities, such as Cali, have returned to the cadastral system while Bogotá has modified the system as explained below.

Until 2000, the self-assessed value established by a taxpayer in Bogotá could not be less than the value declared in the preceding year indexed by the percentage set by the Central Bank as the inflation target for the taxable year, or the cadastral value of the preceding year indexed by this percentage. When the cadastral value resulted from either *formación catastral* or *actualización catastral* in the preceding year, the valuation taken into account for unified property tax purposes was that thus established. Taxpayers could declare lower values if they could prove to the satisfaction of the tax administration that the real value of property had decreased.

As mentioned earlier, however, this system ran into problems following a severe recession in the land market in Bogotá in 1998–99. The result was that the tax administration received an overwhelming number of petitions asking for authorizations to declare lower values. Consequently, in 2000 general permission was granted to declare lower values, and in 2001 Law 601 changed the provisions regarding the minimum value to be simply not less than the cadastral value. The city council rejected increases in tax rates several times during this period, so the administration raised cadastral values (up to 70 percent in some cases) in order to increase revenues. Nonetheless, a recent estimate is that, on average, cadastral values are 70 percent of market values in Bogotá, compared to 85 percent in Medellín, traditionally thought to be the city in Colombia with the best property tax administration (Giugale et al., 2003).

Tax rate

Local councils (*Concejos Municipales* or *Distritales*) must set the tax rate of the unified property tax within the limits established by the National Congress. The general rule (Law 44 of 1990) is that councils can establish a progressive rate scale from 0.01 percent to 1.6 percent. In setting rates, councils must take into account the social and economic strata of the property,[12] its use, and the date of the last value revision. In addition, 'popular' (low-cost) housing and small rural property used for agricultural production must be taxed at the lowest rate set. On the other hand, land capable of being urbanized but not yet urbanized – land is considered 'urbanized' when it has access to basic public utilities (such as electricity, gas, water and sewerage) – and land that has been urbanized but as yet has no construction, can be taxed at any rate subject to a maximum of 3.3 percent.

Many municipalities impose different tax rates depending on the use of the property. In Bogotá, for example, the tax administration and the environmental authorities can classify property used for industrial purposes as producing a high, medium or low environmental impact. Until such a classification is made, all industrial properties are deemed to produce a high environmental impact, and since none has been made, all industrial properties in Bogotá are so classified. Similarly, Bogotá's Tax Code provides that commercial property is taxed at different rates, depending upon its effects on urban development. The lowest impact is that produced by so-called 'local' commercial property, with a higher impact being produced by 'metropolitan' commercial property. In Bogotá, the mayor of each small locality forming part of the Capital District – these mayors are appointed by the elected Mayor of Bogotá – can define the property that produces an impact within the locality or within a larger area, which is the zone. One result in Bogotá, as in many other Colombian municipalities, is that the tax rate changes with improvements only when such improvements imply a change in the use of the property.

The result of all this is a very complex rate structure – nowhere more so than in Bogotá. Table 24.2 sets out the general rates of the unified property tax applicable in Bogotá in 2000.

Table 24.2 does not by any means tell the whole story. In addition to the regular system for determining the unified property tax, Bogotá has a

Table 24.2   Bogotá: general property tax system, 2001

Type of property	Rate (%)
● Rural	1.6
● Rural/residential	1.6
● Rural/for institutions, public entertainment, or green zones	0.5
● Rural property for agricultural production	0.5
● Zones that are defined as being near to urban zones ('suburbanas')	1.6
● 'Suburbanas'/residential	1.6
● Urban for residence – Strata 1, 2 and 3	
Up to 70 m² of construction	0.4
More than 70 m² of construction	0.5
● Urban for residence – Stratum 4	
Up to 100 m² of construction	0.6
More than 100 and less than 150 m² of construction	0.6
More than 150 m² of construction	0.7
● Urban for residence – Strata 5 and 6	
Up to 220 m² of construction	0.7
More than 220 and less than 300 m² of construction	0.8
More than 300 m² of construction	0.85
● Industrial	
High environmental impact	1.0
Medium environmental impact	0.9
Low environmental impact	0.85
● Commercial	
Local impact	0.8
Zone impact	0.85
Metropolitan impact	0.95
● Financial institutions	1.5
● State enterprises	0.85
● For a civic/institutional use	
Local impact	0.5
Zone impact	0.6
Metropolitan impact	0.65
Educational institutions	0.5
● Land that is susceptible of being urbanized but is not yet, and land that having been urbanized has no construction yet	
less than 100 m²	1.2
more than 100 m²	3.3

'preferential system' applicable to land used for residential purposes that is classified in the two lowest strata (Strata 1 and 2). Under the preferential system, available at the option of eligible taxpayers, the property tax is set equal to a certain number of MDW (minimum daily wages – *salarios minimos diarios vigentes*, as set annually by the national government), depending on the cadastral value of the property. When no cadastral value has been established, those under the preferential system pay the equivalent of two MDWs. The cadastral value taken into account for the purposes of this system is indexed each year by the percentage settled by the Central Bank as the inflation goal for the taxable year. In addition, the law provides for a discount for early payment.

The ranges established for the preferential system are set out in Table 24.3, and the actual rates applied in 2001 are set out in Table 24.4.

Similarly complex rate structures exist in other large cities. In Medellín, for instance, tax rates are set in accordance with cadastral value, the use of the property, and the incorporation of the property into the cadastre. In addition, all common zones of buildings or condominiums are levied at lower rates than the residential units. As is common, cadastral value is indexed by the percentage settled by the Central Bank as the inflation goal for the taxable year. The tax rates applicable in Medellín for 1998 ranged from 0.2 percent for the 'common zone' for the lowest value class for residential property up to 1.3 percent on the highest-class residential properties not incorporated in the cadastre. The rate was similarly progressive for industrial and commercial property (from 0.5 to 1.4 percent) and rural land (0.0 to 0.6 percent). Property 'susceptible to being urbanized' was taxed at rates up to 3.3 percent. Although the rate structures applied in two other large cities, Cali and

Table 24.3 Bogotá: preferential property tax system, rate ranges

Value (pesos)	Minimum daily wages	
	Rate	Without discount
Up to 3 000 000	0	0
3 000 001–7 000 000	1	2
7 000 001–10 000 000	2	3
10 000 001–15 000 000	3	4
15 000 001–22 000 000	6	8
22 000 001–27 000 000	9	11
27 000 001–40 000 000	12	14
More than 40 000 000	18	20

Table 24.4   Bogotá: preferential property tax system, actual taxes, 2001

Value (pesos)	Taxes imposed	
	With discount	Without discount
Up to 4 200 000	0	0
4 200 001–9 800 000	10 000	19 000
9 800 001–13 900 000	19 000	29 000
13 900 001–20 900 000	29 000	38 000
20 900 001–30 700 000	57 000	76 000
30 700 001–37 700 000	86 000	105 000
37 700 001–55 800 000	114 000	133 000
More than 55 800 000	172 000	191 000

Barranquilla, are less complex, tax rates again vary with the use and the strata of the property. For example, residential property in Cali in 1999 was taxed at rates from 0.4 to 1.4 percent and in Barranquilla (in 2000) from 0.3 to 1 percent. A study of 74 municipalites in 1999 found that the average nominal rate of property tax was 0.81 percent (Leibovich and Nuñez, 2002).

As a final note on rates, Law 44 of 1990 establishes that the unified property tax cannot be higher than double the tax determined for the preceding taxable year. This limit does not apply, however, when the increase of the tax derives from an increase in the value of the property due to improvements, or when the property susceptible of being urbanized is either not yet urbanized or even if urbanized, has no construction on it yet.

Administration of the unified property tax
All activities related to the administration of the unified property tax, including enforcement and collection, are assigned to local governments. To the extent possible, the administrative procedures for the enforcement and collection of the tax are the same as those established in the National Tax Code for the administration of national taxes.

As mentioned earlier, some larger municipalities, like Bogotá, have adopted the system of self-assessment. This has many implications from the administrative point of view, as shown below in the discussion of property tax administration in Bogotá (self-assessment) and Medellín (assessment by tax officials).

Self-assessment in Bogotá   The Tax Administration in Bogotá (*Dirección Distrital de Impuestos*) is organized by tax. The Property Tax Office has three units: one for assessment, one for enforcement, and one for collection. The District Tax Administration administers the unified property tax based on the information provided by the taxpayers themselves and by the District Cadastral Office, and the Public Registry Office.[13] Since 1998, Bogotá's cadastral department has been trying aggressively to incorporate and update the cadastral registry. At present, only 3.4 percent of all land in Bogotá has not been incorporated in the cadastre (with an estimated value of 1.6 billion pesos). The current cadastral registry includes over 1.6 million properties, with an estimated value of 65.6 billion pesos, and 54.8 percent of these values have been updated since 1998.

As noted earlier, the general rule in Bogotá is that taxpayers self-assess their unified property tax. The tax must be paid when the tax return is filed with the banks authorized by the District Tax Administration to collect taxes. The tax is usually due in July, although different deadlines are set for different groups of taxpayers (natural persons and corporations and by TIN, tax identification number). A discount of 15 percent was given to those who paid earlier; this was later reduced to 10 percent. High interest rates are also charged on late payments. Both measures encourage timely payment.

The District Tax Administration has two years to audit the unified property tax returns, and five years to assess the tax of non-filer taxpayers. The first stage is to send letters to the taxpayers inviting them to comply voluntarily. Reportedly, about 15 percent of the tax gap related to the unified property tax is collected at this 'persuasion' step. If taxpayers do not comply voluntarily, the Administration begins the procedures to audit and/or collect the tax. At this collection step, the tax gap is reduced by about 20 percent.

As of 31 October 2001, the accrued liability for the unified property tax in Bogotá (including amounts for prior years) was 84.8 billion pesos, compared to collections of 339.6 billion for the taxable year 2001.

Official assessment in Medellín   In Medellín, Colombia's second-largest city, in which, as mentioned earlier, the property tax is usually considered to be perhaps the best in the country, the unified property tax is assessed by the Cadastral Division of the municipal Treasury Department. This Division both determines the tax base and assesses the tax. Taxpayers can ask the Cadastral Division to correct the assessed value when there has been a change in the use of the property or in its physical characteristics, or an appreciation in the value of the property. Once the tax is calculated, the Cadastral Division sends a bill to the taxpayer. The taxpayer can either pay the tax or file a petition asking for a reconsideration of the determination of the tax. The tax can be paid directly to an office of the Municipal Treasury or to a bank authorized to collect taxes.

Reforms

There have been two major reforms to the taxation of land in Colombia during the past ten years. The first important reform, as already discussed, was the fusion in the unified property tax of four earlier taxes. This reform was introduced to simplify the administration of taxes on land, and to avoid the possibility of taxing the same factors twice (as did the socioeconomic strata tax).

A second reform was the introduction of the self-assessment system. To prevent undervaluation, self-assessed values are not to be less than the indexed value of the previous year or the value obtained by multiplying the area of the property by the value set by the Tax Administration as the minimum presumptive base. Law 14 of 1983 had mandated the update of the cadastral registry by 1989, but this had not been accomplished. The main reason for introducing the self-assessment system was to update the cadastral registry. By asking taxpayers to estimate the value of their property and by allowing them to take this value as a basis for the purposes of income and capital gains tax, it was hoped that the values would be closer to commercial value. At least in the case of Bogotá, this system did result in both an increase in valuations and in local revenues. Law 44 of 1990 again ordered the update of the cadastre registry. So did Law 223 of 1995, which required this update to be completed by 1999. Law 44 of 1990 also changed the range of tax rates, establishing a higher rate at 1.6 percent of the base for land used for purposes different than the simple possession of property, and one of 3.3 percent for property not used for the performance of an economic activity (the *lotes urbanizables no urbanizados* and *lotes urbanizados no edificados*, which are supposedly held solely for speculative purposes).

With the exception of the self-assessment system, the reforms introduced by Law 44 of 1990 were adopted relatively quickly by almost all municipalities. The first municipality to introduce the self-assessment system was Bogotá, in 1994. The shift from one system to another thus did not take place at once, even in Bogotá. Moreover, as the preferential system applicable to residential property discussed earlier suggests, it was not all that radical a shift in any case.

*Impuesto de plusvalía (*land value increment tax*)*

A second major change to land taxation in Colombia, not earlier discussed, was the introduction of the *impuesto a la plusvalía* in Law 388 of 1997 (Jaramillo, 2001). The rationale for this tax was stated as follows (Art. 73):

> The right that public entities have to participate in the appreciation of property, that is the consequence of urban actions related to the use of the soil and the urban space area, increasing the exploitation of the land and generating benefits.

This concept was first introduced in Law 9 of 1989, but this tax did not function well, particularly because no provision was made to coordinate it with related levies such as the valorization contribution discussed earlier. The tax created by Law 388 of 1997 is based on the concept of *plusvalía* established in Article 82 of the Constitution that provides for the participation of public entities in the appreciation of property derived from their performance as urban authorities.

The 'urban actions' to which Law 388 of 1997 refers to are those related to land use plans of public entities, in other words administrative decisions related to the use of the land included in the master plans (*planes de ordenamiento territorial*) that must be established by every municipality. Although local governments, as the public entities in charge of urban development, can introduce specific rules applicable to the land value increment tax within their territory, the concepts of 'change of use,' 'exploitation of the soil,' 'occupation index,' and 'construction index' for the purpose of the tax are regulated by the National Government. In general, the administrative decisions that constitute 'urban actions' for the purposes of this tax are authorizations to change the use of the land for a more profitable one and to increase the levels of exploitation of the soil by permitting larger areas for construction. Among the 'urban actions' (regulated by Decree 1599 of 1998) are:

- changes in classification from rural to urban or suburban;
- changes in the use of the property (by changing the use of all property located in a certain zone of the municipality jurisdiction);
- increases in the level of exploitation by increasing the 'occupation index' (the proportion of land on which construction is allowed) or the 'construction index' (the relation between the area of the construction and the area of the land), or both; and
- the construction of public improvements, contemplated in the master plan, that are not financed by valorization contributions.

The master plan is supposed to specify the areas that benefit from these 'urban actions' that are considered to generate 'surplus value' or land value increments for purposes of this tax.

The owners or occupiers of property are liable for the land value increment tax. The tax base is the amount of the appreciation of land value, as calculated by the difference between the commercial value of the property before the 'urban actions' that affect it and its commercial value after those 'urban actions.' These before-and-after values can be determined either by the IGAC, local cadastral authorities, or private firms registered with associations of real estate agents. 'Commercial value' is defined, conventionally, as 'the most probable price by which the property would be sold in a market in which the seller and the buyer would act freely, knowing the physical and legal conditions that affect the property.' The tax is assessed by local tax authorities based on the valuation made by the entities in charge of establishing the before-and-after commercial value of properties. The tax assessments are to be published in three editions of a popular newspaper within the local jurisdiction and also to be available for viewing in the mayor's office. If taxpayers do not appeal, the tax assessment is registered in the Public Registry Office.

Municipal councils can establish the rate of the tax in the range between 30 and 50 percent of the appreciation of the property. In doing so, they must take into account the economic conditions of the property owners affected.

The appreciation is recognized and the tax becomes due when any of the following events occur:

- The taxpayer asks for a license for the urbanization or the construction of the property.
- There is an effective change in the use of the property.
- There is a transfer of the property.
- The title of the right to construct on the property is sold.

The tax may be paid in cash, or by transferring a portion of the property affected by the appreciation (or another property), or shares or rights to participate in a project for the construction or the urbanization of the appreciated property, or by the construction of public goods or the provision of public utilities.

The land value increment tax is levied notwithstanding the existence of other taxes on the value of property. However, whenever a valorization contribution – which, it will be recalled, differs because it is based on the cost of public works – has been imposed, the factors taken into account in its determination cannot be considered in calculating the appreciation that gives rise to the land value increment tax.

All this sounds interesting, and has aroused considerable attention among those who deal with land taxation around the world. However, it is as yet far from clear that this complex new levy can or will amount to much in Colombian conditions. In Bogotá, for example, the *plusvalía* was rejected by the city council and seems unlikely to be applied in any general form. On the other hand, there continues to be substantial interest in possible application of the general approach – in effect, of sharing benefits between private and public participants in urbanization projects – in particular cases (Maldonado-Copello and Smolka, 2003). Whether Colombian cities can make effective use of this complex new urban land policy instrument remains to be seen, however.

A final note

In contrast to the relative pessimism of this last statement, however, this brief account of some aspects of land taxation in Colombia can be ended on a surprisingly positive note. Quite apart from the dramatic increase in the relative importance of the property tax mentioned at the beginning of this chapter, Bogotá has recently been the scene of one of the most startling phenomena of modern times – indeed, one that is almost inconceivable in the context of Colombia – namely, the voluntary payment of additional taxes by a surprisingly large number of citizens. In 2002, facing a fiscal crisis, the Mayor of Bogotá established a voluntary surtax of 10 percent of property tax that citizens could pay to the municipal government if they wished to do so. Amazingly, about 10 percent of property taxpayers (about 45 000 persons) did pay this surtax, completely voluntarily, over the course of the next few months. As one who did so said (in a private conversation), 'For the last ten years, this city has been run really well, under three different mayors. I want to keep it that way.' Few local governments in few countries have ever received such a vote of confidence.

Notes

1. A draft of much of the material in this chapter was prepared by Natalia Aristizabal, Contraloria General de la Nacion, Bogotá, while she was at Harvard Law School. We are also grateful to Jose Leibovich, Olga Lucia Acosta and Juan Gonzalo Zapata for useful comments and material.
2. This finding is confirmed in a more recent report (Zapata and Chaparro, 2003).
3. See also Zapata and Chaparro (2002). Zapata and Chaparro (2002a) analyse the case of Bogotá in more detail.
4. Only the percentage shares for the first two taxes are shown, because (not all) the revenues from the last two flow to the local budget, as discussed later in the text.
5. This Office is distinct from the Cadastral Office and has a different land registry. It is supposed to inform the latter of any changes in property title.
6. This amount cannot be less than any of the following amounts: the valuation made by the Cadastral Office, the self-valuation made by the taxpayer for property tax purposes, the value of the sale, or the value of the adjudication, depending on the case.
7. That is, contributions can be national, departmental, or local, depending upon which actually carries out the public works.
8. See World Bank (1989) for fuller discussion of the pre-1990 system. Ahmad et al. (1995) outlines the post-1990 system.
9. This index cannot be less than 70 percent or more than 100 percent of the change in CPI from 1 September of the previous year to 1 September of the present year. In practice, however, an earlier similar proviso (in Law 14 of 1983) was not followed and the index applied throughout the 1980s was consistently lower than that specified by law (World Bank, 1989).
10. Cali adopted the self-assessment system in 1995 but switched back to the cadastral system in 1998.
11. The self-assessed value can be used for income tax and capital gains tax purposes if the self-assessed value was reported in the income tax return before the disposition of the property.
12. The law provides for six social and economic strata, with number one as the lowest and six as highest.

13.   Since to be complete and enforceable all transactions regarding the disposition of property or any right over a land must be registered with this office, it is common for the Registry Office to have more updated and accurate information than the Cadastral Office.

References

Ahmad, Ehtisham et al. (1995), *Colombia: Reforming Territorial Taxation and Transfers*, Washington: International Monetary Fund.

Guigale, Marcelo M., Olivier Lafourcade and Connie Luft (eds) (2003), *Colombia: The Economic Foundation of Peace*, Washington: World Bank.

Jaramillo, Samuel (2001), 'La experiencia colombiana: la contribución de valorización y la participación en plusvalías,' Cambridge MA: Lincoln Institute of Land Policy.

Leibovich, Jose and Jairo Nuñez (2002), 'Land Taxation in Colombia,' Bogotá, October.

Maldonado-Copello, Maria Mercedes and Martim O. Smolka (2003), 'Using Value Capture to Benefit the Poor: The Usme Project in Colombia,' *Land Lines* (Lincoln Institute of Land Policy), July, pp. 15–17.

World Bank (1989), *Colombia: Decentralizing Revenues and the Provision of Services*, Report No. 7870-CO, October.

World Bank (1996), *Colombia: Reforming the Decentralization Law*, Report No. 15298, April.

Zapata, Juan Gonzalo G. and Juan Camilo Chaparro C. (2002), 'Estructura del financiamiento y del gasto de los municipios con menos de 30.000 habitantes. Primer informe,' Bogotá, July.

Zapata, Juan Gonzalo G. and Juan Camilo Chaparro C. (2002a), 'Sostenabilidad de las finanzas públicas de Bogotá 1990–2009,' *Coyuntura Económicas*, vol. 32 (enero–junio), 71– 101.

Zapata, Juan Gonzalo G. and Juan Camilo Chaparro C. (2003), 'The Income and Spending Structure and Fiscal Dependency of Municipalities with Less Than 30,000 Inhabitants,' Bogotá, January.

25 Taxes on land and property in Argentina

Ernesto Rezk

Argentina is a three-tiered federation: in addition to the national government, there are 23 provinces plus the autonomous city of Buenos Aires and 1175 municipalities.[1] Each layer of government is constitutionally endowed with ample fiscal powers and spending functions, but property and land taxes are basically at the subnational level.

Property tax revenues are roughly $1.1 billion annually, $0.66 billion at the provincial and $0.44 billion at the municipal level respectively. In percentage terms, this annual revenue represents 1.1 percent of GDP (0.65 percent levied by provinces and 0.45 percent by municipalities). Property and land taxes yield a by no means negligible 5 percent of all tax revenues in Argentina.

As shown in Table 25.1, in terms of provincial own fiscal resources, property and land taxes are second only to the turnover tax, contributing in the period 16 percent of consolidated provincial fiscal revenues compared to almost 57 percent contributed by the latter. The second and third columns of the table show that the collection of the tax is concentrated in the main provinces (City of Buenos Aires, Buenos Aires, Córdoba, Mendoza and Santa Fé), which together account for almost 90 percent of the total yield. At the municipal level, this tax is by far the most important fiscal resource, amounting to 35 percent of municipal fiscal revenues.

As mentioned above, constitutional arrangements in Argentina permit overlapping of fiscal sources, since the use of one tax or a tax base by one government level does not preclude its use by others. Both provinces and municipalities use the land tax, and each has full power to determine and assess the tax base, to set the rates, and to administer the tax. In addition, the tax on personal goods levied by the national government also adds to the taxation of property since land and houses enter the tax base together with all other assets of any kind. Collection of this tax amounts to US$200 million annually and represents around 0.20 percent of GDP.

Provincial property taxes normally impact on urban properties (located in cities, towns or villages) as well as on rural land, or land for agricultural purposes, whereas only buildings or vacant lots situated within the boundaries of a municipality are reached by local taxes. As shown in the table, several provinces gave up to their municipalities the collection of the tax on urban property and retained only rural land taxation. In the case of urban property, when there exists tax overlapping, provinces and municipalities

Table 25.1   Argentina: provincial own fiscal revenues, 1995–2002

Provinces	Province share in all provinces fiscal resources	Turnover tax share	Property and land tax share	Car tax share	Others (stamp duties 6.6%)
City of Buenos Aires	0.234	0.670	0.184	0.092	0.054
Buenos Aires	0.370	0.480	0.144	0.091	0.285
Catamarca	0.003	0.681	0.103	0.090	0.126
Chaco	0.009	0.782	0.025[b]	[a]	0.193
Chubut	0.010	0.7939	0.0001[b]	[a]	0.206
Córdoba	0.106	0.549	0.258	[a]	0.193
Corrientes	0.006	0.723	0.139	[a]	0.138
Entre Ríos	0.034	0.510	0.240	0.100	0.150
Formosa	0.002	0.770	0.038[b]	[a]	0.192
Jujuy	0.005	0.660	0.135	[a]	0.205
La Pampa	0.009	0.463	0.176	0.148	0.213
La Rioja	0.002	0.625	0.096	0.145	0.135
Mendoza	0.029	0.564	0.121	0.125	0.190
Misiones	0.014	0.649	0.119	0.022	0.210
Neuquén	0.014	0.766	0.080	[a]	0.154
Rio Negro	0.012	0.568	0.162	0.107	0.163
Salta	0.009	0.752	0.051	[a]	0.197
San Juan	0.005	0.595	0.084	0.102	0.219
San Luis	0.009	0.604	0.157	0.064	0.175
Santa Cruz	0.004	0.827	[b]	[a]	0.173
Santa Fé	0.090	0.586	0.230	0.009	0.175
Santiago del Estero	0.006	0.607	0.102	0.068	0.223
Tucumán	0.014	0.577	0.118	0.088	0.217
Tierra del Fuego	0.004	0.948	0.002[b]	[a]	0.050
All provinces, average		0.568	0.163	0.074	0.195

Notes:
[a]   Levied by municipalities.
[b]   Levied by municipalities; provinces collect only the tax on rural land.

Source: Informe Económico Regional, Secretaría de Programación Económica y Regional, Buenos Aires, Argentina.

generally follow similar land and building assessment procedures in order to determine the tax base.

To start with, every newly built property, or building improvement, must be declared at the Cadastral Office,[2] which, on the basis of the value of the land, year, area and quality of the construction, produces the fiscal valuation. This original assessment is in turn subject to periodical adjustment in order that fiscal valuations keep pace with the evolution of market values. Experience suggests that in general the tax base is 60–70 percent of market value. To obtain the tax base, provincial and municipal tax offices in turn adjust the fiscal valuation of houses with tax coefficients annually set by Legislatures and Municipal Councils respectively.[3] Although larger municipalities generally have their own cadastral and tax offices, they usually cooperate with the corresponding provincial offices. Smaller local governments, that cannot afford to have their own cadastral departments, usually receive support from provincial governments or resort to simpler methods for fiscally valuing properties, as for instance a local assessment procedure (*avalúo*).[4]

Although the reassesssment process is supposed to be continuous, regularity is not always the rule and the performance of subnational governments varies. In some cases, provinces and municipalities are keener to protect tax bases by permanently enhancing ways of capturing building improvements and of securing information on new constructions, whereas in others fiscal valuations lag well behind market values due to the lack of effective managerial and administrative controls upon improvements or new construction.[5] It is also worth noting that, even when the same properties are subject to provincial and municipal taxation, the fiscal performance of local governments normally ranks higher than that of provinces.

Determination of tax base for the provincial tax on rural land is carried out on the basis of the location, area, ground fertility, and alternative economic uses, with the assessment being in charge of technical bodies called 'juries' made up of representatives of the public and the private sector.

Both provinces and municipalities have formal appeal processes. As the valuation of properties assumes existing records on land and built areas, as well as data on the quality and area of the construction, the year and area of improvements, and the per m^2 market value of real estates, owners have the right to lodge complaints (*recursos de queja*) against determined fiscal valuations with the Cadastral Office, based on allegedly mistaken assigned category or wrong information used in assessing properties.[6] Taxpayers often consult this information, especially with respect to the built area. In the case of rural land an additional instance is open to owners through the plea for the unimprovement acknowledgement (*reconocimiento de la desmejora*), whereby a reduction of the tax base is granted on the basis of the proven damage caused by natural phenomena (floods, droughts, fires and so on) to agricultural lands' productive capacity.

Due to the federal institutional set-up and the constitutional acknowledgement of local governments' autonomy, provinces and municipalities are empowered to enact taxes, tax bases and tax rates, through provincial legislatures and municipal councils respectively. In practice, tax rates fall within a wide range reaching in some cases 1.7 percent, although modal values are between 1 percent and 1.2 percent for provincial taxes on urban property, whereas most municipal tax rates fall within the interval 0.7–1 percent. A feature worth noting is that while many subnational governments apply a uniform tax rate, others have a progressive system whereby the tax base is split up and its components successively reached by a set of graduated tax rates.[7] Likewise, many subnational governments tend to discourage the prolonged existence of vacant lots either by increasing the uniform tax rate or by extending the progressive system to which urban properties are subject.[8]

Owing to the fact that the assesssment of land and buildings by provincial and municipal Cadaster Offices is aimed at getting the property's fiscal valuation and the latter, once adjusted by the corresponding annual tax coefficients set by the legislature or local council, becomes the property's unique tax base, there are not separate tax rates for land, building or improvements.

The tax rate scheme applied to rural and agricultural land differs in that provincial governments usually resort to personal progressive mechanisms; that is, rural properties are not only normally subject to a uniform tax rate,[9] but in addition the sum of all rural estates' tax bases from the same owner – above an annually set threshold – are subject to graduated additional tax rates ranging between 1 and 9 mills.

The dual operating framework for property taxes in Argentina, under which the identification of sites and ownership, the determination of the fiscal valuation and through it of the tax base, rests in the hands of the cadastral departments, whereas the billing and collection of the tax is the responsibility of tax administration departments, makes the system highly dependent upon the quality of registration, in terms of the completeness, adequacy and availability of up-to-date building information, as well as on the managerial capability of the departments in charge of levying the tax. Experiences differ widely among subnational governments as some provinces and municipalities are firmly committed to enlarging their tax bases (for example through aerial surveys) or to making more efficient and effective their tax administration, while others are neglecting the technical aspects of the cadaster or not directing enough effort or resources to proper collection enforcement, not to mention the opposition of many governors and mayors, on political grounds, to raising tax bases in line with market values.

In order to measure the performance of property taxes in Argentina, taxpayers' degree of compliance rather than evasion is the aspect to be looked at, in relation to a tax whose tax base is by and large objectively determined and the subject to be billed (the property owner) perfectly identified. In this connection, allowing for exceptional cases of almost perfect tax compliance or very low tax compliance, in the latter case sometimes due to natural disasters mainly affecting rural lands, diverse estimates indicate that 20–25 percent of taxpayers fail to pay their property tax bills. Among the reasons explaining this important resource loss for subnational governments, the critical economic situation has come to the forefront as many house-owners facing economic strains decide to postpone the payment of the tax (instead of postponing consumption), hoping that tax arrears will be forgiven in the future. In doing so, taxpayers have behaved rationally as provinces and municipalities have permanently favoured bad tax compliers, and encouraged moral hazard situations, by extending the payment period for tax arrears and reducing applicable interest rates.

Lack of know-how, insufficient computational support and scarce managerial experience in many tax departments, particularly in municipalities, also help explain poor compliance performance. Although provinces and municipalities bill their taxpayers once a year, or give them the possibility of monthly, bimonthly or quarterly payments, the administrative and legal machinery aimed at ensuring higher tax compliance is still cumbersome and ineffective in many cases, thus jeopardizing efforts to build 'fiscal conscience' among taxpayers.

In addition to the property taxes, provinces and municipalities may also finance certain public works by *contribuciones de mejoras* (betterment taxes) when those works raise land values. As a rule, the governments identify certain categories of beneficiaries and share part of the cost of construction among them in proportion to estimated benefit.

Finally, a national tax is imposed on land transfers at a rate of 1.5 percent of sales price. This tax is payable only by individuals, not legal entities, and is aimed at capturing capital gains. If the seller is a firm or corporation, the sales price is added to gross receipts for purposes of calculating income and corporation taxes.

Notes

1. Over 2000 if smaller local units called *comunes* are accounted for.
2. The provincial and municipal cadastral offices, also known as Property Survey Rating Departments, are in charge of registering the quantity, value and ownership of real estate.
3. Every province enacts its own cadastral law establishing adjustment coefficients. In general, fiscal valuations are adjusted annually.
4. Smaller municipalities directly relate the tax to the lineal metres of real estate frontage, the rationale being that the more metres the property front has, the more municipal services it receives.
5. It is not difficult to find, even in large cities, that luxurious estates remain on the roll for years as 'vacant lots'.
6. It goes without saying that owners accompany the complaint with data, records and any other valuable information supporting their claim.
7. Córdoba uses this progressive scheme whereby the tax base is subject to tax rates ranging from 1.3 percent to 1.7 percent, although the provincial government has currently granted a reduction of 30 percent applicable to all tax rates.
8. Referring again to Córdoba, in the case of vacant lots, tax rates' minima and maxima values are 2 percent and 2.40 percent, respectively,
9. In Córdoba 1.2 percent (actually 0.84 percent due to the temporary 30 percent reduction).

26 Property tax in Chile

Ignacio Irarrazaval

Chile is a unitary country divided into 13 regions, 51 provinces and 341 communes. In each region, the central government appoints an 'Intendente' who is the President's representative for the region and coordinates all the ministerial branches at the regional level. Each ministry, such as education, has its Ministerial Secretariat at the regional level. Additionally, the Intendente is accountable to a regional council of 10 to 18 people appointed indirectly from municipal councilors. The main function of this council is to allocate the national intergovernmental transfers for investment within the region.

At the provincial level, there is a governor who is also appointed by the central government with the principal task of administering public order. The commune territory is administered by the municipality, which is headed by an 'Alcalde'. Both alcaldes and municipal councilors are elected by universal vote.

Chile has a very strong centralized tradition inherited from the Spanish colonial era. In the last two decades however, successive governments have instituted a variety of decentralization initiatives. One result is that today 50 percent of total public investment is decided at the regional level.

The property tax (*impuesto territorial* or *contribución a las bienes raíces*) is a national tax in Chile. It is assessed and administered by the national government. Although all the revenue from the tax goes to municipalities, it is important to note that only 40 percent of the revenues collected from the tax goes to (remains) in the municipality where the property is located. The remaining 60 percent is directed to the Municipal Common Fund, a national revenue-sharing system that is distributed according to a socioeconomic formula. Industrial and commercial taxes and vehicle licenses also contribute to the Municipal Common Fund.

As shown in Table 26.1, property taxes (including the portion redistributed through the Municipal Common Fund) account for about 35 percent of municipal revenue (excluding conditional transfers) in Chile, although only about 0.7 percent of GDP. These figures have not changed much over time: from 1980 to 1990, for example, the GDP share varied from 0.6 percent to 0.9 percent and the share of total revenue (not just municipal revenue) from 2.5 percent to 4.0 percent.[1]

Table 26.1 Chile: municipal own revenue, 1990–99 (millions of US$, year 2000)

Year	1990	1991	1992	1993	1994	1995	1996	1997	1998	1999
Total revenue	564.2	665.8	808.9	876.4	928.8	1054.0	1136.4	1272.3	1329.6	1419.0
Land taxes	212.9	269.1	303.8	329.4	6.0	352.8	402.2	443.4	468.8	498.2
Land tax/tot. mun. rev. %	37.7	40.4	37.6	37.6	0.6	33.5	35.4	34.8	35.3	35.1
Land tax/GNP %	0.5	0.6	0.7	0.7	0.6	0.6	0.7	0.7	0.7	0.8

Notes:
Exchange rate (considering average 'observed price' of the US$ for the year 2000): US$1 = $572.68
* Excludes central government transfers to finance education and primary health care.

Source: Estadísticas de las Finanzas Públicas 1991–2000
Dirección de Presupuestos – Ministerio de Hacienda
www.dipres.cl

Tax base

The property tax in Chile is regulated by Law 17,235 of 1969, as modified. It is levied directly on the property, regardless of ownership or occupancy. There are two distinct tax bases – agricultural land and non-agricultural land.

Agricultural land (first series)

Agricultural land comprises all plots that are used mainly for agricultural or forestry. Its value for tax purposes (fiscal value) is based on the value of land and the value of improvements above US$8271.[2] In assessing the value of agricultural plots, the Internal Tax Service (*Servicio de Impuestos Internos*, SII) considers the following elements:

- Tables that classify the land according to its actual use. These tables distinguish classes I to IV with irrigation and I to VIII with no irrigation. The unitary values for each class of soil are published in the Official Registry (*Diario Oficial*).
- Maps and tables of location that consider the type of roads and distances from services.
- Table of values that combine the two previous elements.

Non-agricultural land (second series)

The non-agricultural tax base, which includes both land and improvements, is much more important than the agricultural land tax base in Chile. In 1990, for example, the 2.2 million non-agricultural properties (out of a total of 2.7 million) accounted for 83 percent of all properties and 77 percent of property tax liabilities.[3]

- For each municipality the SII elaborates maps of land values, showing the value of land according to location and the surplus value (*plusvalía*), according to the use made of the land. The fiscal value of land is obtained by multiplying the area of the land by the unit cost of a square meter. The unit value depends on the block (*manzana*) in which the plot is located.
- Constructions are valued in accordance with the structural material, design quality and finishing details. These parameters are combined in special tables to obtain the value of construction per square meter. These tables are published in the Official Registry. A special coefficient is applied to the unit value per square meter according to the type of municipality. A depreciation factor considering the age of the building is also taken into account, with the limit that cumulative depreciation cannot exceed 25 percent of a building's fiscal value.

The law mandates that the period between two consecutive assessments should not be longer than five years or shorter than three years. However, it is common to find that, using presidential power, assessments have been postponed. The last general reassessment was in January 2000, although municipalities were given some freedom with respect to when they introduced the new values. Since the 2000 reassessment, over 200 of Chile's 345 municipalities have updated their cadastres.

Between reassessments the value of land may vary according to physical changes that are registered in the local municipality. In effect, this is a system of self-declaration, subject to verification by the government. Notaries have to make periodic reports to SII for income tax control purposes, and this information is of course also available for property tax purposes. The SII annually conducts some 400 000 alterations of the cadastre based on new properties, property improvements, division of properties, changes of owners or changes of use. In addition, values are updated every six months in accordance with changes in the consumer price index.

The national tax administration (SII) is responsible for assessment since the tax is a national tax. Since all revenues are earmarked for local governments, however, many municipalities are keen to complement the SII teams with local government officials. Over 400 such officials have been trained (by SII) for this task.

A 1998 study reported that fiscal values on average were about 80 percent of market value.[4] An earlier study in 1994 put the assessment value/market value ratio lower, at 25 percent for agricultural properties and 45 percent for other properties.[5] Even after the 2000 reassessment, it is generally thought that the assessment of property remains below market values.

Tax rates
In the case of agricultural land the general tax rate is 2 percent. For non-agricultural property there are two tax rates: 2 percent for residences assessed at less than US$54 962, and for others, 1.4 percent plus a national surcharge of 0.025 percent earmarked to finance firemen. Since tax rates are set nationally, local governments have no autonomy in this respect.

In those municipalities that have introduced the new (2000) reassessment, properties with an assessed value of less than US$14 315 are exempted from property tax. In the case of agricultural properties, land with a value of less than US$2656 is exempt, but only if the value of improvements is less than US$7696. In addition, as a general rule government properties as well as those used for education, sports, religion and local neighborhood associations are exempted. Charitable foundations and most non-profit organizations are exempted from 50–75 percent of the tax. Agricultural properties with an approved forest management plan are exempt. In total, over two-thirds of properties registered in the fiscal cadastre are exempted from the tax.

Tax administration

The property tax is administered throughout Chile by the national tax administration. The actual collection of the tax, however, is the responsibility of the Treasury (*Tesorería General de la República*). The tax is billed in four installments and may be paid at most commercial banks. The bill contains the identification of the property, and the identification of the owner. The property identification number (*Rol de avalúo*), contains the number of the block (*manzana*) where the property is located and the number of the property. The bills are sent to the property unless another address is required. In the case of agricultural properties or empty plots the bills are sent to municipalities. In this connection, it is interesting to note that the failure to receive a bill is no reason for non-payment, since bills can be obtained in any office of the SII or over the internet.

There are a number of procedures for complaints against assessments or administrative errors. Valuations can be appealed to the regional director of SII, and further objections can be taken to the Special Appeals Court on Property Valuation, and to the Supreme Court. In 1990, only 16 000 appeals were filed (1.3 percent of declarations).[6]

Although current information about arrears could not be obtained, the collection rate in 1991 was reportedly 96 percent, owing in part to a 1990 amnesty. The collection rate in the year before the amnesty was only 71 percent.[7] Delinquency notices are sent out within three months of the due date, then judicial collection notices one month later. If delinquency is not cleared, the Treasury can attach, seize and auction property to settle tax liabilities. There are frequent notices in local papers of auctions of property to pay property taxes.

A final note

The present property tax is the result of a sustained reform effort for a period of several decades. Once the property tax law was established in 1969, many further statutory and administrative reforms took place up to 1987, when a mandatory ten-year revaluation of non-agricultural property was launched. Although this effort to update values in the face of dramatic changes was not fully successful, there is little doubt that, as one observer said, Chile has a 'relatively efficient and equitable property tax system.'[8] This state of affairs was not cheap to achieve. In 1985, for example, the property tax was estimated to be the most expensive tax administered by SII, accounting for only 3.5 percent of revenue but 20 percent of field personnel and 40 percent of computer programming maintenance and operations. Another estimate for

1991 put the cost of property tax administration at 2.2 percent per dollar of tax revenue.

Notes

1. Reportedly, property taxes in this period accounted for close to half of own-source munici-pal revenue, and over 70 percent in smaller municipalities (Rosengard, 1998, pp. 102–3).
2. Figures are in 2001 US$, using the exchange rate of 1US$ = Chilean pesos 656.2.
3. However, there were very extensive exemptions, so that fewer than a million properties were taxed in that year (158 000 agricultural properties – 35 percent of the total – and 749 000 non-agricultural properties – 33 percent of the total). See Rosengard (1998), p. 104.
4. Rosengard (1998), p. 87, n. 6.
5. Youngman and Malme (1994), p. 106.
6. Rosengard (1998), p. 104.
7. Youngman and Malme (1994), p. 112.
8. Rosengard (1998), p. 85. This paragraph is based largely on this book and on the account of Chile in Youngman and Malme (1994).

References

Rosengard, J.K. (1998), *Property Tax Reform in Developing Countries*, Boston: Kluwer.
Youngman, J.M. and J.H. Malme (1994), *An International Survey of Taxes on Land and Buildings*, Deventer: Kluwer.

27 Property taxes in Mexico[1]

Richard M. Bird

Mexico is a federal country, with 31 states and a federal district (Mexico City). It also has 2430 local governments. Since a constitutional reform in 1983, the property tax has been a local tax. At present, the property tax (*predial*), is the single most important source of own-tax revenue for local governments. The base and rate of this tax are generally set by the state, not by the local government, however.[2] There are wide variations from state to state in the importance of this tax. Variations within states are equally great, with many rural areas not even collecting the tax.

For Mexico as a whole in 2000, the property tax accounted for 5.6 percent of total revenues and for 58.7 percent of municipal taxes (Chavez-Presa, 2002). Local governments in some states, such as Nuevo León, financed about 25 percent of their expenditure with their own taxes but in other states, such as Chiapas, the figure was 5 percent or less (Giugale and Webb, 2000).[3] As a percentage of GDP, property tax collections in 2000 were 0.21 percent, with different states ranging from 0.06 to 0.28 percent, and the federal district reaching a high of 0.44 percent. In 1999, all municipal taxes (excluding the federal district) amounted to only 0.14 percent of GDP and property taxes accounted for 64 percent of this amount (or 0.09 percent of GDP) (Mayer-Serna, 2001).[4]

Unfortunately, there is no centralized source of information in Mexico on local finance, so we are only able to present here some scattered and not necessarily representative data. Table 27.1 does show, as mentioned earlier, that variations within states are important. Reportedly, smaller municipalities are generally more dependent on property tax revenues, at least when they are urbanized to some extent. The relative importance of the different taxes shown in Table 27.1 may be compared with some aggregate data which indicate that in 1997, when total property taxes amounted to 9 billion pesos (in 1999 pesos), or 75.6 percent of total land taxes, compared to 68.4 percent for the three municipalities shown in Table 27.1. The land transfer tax in the same year yielded about 1.3 billion pesos (10.9 percent), and development charges only about 0.6 billion pesos (5.1 percent).[5]

Tax base

The tax base for land and property is the assessed value determined in different ways in different states by the State Land Registry and the local

*Table 27.1   Mexico: taxes on property, selected municipalities, 2001 (as %
of local revenue)*

	San Nicolas, N.L.*	San Pedro, N.L.**	Monterrey, N.L. ***	Average of the three
Property tax	21.2	28.6	17.8	22.5
Land transfer tax	3.3	11.2	4.6	6.4
Development charges	1.7	1.2		0.9
Total 'land' taxes	26.2	50.0	22.4	32.9

Notes:
  * San Nicolas de los Garzas, Nuevo León, first two quarters of 2001.
 ** San Pedro Garza Garcia, Nuevo León, first three quarters of 2001.
*** Monterrey, Nuevo León, first two quarters of 2001.

Sources: From information available on municipal web sites (sanicolas.gob.mx, sanpedro.gob.
mx, monterrey.gob.mx).

Table 27.2   Administration of property tax in Mexico (% of total)

Administrative function	State	Municipality	Both	Decentralized entity
Taxpayer registry	62	29	3	6
Tax collection	10	90	0	0
Tax control	49	45	6	0
Oversight	47	48	5	0
Billing	43	56	1	0
Cadastral registry and update	64	13	22	1
Formation of cadastral value tables	65	16	13	6
Assessment	62	17	16	5

Source: Calculated by Uri Raich from information in Zarzosa-Escobedo (2000).

treasury department, which are jointly responsible for an annual assessment.
As shown in Table 27.2, in almost two-thirds of the states, assessment is the
responsibility of a state agency, the name of which varies from state to state
(Zarzosa-Escobedo, 2000). The assessed value of the land is usually less than
the market value. A 1997 study reported that in 1985 assessed values were on
average less than one-fifth of market values, although by 1995 they had risen
to about 50 percent of market values.[6] Although the 1999 constitutional

reform required the state legislatures (together with municipalities) to update the value of land – not buildings – to market values, on average the estimated relation of assessed (cadastral) to market values was only 43 percent, with state ratios varying between 8 percent and 90 percent (Zarzosa-Escobedo, 2000).

Cadastres are based in part on a national cartographic study provided by the federal government (*Instituto Nacional de Estadística, Geografía e Informática Estadistica, INEGI*) in coordination with state and local governments. For rural and agricultural lands, land use determines the assessed value, subject to the constraints established by state and municipal law. For example, if land is given by the government to peasants in some states it is not taxed at all and in others they will pay a fixed amount. Buildings are assessed on the basis of unit values of construction.

Exemptions vary from state to state but generally include properties owned by all levels of government, although the 1999 constitutional reform abolished the previous exemption of the property of state-owned enterprises (*paraestatales*). States also offer lower rates to properties dedicated to education and activities of public benefit as well as to those occupied by handicapped and senior citizens.[7]

Assessed values are indexed annually by the consumer price index. In addition, if a taxpayer wishes to update his property value he can do so on transfer by stating the value in the *escritura* (public document that transfers property). Owners of commercial and industrial activities are more likely to wish, for various purposes (for example for use as collateral), to declare market values than are residential owners. Public notaries are required by law to inform the Land and Property Register office about all transfers of property; notaries are the primary source of ownership information.

Tax rate

The tax rate varies from state to state and from one local government to another. It is seldom very high, and most taxpayers pay minimal amounts. In the state of Puebla, for example, a rate of 2 mills (0.2 percent) is applied to the assessed value of land and improvements, with the same rate applied in rural and urban areas. The rate is established by each state legislature. The tax rates in the federal district (in 1999) varied from 0.131 percent to 0.647 percent of cadastral value, with rural land used for agricultural purposes normally subject to 50 percent of these rates. On the other hand, the tax on unimproved land (with buildings covering less than 10 percent of the total area) is increased by a 100 percent surcharge (IBFD, 1999). More generally, rates in the various states appear to vary from 0.01 to 0.30 percent, depending largely upon the location and use of the property (Perlo-Cohen and Zamorano-Ruiz, 1999). Zarzosa-Escobedo (2000) indicates that the tax rate on urban land varies between 1.2 and 20 mills, with the rates being generally highest in the states with weak and out-of-date tax bases. Twenty-one of the 31 states apply uniform rates; the other ten have progressive rates.

Tax administration

While, as Table 27.2 shows, there is considerable variation in administration from state to state, in many cases the state government annually provides tax bills to the local governments, which in turn distribute them to taxpayers. Payment can be made to the local treasury or, as the case may be, to a bank authorized for the purpose. Local treasury offices are often responsible for tax collection, although local governments can contract with the state government to look after tax collection. Although collections are supposed to be reported to the state ministry of finance, the local government generally keeps the money it collects and is responsible for enforcement.

If a taxpayer wishes to challenge the official assessment, he may appeal to the fiscal authority, which then has four months to respond. If it denies the petition, the taxpayer may then appeal to the judicial branch, providing he pays the disputed amount first. Court procedures take up to two years. In reality, however, few appeals are launched since the tax amounts are generally so small.

Record-keeping is usually manual at the local level. Only the larger local governments have the capacity to use modern information technology. One result of the lack of uniformity, consensus, cooperation and coordination in the sharing and collection of information is the lack of information on arrears.

Other taxes

In addition to the property tax, land transfer taxes, levied as a percentage of transaction value, are a source of local revenue. The rate of this tax is established by the states. Before being turned over to the states in 1995, the federal tax was levied at 2 percent, reduced for land held longer.[8] Local governments administer the land transfer tax in 73 percent of municipalities. Except for a very few municipalities that do not impose this tax, the state administers it in the remaining cases. Finally, development charges (*Construcción y Urbanizaciones* and *Nuevos Fraccionamientos*) may be levied. These charges are generally either fixed amounts or an *ad valorem* levy based on the zone where the land is located or the final use of the land. Again, in most cases (86 percent) charges are imposed by the local rather than the state government, although almost 8 percent (185) of municipalities do not impose such charges at all.

Although betterment levies may be imposed on persons who benefit from public works, with the revenue going to the relevant executing agency, for example for hydraulic works, the National Water Commission (IBFD, 1999), 61 percent of municipalities do not impose such levies. Finally, there is the *impuesto de plusvalía*, a tax on value increments attributable to public works or for other reasons. Only seven states appear to have such a tax, and in none of them has it amounted to much owing to serious implementation problems.

An interesting experiment
As noted above, property taxation in Mexico can vary substantially from state to state. Some information from three jurisdictions – the federal district, Nueva León, and Puebla – was reported above and in Table 27.1. This note adds some additional information on the city of Mexicali, located on the US border in the state of Baja California Norte (Perlo-Cohen and Zamorano-Ruiz, 1999).

Until 1989, Mexicali, like the rest of Mexico, taxed both land and buildings at rates from 0.85 percent for housing to 1.05 percent for non-residential uses. In addition, vacant lots were subject to a rate of 3.0 percent. The tax was based on valuations provided by the state, based on a 1957 valuation. In 1987, the municipality itself undertook a general revaluation. More importantly, in 1989 a dynamic new mayor introduced a new tax system under which only land would be taxed. The new values were to be established by a municipal valuation commission, which included private representatives, utilizing (in effect) a model of land rent gradients (that is, with unit values decreasing with distance from specified high-value locations). At the end of 1989 the proposed new system was approved by the state legislature, although only with lower rates of 0.6 percent on residential land and 0.8 percent on non-residential land.

The cadastre in Mexicali was by no means up to date in 1989, with only 58 percent of properties being registered, and many other changes and improvements in tax administration were also needed. Nonetheless, the reform was implemented in 1990, and collections from the property tax increased substantially. Other taxes based on land, such as the land transfer tax, also showed a significant increase. The assessment/market value ratio rose from an estimated 10 percent to 60 percent and a substantial number of new properties were incorporated in the tax roll (a 13 percent increase in one year). These changes, perhaps because of the charisma of the mayor and his appealing programs, were generally accepted by the population.

Following this initial, and striking, success, Mexicali continued to develop its system over the next decade, with varying emphasis and aims, as different municipal governments came and went every three years. The cadastre was not kept as up to date as it should have been: in 1996, a study found many errors and deficiencies in the register – for instance, 22 percent of lots were located incorrectly. Nonetheless, average property tax collections in the city continued to outstrip both those in the state and in the country as a whole. In 1989, property taxes provided 19.6 percent of municipal own revenues; in 1990, this share leaped to 33.5 percent, and in 1998, the corresponding figure was still 28 percent. Mexicali's share of total property tax collections in the state rose from 30 percent to 60 percent.

Notes

1. A first draft of the material in this chapter was prepared by David Santoyo-Amador, now of Baker McKenzie, Ciudad Juarez, Mexico, when he was at Harvard Law School in 2001–2002. The present version has benefited from comments by Laura Sour, CIDE, Mexico City, and especially from comments and material from Uri Raich, Massachusetts Institute of Technology.
2. As OECD (1999) notes, it is not entirely clear how much freedom municipalities in Mexico have with respect to determining property tax rates. In some instances – as in the Mexicali case discussed in the addendum to this chapter – they may have such freedom, but in general local taxes are essentially set by state law.
3. These figures exclude the federal district (*Distrito Federal*, DF), which accounts for almost half the property taxes in Mexico (for example 46.4 percent in 2001). Unlike most states, the DF continually updates its cadastre and makes much greater efforts to improve compliance.
4. As mentioned in the previous note, almost half of all property taxes are collected in the DF. For a detailed history of property tax collections, by state, for the 1980s, see Perlo-Cohen and Zamorano-Ruiz (1999). For the most part, the relative importance of the tax has declined over this period.
5. The 1997 aggregrate figures are estimated from graphical depictions in Zarzosa-Escobedo (2000).
6. Even in the latter year, however, in some cases, cadastral values were so low that the costs of maintaining the cadastre exceeded property tax collections (Delgado and Perlo, n.d.).
7. Unlike some Latin American countries, Mexico does not exempt properties of religious organizations.
8. Mexico has no inheritance tax. There is, however, capital gains tax on gains realized from the transfer of immovable property. In addition, transfers are subject to value-added tax (IBFD, 1999).

References

Chavez-Presa, Jorge A. (2002), 'Impuesto predial: la alternativa al problema financiero de los municipios,' presentation at Encuentro de comisiones de hacienda, finanzas y presupuesto de los congresos estatales rumbo al Seminario de Federalismo Hacendario, Ciudad de Puebla.

Delgado, Alfredo and Manuel Perlo (n.d.), 'El estado del conocimiento sobre el Mercado del suelo urbano en México,' Cambridge, MA: Lincoln Institute of Land Policy.

Giugale, M.M. and S.B. Webb (eds) (2000), *Achievements and Challenges of Fiscal Decentralization: Lessons from Mexico*, Washington, DC: World Bank.

International Bureau of Fiscal Documentation (IBFD) (1999), Mexico, Supplement No. 115, Amsterdam, March.

Mayer-Serna, Carlos Elizondo (2001), 'Impuesto, democracia y transparencia,' *Cultura y rendición de cuentas*, No. 2, México City: Auditoría Superior de la Federación, Cámara de Diputados, November.

OECD (1999), *Taxing Powers of State and Local Government*, Paris: OECD.

Perlo-Cohen, Manuel and Luis R. Zamorano-Ruiz (1999), 'La reforma al sistema fiscal sobre la propiedad inmobiliaria en Mexicali, 1989–98,' Cambridge, MA: Lincoln Institute of Land Policy.

Zarzosa-Escobedo, Jose Antonio (2000), 'Evolución de las contribuciones inmobiliarias en México,' paper presented at Seminar on Las Finanzas Locales y los Impuestos Inmobiliarias, Tijuana, June.

28 Property taxes in Nicaragua[1]
Richard M. Bird

Nicaragua, like its neighbors in Central America, is essentially an agricultural country with a small manufacturing sector. Its political history in recent decades has been somewhat unusual, with a long-established (Somoza) dictatorship being overthrown in the 1970s by a left-wing (Sandinista) government, which in its turn was replaced in 1990 by a more centrist regime, which has since weathered three democratic elections. One legacy of this history is that Nicaragua's tax ratio is relatively high for the region – 23.9 percent of GDP in 1995–99 compared to a regional average of 16.5 percent, for example. Moreover, Nicaragua is unusual in Central America in that its local taxes are also relatively high – over 2 percent of GDP in 1995, compared to as little as 0.2 percent in some of the neighboring countries such as Guatemala and El Salvador. Local taxes accounted for 17.4 percent of total government revenues in 1995.

There are 151 municipalities in Nicaragua. There is no intermediate level of government. Most municipalities are small, rural and poor. Local taxation is dominated by the capital, Managua, which accounts for 53 percent of all local revenues. Mayors and councils are elected for a four-year period. Municipal taxes are governed by a national law (Plan de Arbitrios, Decree 455 of 1989 for other municipalities and Decree 10-91 for Managua).

Despite the relative importance of local revenues in general, property taxes are less important in Nicaragua than in any other country in the region, accounting for only 6.4 percent of local tax revenues in 1995 (6.8 percent in Managua and 5.7 percent in other municipalities).[2] Most local revenues came from sales taxes, followed in importance by a business tax, and then, third in order, by the property tax. Additional small charges on property are imposed for '*obras y construcciones*' (essentially building licenses). A tax of 1 percent is levied on real estate (presumably that held by corporations) as an additional corporate tax.

The property tax
The property tax was created as a national tax in 1962, with a 25 percent share going to local governments. However, the failure to establish an up-to-date national cadastre ensured that this tax never yielded much revenue. Having failed as a central government tax, the property tax was transferred to

the municipalities in 1992. Matters did not improve following this change, however. The present tax is governed by Decree 3-95 of 1995.

Tax base

The base of the property tax (*impuesto sobre bienes inmuebles*, or *predial*) is the value of land, buildings and permanent improvements. The tax is imposed, in order, on owners, users, or possessors of title (with respect, for example, to public properties occupied by third parties).

The tax is based on cadastral value, self-declared value, or estimated value, in order of preference:

- Cadastral values are the responsibility of the Fiscal Cadastre of the national tax administration (DGI, *Dirección General de Ingresos*) but they may also be based on values established by experts contracted by the municipality. In the latter case, the valuation methods employed must be approved by the National Cadastral Commission.
- Self-declared values are those based on the characteristics of the property and unit cost factors (for land, buildings, other constructions, permanent cultivations, and fixed machinery) as established by the municipality, again subject to approval by the National Cadastral Commission.[3]
- Estimated values are also self-declared but are based on the higher of book or acquisition value, adjusted by depreciation. Estimated values are not subject to the 80 percent rule mentioned below.

Values are to be adjusted annually on the basis of the CPI.

Assessed values seem to be well below market values, and it appears to be very difficult to keep values up to date.[4] Managua, for example, attempted in 1995 to utilize new values following a cadastral study but was unable to do so owing to taxpayer resistance. Moreover, additional exemptions were incorporated in the law in 1995, weakening the tax even further. Nonetheless, with external assistance efforts have continued, albeit as yet largely unsuccessfully, to update cadastral values.

Tax rate and exemptions

The tax rate is 1 percent of the taxable value, but since taxable value is set at 80 percent of the cadastral value (or, as the case may be, self-declared value), the rate is really 0.8 percent. Residential properties less than 10 000 cordobas (in general) or 40 000 cordobas (in Managua) are exempt. In rural areas, this exemption may include up to 1 hectare of land. Other exemptions include indigenous communities, associations of municipalities, agricultural cooperatives during their first two years, non-profit welfare and social assistance

organizations, houses occupied by pensioners, universities and higher technical institutions, cultural, scientific, sport and artistic institutions, unions and
professional and business (non-profit) associations, and enterprises operating
in 'export-free zones.' Decree 3-95 provided that municipal councils could,
within limits, grant additional exemptions subject to the approval of the
Minister of Finance, but this has apparently been cancelled by Law 261 of
1997, which prohibits municipalities from granting exemptions. Law 306
exempts 'tourist investments' in building and improving hotels, motels,
campgrounds, and so on from real estate taxes for up to ten years.

Tax administration

The administration of the property tax was devolved to municipalities in
1995. Taxpayers are supposed to file a declaration in the first quarter of the
year for the previous year, using forms supplied by the municipality. If the
tax is paid at that time, there is a 10 percent discount. Otherwise, 50 percent
of the tax must be paid in the first quarter and the balance no later than 30
June. Taxpayers may consolidate all properties in any one municipality for
purposes of declaration. If a property is divided between owners, a single
declaration is to be presented.

Reportedly, many smaller municipalities do not even collect the tax owing
to lack of knowledge or technical capacity. The situation has not been helped
by a long-standing tradition, under both the Somoza and the Sandinista
regimes, of not paying property taxes.

Additional problems in administering the property tax arise in many areas
as a result of the insecurity and confusion of land titles, which, among other
things, makes it difficult to know who is supposed to pay the tax.[5] Often,
there is not even a rudimentary cadastre on which to base the administration
of the tax. The attempt to utilize a 'self-assessment' system to replace the
(missing) official cadastre has not functioned well in part because of the
exemption of small properties but more fundamentally because there is no
verification or enforcement system. Efforts currently under way to register
secure titles should produce both a better basis for the fiscal cadastre and a
larger tax base: one recent study, for example, reports that values for land that
is registered are 30 percent higher than for unregistered land (Deininger and
Chamorro, 2002).

A 1997 reform proposal would have exempted residential properties valued at less than C$50 000 in Managua, and less than C$30 000 elsewhere,
subjecting other residential properties to a progressive rate (0.5 and 1 percent) and other property to a rate of 1 percent. But the poor state of cadastral
information and the weakness of tax administration – paying local taxes in
Nicaragua has been described as 'a voluntary act' – means that such proposals are unlikely to be successfully implemented, even if they were approved.

For this reason, experts at the time suggested that it would be much more feasible and in all likelihood more equitable to impose a single rate of 0.5 percent, with no exemptions. In fact, as noted earlier, the current tax imposes a single rate of 0.8 percent (in effect) but with many exemptions.

Notes

1. We are grateful to Julio Francisco Baez Cortes for supplying useful material for the preparation of this chapter.
2. For the 1995–99 period, a recent IMF study reports property taxes in Nicaragua are less than 0.05 percent of GDP; compared to 0.2 percent in 1990–94 (Stotsky and WoldeMariam, 2002), but it appears that local taxes are not included in these figures.
3. The Nicaraguan Institute of Land Studies (INETER, *Instituto Nicaraguense de Estudios Territoriales*) is supposed to provide technical support to municipalities with respect to cadastral matters.
4. Tax values are used as the basis for compensation claims with respect to expropriated property. As mentioned later, land claims have for the last decade been one of the most complex and controversial issues in Nicaraguan politics, which has not made it any easier to establish a good property tax valuation system.
5. To illustrate the state of affairs, the area of land under claim for 'restitution' reportedly exceeds the entire land area of Nicaragua! Of course, secure titles are important for many reasons besides providing a better base for the property tax. See, for example, the discussion in Deininger and Chamorro (2002) and Bandiera (2002).

References

Baez Cortes, Theodulo and Julio Francisco Baez Cortes (2001), *Todo sobre Impuestos en Nicaragua*, 5th edn, Managua: Instituto Nicaragüense de Investigaciones y Estudios Tributarios.

Bandiera, O. (2002), 'Land Distribution, Incentives, and the Choice of Production Techniques in Nicaragua,' CEPR Discussion Paper No. 3141, January.

Deininger, K. and J.S. Chamorro (2002), 'Investment and Income Effects of Land Regularization: The Case of Nicaragua,' World Bank, January.

Martinez-Vazquez, Jorge (1997), *Principios para una Estrategia de Descentralización Fiscal en Nicaragua*, Managua: USAID, Junio.

Perez, M. Jose Antonio (1998), *Sistemas Tributarios de los Gobiernos Locales en el Istmo Centroamericano*, Serie Política Fiscal 107, Santiago de Chile: CEPAL.

Stotsky, Janet G. and Asegedech WoldeMariam (2002), 'Central American Tax Reform: Trends and Possibilities,' IMF Working Paper WP/02/227, Washington, December.

Index

abatement *see* exemption
accountability 12, 33, 39, 88
administration, of property tax 41–47
  centralization of 65, 231
  in China 171–72
  in Germany 98
  in Guinea 208–9
  in Hungary 226–30
  in India 136–41
  in Indonesia 121, 125
  in Mexico 293
  in Tanzania 192–3
  in UK 84, 86–7
administrative costs 14, 64
  in Hungary 233 nn. 6, 10
  in Indonesia 122
  in Mexico 297
aerial survey, in Tanzania 193
agricultural land, taxation of 27, 34–5,
    39–41
  in Australia 94
  in Canada 40
  in Chile 288–9
  in Germany 99, 101
  in Guinea 205
  in Hungary 226
  in Japan 110, 113
  in Kenya 187 n.4
  in Mexico 294
  in Philippines 39–40, 153
  in Poland 255–6
  in Russia 238, 239
  in Tunisia 213, 215–6
  in Ukraine 247, 249
  see also farms; rural areas
Alberta, 73
amnesty
  in Argentina 285
  in Chile 290
annual (rental) value (ARV) *see* rental
  value
appeals 44–5, 46
  in Argentina 283
  in Canada 74, 75

  in Chile 290
  in Colombia 270
  in India 139, 140
  in Japan 111
  in Mexico 295
  in Philippines 155
  in Russia 244
  in South Africa 202
  in Tanzania 191
  in Tunisia 216
  in Ukraine 248
acquisition tax *see* transfer tax
Andhra Pradesh 131, 136
appraisal
  in Hungary 228
  in Indonesia 119, 122
  in Tanzania 192
  see also assessment; valuation
area
  compared to market value, 30–31
  as tax base 22–3, 26–7
    in China 166
    in Germany 104
    in India 146
    in Kenya 178–9
    in Poland 254, 258 n.6
    in Tunisia 27, 210, 214
    in Ukraine 250–51
  see also unit value
Argentina 37, 281–5
arrears 8, 47, 48–9
  in Argentina 284–5
  in Canada 75
  in Chile 289
  in Germany 104, 106 n.7
  in Hungary 229
  in India 140–41
  in Poland 255
  in Russia 244
  in Tanzania 197 n.10
  in UK 85
Assam 136
assessed value/market value ratio 7
  in Argentina 283

in Chile 289
in Mexico 293–4, 296
in Philippines 156
assessment 42–5
    centralization of 42–3, 44–5
        in Canada 73–4
        in Colombia 269
        in Hungary 59
        in India 140
    frequency of 43, 44–5, 77
    inequities in 75
    see also valuation
assessment ratios, differentiated
    in Indonesia 120, 124, 125
    in Philippines 153–4
    see also rates, differentiated
Australia 5, 13, 53 n.4, 91–7
autonomy *see* local autonomy

Bahl, R. 9, 12, 16 nn.4, 8
Bangkok 159, 161, 162
Bavaria, 104
benefit tax, property tax as 10–11, 15,
        33, 36, 203 n.3
    in Tunisia 213–5
    see also betterment tax; service
        charges; water rates
betterment tax 50–51, 52, 53
    in Argentina 285
    in India 149
    in Mexico 295–6
    in Poland 256
    in Tanzania 192
    see also development charges; land
        value increment tax; special
        assessments; valorization
Bihar 136
Bogota 32, 63, 265–6, 278, 279
Bombay *see* Mumbai
British Columbia 71, 73, 78, 79, 80 n.2
Budapest 219, 223
Buildings, as tax base 19, 22–3
    in Hungary 225
    in India 134
    in Tanzania 190
    see urban outlining tax
building and construction licenses, fees
        50–51
business taxes, local 20–21
    in Argentina 282–83

in China 165, 169, 171
in Colombia 265
in Germany 99
in Guinea 205–8
in Hungary 219, 223
in Kenya 183
in South Africa 200
in Tunisia 210–11, 213, 215
in UK 85–7
see also non-residential property

Cadastre 41–2, 61
    in Argentina 282–3, 285 n.2
    in Chile 289
    in Colombia 269–70, 275
    in Guinea 208–9
    in Hungary 228–9
    in Indonesia 126–7
    in Kenya 179, 186
    in Latvia 260
    in Mexico 296
    in Nicaragua 298–9
    in Poland 254, 257
    in Tanzania 193
    in Tunisia 211–12
    see also titles
Cali 265, 269, 270, 274, 279 n.10
California 65 n.2
CAMA (computer-assisted mass
        appraisal) 74
    in South Africa 202
    see also appraisal
Cameroon 205
Canada 5, 9, 13, 33, 40, 54 n.14, 69–80
    see also Ontario
capacity, technical 60, 61, 64
    in Hungary 227
capping, of rates
    in Ontario 76
    in UK 86, 88
    see also rates, limits on
capital gains tax 50–51
    in Australia 96
    in Germany 105–6
    in Japan 112, 113
    in Mexico 297 n.8
    in South Africa 203
    in UK 89
capital value 82
    in India 129–30

in Indonesia 118
see also market value
capitalization of property tax 10–11, 24
carpet area 131
cess
  in India 134–5, 149
  in Kenya 177
  in Tanzania 196 n.3
Chennai 140–41
Chiapas 292
Chile 13, 65, 286–91
China 165–74
city planning tax, Japan 107, 108
classification of properties 63
  see also assessment ratios
clearance certificates, as enforcement
    mechanism 47
  in Kenya 181
collection of property taxes 46–9
  centralization of 48–9
  see also administration
collection-led reform, Indonesia 125
  see also valuation-led reform
Colombia 32, 43, 52, 53, 58, 60, 62,
    265–80
comparative sales approach 28
  in Hungary 228
  in Philippines 154
  in South Africa 201
communal tax (Hungary) *see* poll tax
community charge (UK) 82, 88
Conakry 205, 207–8, 209
Cordoba (Argentina) 285 nn. 7–9
cost approach *see* depreciated cost
council tax (UK) 28, 62, 81, 82–5,
    88–9
credit, property tax 63
  see also reliefs

Dar es Salaam 191–6, 197 n.8
De Cesare, C. 14
De Soto, H. 42
Delhi 132, 134, 136
depreciated cost approach 28
  in Chile 288
  in Indonesia 120
  in Philippines 154
  in Russia 240–41
  in Tanzania 191
development charges 52, 53

in Australia 96
in Canada 79–80
in Mexico 295
see also betterment tax

earmarked revenues
  in Chile 289
  in Colombia 268
  in India 150
  in Philippines 157
East Germany 99, 100, 101, 106 n.7
effective rates of property tax 7, 16
  in Colombia 265–66
  in Indonesia 37, 123
  in Japan 113
  in Philippines 38, 156
  in Tokyo 17 n.11, 113
El Salvador 298
elasticity of property tax 12, 14
  in Colombia 266
  in Germany 103
  in Philippines 156
enforcement of tax 47
  in Colombia 275
  in Hungary 229–30
  in Kenya 181
  in Philippines 155–56
  in South Africa 203
  in Tanzania 194
  see also clearance certificates; forced
    sales; sanctions
enterprise tax *see* business taxes; non-
    residential property
exactions *see* development charges
exemptions 14, 25–26
  in Australia 92, 93
  in Canada 71
  in Chile 289, 291 n.3
  compared to grants 26
  in Germany 98
  in Hungary 225–6, 232
  in India 137
  in Japan 110
  in Latvia 261
  in Nicaragua 299–300
  in Philippines 153
  in Poland 255
  in Russia 241
  in South Africa 201
  in Tanzania 190

in Thailand 159, 161, 163
in Tunisia 214
in Ukraine 248
in UK 83–4, 86
see also reliefs; valuation deduction

fairness *see* incidence
farms, taxation of 15, 34–5
in Canada 70–71
in China 168, 170, 172
see also agricultural land
Fischel, W. 10
forced sales 47
in Chile 290
see also seizures
forest tax 20
in Germany 98
in Philippines 153
in Poland 256
in Russia 238
in Ukraine 251 n.5
freeze, in tax burden 63–4
in Ontario 63, 76
in UK 63, 89

GDR *see* East Germany
George, H. 11, 24
Germany 1, 9, 54 n.14, 98–106
Guatemala 298
Guinea 42, 205–9
Gujarat 131, 136, 137

Haryana 131
Hesse 104
Himichal Pradesh 131
Hoff, K. 40
Hood, C. 52
housing, taxes on 11
in China 166, 169, 171
in Japan 110
see also owner-occupied residences;
residential
Hungary 31, 42, 43, 58, 61, 62, 219–35,
261 n.2

idle land tax 37
in Germany 106 n.6
in Philippines 157
see also vacant land
improvements, as tax base 19, 22–23, 24

see also buildings
incentives, to business
in Canada 75
in Thailand 161
incidence of property tax 11, 24, 30, 65
in India 142
income approach 28, 32
indexing of valuations 43
in Argentina 283
in Colombia 269, 273, 279 n.9
in Germany 100
in Kenya 180
in Mexico 294
in Nicaragua 299
in Russia 238, 242
in UK 85
India 29, 30, 53, 129–51
Indonesia 7, 37, 58, 60, 61, 63, 117–28
information, problems in collecting 46
in Guinea 205
in Kenya 181
in Mexico 292
in Tanzania 189
in Thailand 162
in Ukraine 251 n.2
information system
in Kenya 60, 183–4
in Indonesia 121–3, 125–7
inheritance and gift taxes 47, 50–51
in Germany 101
in Japan 112
in Poland 257
in Russia 241–2
in South Africa 203
in UK 89
see also transfers
Ishi, H. 113

Jakarta 122
Japan 17 n. 11, 54 n.14, 107–114

Karnataka 131–2
Kenya 42, 58, 60, 61, 62, 177–88
Kerala 136
Khan, M. 40
Krakow 255
Kyiv 247

Latvia 5, 13, 42, 65, 259–61
land, as tax base 14, 19, 22–3, 24

in Australia 92–3
in Indonesia 124
in Kenya 178–9
in UK 89
land charges *see* land rent
land rent, as substitute for tax
in Russia 238
in Tanzania 190, 197 n.5
in Ukraine 247
land use, tax effects on 15–6, 24, 37, 38,
    47, 52, 154
land value increment tax 16, 50–51, 52,
in Poland 256
in UK 89
see also Plusvalia
land value tax 11, 16, 52
in Australia 93, 94
in Germany 104
in Indonesia 120
in Japan 113
in Latvia 260
in Thailand 161–62
see also site value tax
leverage ratio, in Germany 99, 102
local autonomy 8, 13
in Hungary 219–20
in Latvia 259
in Philippines 152
in Russia 236
in setting rate 34–35, 128
in Thailand 163
in Ukraine 246
local improvement charges *see* special
    assessments
local tax defined 13
London 81

machinery, as tax base 19, 22–3
in Canada 70
in Germany 99
in Philippines 154–5
in Poland 254
see also tangible business assets
Madhya Pradesh 131
Malawi 197 n.7
Managua 298–300
Manila 152, 157 n.2
Manitoba 73
Marharastra 132, 134, 137, 146, n.7,
    148–51

market value assessment 22–3, 28, 59
in Canada 59
compared to area, 30–31
in Hungary 230
in Indonesia 60
in Thailand 163
in UK 59
see also capital value; rental value
mass appraisal *see* appraisal; CAMA
Medellin 265, 267, 269, 273, 275
metropolitan areas 39
Mexicali 296–7
Mexico 9, 292–7
Mexico City 15, 292
Mombasa 181
Moscow 244 n.3
Mumbai 131, 132–5, 148–9

Nagpur 149
Nagoya 111
Nairobi 180, 181, 187 n.7
Netherlands 31
New Brunswick 73
New South Wales 91, 92, 93, 94, 95
Nicaragua 9, 298–301
non-fiscal use *see* land use
non-residential property, taxation of 11,
    15, 37, 38–9
in Canada 72, 75, 76
in India 135
in Poland 254, 257 n.4
in Russia 241
in UK 81
Northern Territory 91, 92
notarial fees 47
see also transfers
Nova Scotia 78
Novgorod 237, 244
Nuevo Leon 292, 293

Oldman, O. 15
Ontario 33, 40, 57–8, 59, 61, 62, 63,
    69–80
Orissa 136
Ott, A. 41
owner-occupied residences 38
see also residential

Patente, in Guinea 207–8
Patna 131

Pattaya City 159, 161, 162
payment system
  in Indonesia 122–3
  in Philippines 155
payments in lieu of tax
  in Canada 25
  in India 137
  in Kenya 187 n.5
  in Tanzania 191
penalties, in Tanzania 193–4
  see also sanctions
phase-in *see* transition
Philippines 7, 32, 36, 38, 41, 42, 43,
     152–8
pilot projects
  in Kenya 184
  in Russia 237
Pittsburgh 24
plot tax (Hungary) *see* vacant land
Plusvalia 52
  in Chile 288
  in Colombia 276–8
  in Mexico 296
Poland 9, 253–8, 261 n.2
political will, for reform 61–2
  in Indonesia 126
  in Kenya 181, 184–6
  in Tanzania 196
  in Thailand 164
poll tax
  in Guinea 206–8
  in Hungary 223
privatization, incentive to 13
privatization of collection, in Kenya 181
progressivity *see* rates; incidence
Puebla 294

Quebec 73, 78
Queensland 93

Rajasthan 136
rateable value (India) *see* rental value
rates (UK, Kenya, South Africa,
     Tanzania) *see* property taxes
     passim
rates, of tax 14, 33–8
  in Argentina 283–84
  in China 169–71
  in Colombia 271–74
  differentiated 34–37

  in Colombia 270
  in Ontario 59, 71–72
  in Russia 239
  in South Africa 202
  see also assessment ratios; valua-
     tion bands
graduated or progressive 16, 37
  in Argentina 284
  in Australia 94
  in Colombia 271
  in India 148–50
  in Indonesia 60, 120
  in Mexico 295
  in Nicaragua 300
  in Thailand 162
  see also effective rates
in Hungary 230
in India 132–36
in Indonesia 120
in Japan 110
in Kenya 180
limits on 34–36
  in Canada 72
  in Hungary 59
  in India 130
  in Japan 111
  in Russia 240, 245 n.11
in Mexico 294–95
in Poland 254
in Russia 238–39
in Tunisia 214–15
in Ukraine 247–48
in UK 84
reform, of property taxes 57–66
  in Chile 290–91
  in Colombia 276–79
  in Hungary 231–33
  impact of 62–64
  in Indonesia 123–28
  in Kenya 182–86
  nature of 59–60
  in Ontario 75–77
  preconditions for 60–62
  rationale for 57–59
  in Tanzania 194–96
  in Ukraine 250–51
  in UK 87–89
registry fees and taxes 47
  in Colombia 267
  in Japan 112

see also transfers
reliefs, from property tax 38
  in Argentina 283
  in Australia 95
  in Canada 73
  in Latvia 260
  in Poland 255
  in Russia 239
  in South Africa 201
  in UK 86
  see also credit; exemptions
rent control, effects of 138–40
rental value assessment 22–23, 28–30
  in India 129–32
  in Thailand 161
  in Tunisia 210–13
  in UK 58, 88
residential land, Japan 110
  see also housing
residential property, Indonesia 124
  see also housing
revenue aspects of property tax 5–10,
    14, 20–21, 64, 65
  in Argentina 281–2
  in Australia 91–92
  in Canada 69–70
  in Chile 286–87
  in China 174
  in Colombia 266
  in Germany 102–03
  in Guinea 205–06
  in Hungary 220–22, 224
  in India 142–45
  in Indonesia 117–18, 121, 127
  in Japan 107–09
  in Kenya 177–78
  in Latvia 259–60
  in Mexico 292
  in Nicaragua 298
  in Philippines 156
  in Poland 253
  in South Africa 199–200
  in Tanzania 189–90, 195
  in Thailand 159–60
  in Tunisia 212
  in Ukraine 249–50
  in UK 81–82
revenue sharing
  in Indonesia 124
  in Philippines 156

in Russia 239–40, 242–44
Ricardo, D. 47
rural areas, taxation of 52
  in Argentina 281, 283
  in India 146 n.4
  in Indonesia 120
  in Kenya 179
  in South Africa 200–201, 203 n.2
  in Tanzania 190
  see also agricultural land; farms
Russia 226–45

St. Petersburg 244 n.3
sanctions
  in Hungary 229
  in Indonesia 124
  in Tunisia 216 n.3
self-assessment 13, 31–3
  in Colombia 60, 63, 270–71, 274–6
  in Hungary 227
  in Nicaragua 299–300
  in Philippines 154, 157 n.1
  in Poland 255
  in Thailand 163
  in Tunisia 216
  in Ukraine 248
seizures
  in Indonesia 125
  in Philippines 155
service charges, India 132, 134, 137,
    148–50
Sfax 210
simplified taxes, in Ukraine 248–9
site value tax 19, 24, 25
  in Australia 93
  in India 129
  in South Africa 201, 203 n.3
  see also land value tax
Skinner, J. 40
South Africa 5, 9, 199–204
South Australia 92, 93, 95
special assessments 52
  in Canada 78
  in Philippines, 157
  see also betterment tax; valorization
speculation, tax on land, in Ontario 78–9
stamp tax 47, 50–51
  in Australia 96
  in Poland 256
  in Ukraine 251 n.6

in UK 89
see also transfers
standard tax, in Germany 99
standard value, in China 167
Strasma, J. 40
Surabaya, 122
Sydney 94, 95

Taiwan 53 n.4
Tamil Nadu 140–41
tangible business assets, in Japan 108,
    112
see also machinery
Tanzania 189–98
tax competition 15, 36, 39
tax effort 8–10
    in Philippines 156
tax exporting 12, 36, 39
tax roll *see* Cadastre
taxpayer education, in Kenya 184
Thailand 32, 37, 42, 159–64
titles, land
    in Australia 95
    in Canada 74
    in Indonesia 119
    in Nicaragua 300
    see also Cadastre
Tokyo 111
Toronto 71, 75, 76
tourism tax, in Hungary 225
transfers, of land, taxes on 47, 50–51
    in Argentina 285
    in Australia 96
    in Canada 78
    in China 168–9, 170–71, 172–3
    in Germany 105
    in Hungary 226
    in India 146 n.4
    in Indonesia 117, 122
    in Japan 108, 112
    in Mexico 297
    in Philippines 157
    in Poland 256
    in South Africa 203
    in Thailand 159, 163
    see also speculation
transition, in property tax reform 59, 61,
    77
    in Canada 75
    in Japan 111

Tunis 210
Tunisia 27, 32, 53 n.7, 210–16
Tver 237

Ukraine 246–52
unbuilt land *see* vacant land
unit values
    in Hungary 59
    in Poland 257
    see also area as tax base
urban outlining tax (Colombia) 266–7
United Kingdom 9, 28, 54 n.14, 58, 62,
    63, 81–90
United States 5, 7, 38, 43, 80 n.3
Uttar Pradesh 131

vacant land, taxation of 29
    in Colombia 276
    in Hungary 225
    in Tunisia 211, 215
valorization, in Colombia 265, 267–68
    see also betterment tax
valuation 13, 24–5
    in China 167–8
    in Germany 100
    in India 137–40
    in Indonesia 119–20
    in Kenya 179–80
    in Tanzania 191–2
    in Thailand 162
    see also appraisal; assessment;
        indexing
valuation bands, in UK 59, 62, 83
valuation cycle 43
    in Australia 95
    in Chile 289
    in Germany 101
    in Indonesia 119
    in Japan 111
    in Latvia 260
    in Philippines 155
    in South Africa 202
valuation deduction, Indonesia 120–21
    see also exemptions
valuation-led reform, in Tanzania 194–6
    see also collection-led reform
value-added tax 47, 54 n.14
    in Mexico 297 n.8
    in South Africa 203
Victoria 92, 93, 95

water rates, India 134, 148–50
wealth tax, in Germany 101, 105
West Bengal 136
Western Australia 93, 96 n.3

Youngman, J. 63–64

Zilla Parishad 150–51
Zodrow, G. 11